NO LONGER PROPERTY OF
SEATTLE ~~~~~ ~~ ~~~~~~

D0000663

About the author

Carol Dyhouse is a social historian and currently a
research professor of history at the University of
Sussex. Her most recent book, *Glamour: Women,
History, Feminism*, was published by Zed Books in
2010. Longer-term, her research has focused on
gender, education and the pattern of women's lives
in nineteenth- and twentieth-century Britain. Her
books include *Girls Growing Up in Late Victorian
and Edwardian England*; *Feminism and the Family in
England, 1890–1939*; *No Distinction of Sex? Women
in British Universities, 1870–1939*; and *Students: A
Gendered History*.

GIRL TROUBLE

PANIC AND PROGRESS IN THE HISTORY OF YOUNG WOMEN

Carol Dyhouse

Zed Books
LONDON | NEW YORK

Girl trouble: panic and progress in the history of young women was first published in 2013 by Zed Books Ltd, 7 Cynthia Street, London N1 9JF, UK and Room 400, 175 Fifth Avenue, New York, NY 10010, USA

www.zedbooks.co.uk

Copyright © Carol Dyhouse 2013

The right of Carol Dyhouse to be identified as the author of this work has been asserted by her in accordance with the Copyright, Designs and Patents Act, 1988

FSC
www.fsc.org
MIX
Paper from
responsible sources
FSC® C013604

Set in Monotype Plantin and FFKievit by Ewan Smith, London NW5
Index: ed.emery@thefreeuniversity.net
Cover design: www.kikamiller.com
Printed and bound in Great Britain by CPI Group (UK) Ltd, Croydon, CRO 4YY

Distributed in the USA exclusively by Palgrave Macmillan, a division of St Martin's Press, LLC, 175 Fifth Avenue, New York, NY 10010, USA

All rights reserved. No part of this publication may be reproduced, stored in a retrieval system or transmitted in any form or by any means, electronic, mechanical, photocopying or otherwise, without the prior permission of Zed Books Ltd.

A catalogue record for this book is available from the British Library
Library of Congress Cataloging in Publication Data available

ISBN 978 1 78032 494 4 hb
ISBN 978 1 78032 493 7 pb

CONTENTS

ILLUSTRATIONS

ACKNOWLEDGEMENTS

I owe thanks to the many librarians and archivists who have facilitated the research on which this book is based. In particular, I would like to record my appreciation of the helpfulness of staff in the British Library (both at St Pancras and at the newspaper division in Colindale), in the Library of the University of Sussex, and in the National Archives. Thanks also to staff at the County Record Offices in Warwickshire and East Sussex. Archivists at the Salvation Army Heritage Centre, the Women's Library, and Tower Hamlets Local History Library guided me towards some rich material. At Whitelands College, now part of the University of Roehampton, Gilly King was exceptionally hospitable and enthusiastic in explaining Ruskin's legacy and the history of the college.

The team at Zed Books has once again turned the publication process into a pleasure. My thanks to all of them. I am grateful to Pat Harper for her meticulous copy-editing and to Ewan Smith for his skills in production. Warm thanks, also, to Maggie Hanbury and her colleagues at the Hanbury Agency.

For permission to reproduce images I am indebted to the British Library, Whitelands College at the University of Roehampton, Getty Images, Tom Phillips, Tony Beesley and Julie Longden, Gabriel Carnévalé-Mauzan, PA Wire, and IPC+Syndication. Every effort has been made to trace and to acknowledge copyright holders of the illustrations reproduced in this book. The author and publisher apologise for any unintended errors or omissions in this respect. If brought to their attention, any such errors will be corrected in future editions.

This book is the product of research that I have carried out over a long period of time. It isn't an easy matter to compile a list of all the people who have helped me to bring the work into shape over the years, so I have to be selective, and to hope that anyone who feels left out will forgive me. As ever, my fondest debt is to my immediate family: to Nick and to our daughters Alex and Eugénie von Tunzelmann. Their positive thinking, their critical intelligence, and their encouragement in the face of my tendency to quail have been both heartening and indispensable. Then there are friends whose generosity and support I value immensely: most of these are scholarly types and they have always been ready to discuss ideas with me. My thanks to Jenny Shaw, Marcia Pointon, Claire Langhamer, Lucy Robinson, Pat Thane, Hester Barron, Naomi Tadmor, Selina Todd, Lesley Hall, Penny Summerfield, June Purvis, Penny Tinkler, Hera Cooke, Stephanie Spencer, Lucy Bland, Joyce Goodman, Ruth Watts, Sally Alexander, Anna Davin, Jane Martin, Ulrike Meinhof and Amanda Vickery. Thanks also to Ros McLintock and Monica Collingham, both of whose friendship and support go back for many years. Monica's enthusiasm for local history in Tower Hamlets led me to the riches of the Edith Ramsay Collection. Colleagues at the universities of Sussex and Brighton continue to be important in so many ways: as well as those already mentioned, I have profited from discussions with, and encouragement from, Ian Gazeley, Jim Livesey, Paul Betts, James Thomson, Vinita Damodaran, Saul Dubow, Beryl Williams, Ben Jones, Becca Searle, Lucy Noakes, Maurice Howard, Vincent Quinn, Sian Edwards, Lesley Whitworth, Jill Kirby, Sian Edwards and Chris Warne. As well as making insightful comments, Owen Emmerson reminded me about the depiction of white slavery in *Thoroughly Modern Millie*. Thanks to Miriam David, Gaby Weiner and Alexandra Allan for helping to keep me in touch with recent work in gender and education. Andy Smith was generous in lending some hard-to-get books. James Thomson put up with me in a shared office and helped me to negotiate in French with copyright holders. I must also thank the staff in the University of Sussex's IT Centre, without whose support I simply could not have managed. They were unfailingly brilliant when I panicked over technical stuff. So, thanks to Paul Allpress, and particularly to Alex Havell and Claire Wallace, Luke Ingerson, Miles Dymott and Neil Forshaw. Gill Powell patiently explained the tricky business of how to get the bibliography to follow the endnotes.

INTRODUCTION

Are girls better off today than they were at the beginning of the twentieth century? Conditions vary widely across the globe. In parts of the world girls suffer disproportionately from poverty, lack of education, and appalling levels of sexual violence. But there can be no doubt that in some countries, at least, they have more opportunities, more choices and infinitely more personal freedom than ever before. Does this mean that we can afford to be optimistic about the impact of modernity on girls? Have young women emerged as winners rather than losers in modern history?

These are large questions and beg larger ones. This book is more modest in its remit and focuses primarily on Britain, although it is informed by writing and ideas about girlhood from North America, Australia and Europe. Many of the issues and themes which are dealt with will be familiar to readers outside these regions: controversy about whether girls should be seen as the victims or beneficiaries of 'progress' have had a very wide currency.

In what ways are girls better off in Britain now than they were in Victorian times? Whereas in the past girls were schooled for home duties and pushed into domestic service, they are now educated along much the same lines as boys. And they do extremely well in education, at both school and university levels. As far as work opportunities go, young women have many more options than their mothers had, and certainly vastly more choice than their grandmothers. Many liberties are taken for granted:

political rights, the freedom to move about the city, to drive cars, to operate bank accounts, to enter into contracts, to take out loans and to manage financial affairs. All this would have been unimaginable in the 1890s, and even in the 1950s and 1960s bank managers (then all male) routinely refused to grant young unmarried women the mortgages that would have allowed them to own their own homes. Up until the 1970s, opportunities for sexual self-expression were limited. Girls were generally assumed to be in pursuit of husbands. They were expected to remain chaste before marriage, and anything else – especially unmarried pregnancy – brought social shame and a prospect of doom. Today, most girls in Britain have much more control over their bodies and their sexuality.

This is not, by any means, to assert that everything in the garden is rosy. Young women today face many problems. Some of these are new, and some are depressingly familiar. There are still 'double standards' of sexual morality, for instance. Boys have more licence, and they get away with much more. Young women suffer more than men do from bullying, and from sexual violence. And girls are too often expected to be perfect in every way: at school, in work and behaviour, and in the way they look. Subjected to such pressures, they can turn their anger and a sense of powerlessness, or lack of control inwards, resulting in eating disorders and depression.

A great deal of contemporary writing on girlhood has been gloomy in tone. Young women are represented as the victims of all manner of social trends: of capitalism, of consumerism, of body obsessions, of 'sexualisation' and pornography. Girls themselves come under attack for behaving badly: as alcohol-swigging 'ladettes' or as narcissistic 'living dolls'. They may be represented as defenceless innocents or as brainless Barbie-doll impersonators, floating in a fluffy cloud of self-obsession, sparkly pink, and fake tan. Several academic writers have argued that the language of 'girl power', 'empowerment' and 'choice', often used in accounts of the recent history of girls, has served as a smokescreen, obscuring deep-seated inequalities and oppression. Scholars such as Angela McRobbie, Jessica Ringrose, Anita Harris and Marnina Gonick, for instance, have suggested that a liberal discourse of 'freedom' and 'opportunity' can disguise the fact that realistically, there are far too many girls in even the developed world who enjoy very little of either.[1] There is undoubtedly some truth in this, and the economic uncertainties and widening social divisions of the twenty-first century so far give little cause for complacency. The improvements in young women's lives which became noticeable in Britain, particularly after the 1970s, can never be taken for granted: it isn't difficult to find evidence of the 'backlash' which led so many observers to speak of 'post-feminism'.

This book brings together work I have done throughout a longish academic career. This began in the 1970s, when I first became interested in the ways in which, historically, female education functioned as a battlefield for different constituencies, all convinced that they knew what was best for girls. In Britain, Victorian feminists objected to an education designed to groom girls for the marriage market. Their opponents held that too much intellectualism unsexed young women: at best, it turned them into desiccated spinster types; sometimes, it was claimed, it literally shrivelled up their breasts and ovaries, rendering these women infertile.

If social anxieties surfaced around women's struggle for a decent education in the late nineteenth century, in Britain these anxieties paled in comparison with the agitation generated by feminist demands for the vote in the years 1900–1914. The conflicts of this period can realistically be described as a 'sex war', in which both sides showed intransigence and extreme reactions. This war between the sexes escalated around the government's practice of force-feeding suffragettes in prison in 1913. For many women, force-feeding was experienced as torture, or a form of rape.[2] The early twentieth-century panic over 'white slavery', and particularly the alleged kidnapping and trafficking of young girls on city streets in Britain and America, reached its height in precisely the same years. This moral panic reflected the fraught situation of antipathy between the sexes. It brought together an unlikely combination of political groups: evangelicals, social purity workers, feminists and staunch opponents of women's suffrage. Campaigners focused obsessively on the idea of innocent young girls as the defenceless victims of predatory male lust. For some, these stories of white slavery exuded a distinctly erotic appeal.

The book begins with these horror stories about girls being kidnapped on the streets of London. It then moves back in time to trace the ways in which a growth of feminine self-awareness, improvements in education, and a growing political consciousness made their impact upon young women before the First World War. The troubling of social certainties about gender continued through and after the war, as the 'modern girl' established herself on the scene. 'Brazen flappers' horrified conservatives by blowing cigarette smoke in the face of Victorian ideas of feminine constraint and decorum. Young working-class women's determination to live more fully and their ambitions for a better life led them to shun domestic service in favour of new opportunities in shops, factories and offices. This created problems for the servant-keeping middle classes, who whinged incessantly about young girls getting above themselves, and showing too worldly an interest in cheap cosmetics and fur coats. Cinema-going was often blamed for this, in the sense of turning girls' heads. But a shortage of marriageable young men in the aftermath of war also fostered an independent outlook in many single girls. Whether they liked it or not, these young women often had no one else to depend upon.

Respectable society had no answers to many of the predicaments faced by young women, especially those forced to strike out on their own. The Second World War, like its predecessor, proved a catalyst of social change. Chapter 4 shows how, for many people in Britain, the pace of change was itself threatening. Anxieties about young women surfaced in alarm over 'good-time girls', seen as predatory, lusting after foreign men or on the lookout for no one but themselves. There were rumours of these girls batting their eyelids at American servicemen and risking their virtue for nylon stockings. Such concerns carried over into the post-war world. The 1950s was a decade of extraordinary contradictions. The coronation of the young Elizabeth II brought a wave of nostalgia for an idealised past, in which tradition and hierarchy were assumed to have buttressed the British. Dutiful upper-middle-class girls queued to become debutantes, grooming, learning to curtsey, and trussing themselves up for the marriage market. But new conditions were intruding fast, often loudly signalled by American-style consumerism, film and popular music. There was concern lest daughters be seduced by 'crooners', or go after bad boys in leather with slicked hair like Elvis Presley. Then there were Teddy girls, beat girls and Mods.

Harassed fathers were disturbed by the idea of daughters hanging about jukeboxes in coffee bars, or coming across undesirable types in dark and smoky jazz cellars. Would these daughters prove wayward, swerving out of control? Runaway marriages or unmarried motherhood would bring shame on a family's good name. Chapter 5 focuses on the 1960s, unsettled by the Profumo scandal and the teenage revolution.[3] Girls were seen to be behaving in ways which challenged traditional authority and standards of propriety. Increasingly well-educated, they were more often answering back, and threatening to leave – if not actually leaving – home. Chapter 6 explores the ways in which controversies over the 'permissive society' were bound up with unease about changing gender roles, and further, stemmed from fears that girls were behaving precociously and promiscuously, without regard for the consequences. There was a minor moral panic about unmarried, teenage motherhood, but those who fretted most about this were often equally uneasy about young women getting access to contraceptives without their parents' consent.

One of the lasting legacies of the teenage revolution of the 1960s in Britain was the redefinition of adulthood: after the Family Law Reform Act of 1969, young people were regarded as 'coming of age' at eighteen rather than at twenty-one. This defused what had often been an explosive situation in both families and educational institutions. Throughout the 1960s, young people of both sexes had regularly challenged what they had increasingly come to see as unwarranted and 'paternalistic' interference in their private lives. After 1969, students in colleges and universities gained a great deal of personal freedom: the authorities were no longer required to act *in loco parentis* towards them, because eighteen-year-olds were no longer considered 'infants' or 'minors'. Young people over the age of eighteen could henceforward marry without the consent of their parents, should they wish to do so. Those who worked to bring about this reduction in the age of majority had been much influenced by the fact that young people – especially women – were marrying at younger ages than in the past. However, contrary to all expectations, the numbers of teenage brides sharply diminished in the 1970s.

The 1970s in Britain were a watershed. The women's liberation movement, or what became known as 'second-wave feminism', contested almost every aspect of young women's experience. The impact of feminism, and the momentous changes in assumptions about gender and education that characterised the decade are considered in Chapter 6. Chapter 7 moves into the contemporary world. It scrutinises the popular celebration of 'girl power', and asks why so much contemporary writing has represented girls as the casualties, rather than as the beneficiaries, of progress.

This book is first and foremost a history, and while it explores a number of contemporary issues and problems, particularly in the last chapters, it sets out to take a long view. It shows that the history of girlhood in Britain has been deeply troubled. Modern British history has been packed with horror stories about girls. Attention to representations of girlhood in British social history and popular culture shows clearly that the changes in young women's lives since Victorian times have been accompanied by anxiety and social unease. Ideas about femininity, and feminine respectability, have proved a battleground. Expectations about how young women should behave have been contested and uncertain. Settled hierarchies, and often taken-for-granted notions of how men and women should relate to each other, have been regularly disturbed, shaken up, and challenged. For some, this has been a cause for celebration; others have reacted with pessimism or condemnation, anxiety, panic, and even despair.

The Victorian middle class invested heavily in the notion of girlish innocence, holding feminine virtue to be the foundation of a stable home and family life. Social stability was seen to depend on a right ordering of male and female, and on a father's protection of daughters. This protection was envisaged as both moral and economic; it was also, of course, built into politics and sanctioned by the law. Protection was a two-edged sword, and it frequently shaded into control. Feminism, 'new women' and 'modern girls' all challenged patriarchy, and they all brought into question both the efficacy of protection and equally, the need for, and the justice of, control. Girls' demands for greater self-determination and independence spelled trouble. So in each generation, the image of girlhood has been hotly contested, with the 'modern girl' represented at times as a major beneficiary of social change, at other times as symbol, symptom and even the prime agent of social disruption.

In the pages that follow I use the terms 'girl' and 'young woman' interchangeably. 'Girl' was used widely in nineteenth-century Britain, and it was used across class boundaries, unlike 'young lady', which generally excluded the working class. Middle-class writers in the Edwardian era often described girlhood as coming to an end when a young woman first menstruated, or first put up her hair. A decade or so later, girls were more likely to chop off rather than to coil up their tresses. Girlhood was definitely ended by marriage, although colloquially, familiarly (or rudely) women might still be described as 'old girls'. During the twentieth century, even as the age of marriage fell, adult women might refer to themselves as girls – as in 'a night out with the girls'. With the advent of the women's liberation movement there was unease about the term: as applied to young adult women it was widely considered belittling and disrespectful.

Since the last decades of the twentieth century, the term has been reclaimed, somewhat, particularly through discussions of 'girl power'.[4] Adult women were by the 1990s marrying later and later – if they married at all. Reactions to the use of the word 'girl' have often depended on who is using it. I have chosen to use it broadly and affirmatively.

1 | WHITE SLAVERY AND THE SEDUCTION OF INNOCENTS

Where Are You Going To ...? was the deceptively innocent-sounding title of a story which horrified and enthralled British readers in 1913. Originally published as *My Little Sister*, the same story had created shock waves in the USA during the previous year. The book was so shocking that sales had clocked up at the rate of around a thousand copies daily, justifying a fourth edition within a month.[1] The author of the story was Elizabeth Robins, a celebrated American actress then living in Britain. She was a woman of great intelligence, glamour and style. She was also a committed feminist. Robins was determined to publicise the evils of prostitution, and more particularly stories of contemporary trafficking in young women, what was known as the 'white slave trade'. She had carried out intensive research for this book, even to the extent of dressing up in Salvation Army uniform and talking, through the night, with prostitutes working the streets around Piccadilly.[2]

The book told the tale of a pretty maid, 'white and golden', 'dimpled and lovely like a small princess', who fell into the clutches of a group of lustful and immoral men. The reader is left to figure out precisely what happened next, but there is no doubt that we are meant to assume the worst. The story begins with two innocent middle-class girls living in the countryside near Brighton. Their frail and impoverished widowed mother is on her sickbed. The mother decides to send her daughters to stay with their aunt in London. Tipped off by a treacherous dressmaker, a fake aunt is waiting for them at Victoria Station. This 'mysteriously veiled woman', sporting a hat ominously 'boiling over with black ostrich feathers', greets the girls, one the unnamed narrator of the tale, the other her little sister Bettina, (the angelic, white-and-golden one), and whisks them off to a posh brothel: 'one of the most infamous houses in Europe'.

There they are taken to a room of oriental splendour hung in rose silk. The girls are tarted up for display to a male clientele. The fake aunt dresses for dinner in 'a gown all covered with little shining scales, like a snake's skin'. Lest we miss the predatory allusions, we are told that she eyes the girls 'like a huge grey hawk' with 'a full yellow eye, the iris almost black', which turned 'reddish' in the course of the evening. A ghastly collection of male reprobates accompanies the girls at dinner. These men are designated simply as 'the Colonel', 'the Tartar' and so on. One has a hunchback; another is described as blotchy-faced and creepy. After dinner, the men leer over the innocent Bettina, goading her into singing girlish nursery songs ('Where are you going to, my pretty maid?'). Meanwhile Bettina's sister notices that the windows are barred. Her neighbour at table explains that the house was once a private lunatic asylum. Something in the girl's spirit impresses this man, whose dessert she is clearly supposed to become, and he helps her to escape from the house of horror. Half-mad, she blunders through the London streets. Finding refuge in her real aunt's house and seeking help from the police, she desperately searches for Bettina, whom she is never to see again.

Robins's book was one of a clutch of feminist texts claiming to unmask the realities of prostitution, venereal disease and the white slave trade just before the First World War. It should be seen alongside her friend Dr Louisa Martindale's short medi-

cal treatise on the subject, *Under the Surface* (1909), and suffragette leader Christabel Pankhurst's controversial text *The Great
Scourge and How to End It* (1913).[3] All three writers railed against
a double standard of morality and what they saw as the sexual
slavery of women; all three saw votes for women as the first
step towards eliminating such abuses. The books cross-reference
each other: Robins originally thought of titling her story 'What
became of Betty Martindale?'[4] Christabel Pankhurst's *The Great
Scourge* refers to both Martindale and Robins.[5] Robins's text,
with its pantomime villains, reads as gothic melodrama today.
It may strike the reader as curious that in a book intended
to chill the blood with suggestions of the blackest imaginable
excesses of male beastliness, the most obvious villain is female.
Nevertheless, at the time, as a piece of literary propaganda, it
had a powerful impact. Christabel Pankhurst's text has always
proved controversial, particularly over its contention that a large
proportion of Britain's male population of the day were infected
with venereal disease. Some contemporaries and many later
historians have peremptorily dismissed this claim as deluded.[6]
Others have pointed out that Christabel took her information
from supposedly reputable academic and clinical sources at a
time when medical understanding of the disease was far from
perfect. Anxiety over venereal disease was easy to understand.
Before the discovery of sulphonamide drugs and antibiotics,
these diseases were more or less untreatable. A society which
tolerated sexual licence in men, while insisting on wifely innocence, posed particular problems for women.

Christabel Pankhurst saw the powerless wife and the prostitute as linked in a system of patriarchal oppression which
could be described, loosely, as white slavery. Further, *The Great
Scourge* had a specific, contemporary example of white slavery

to trumpet: that of the Piccadilly Flat case.[7] The 'foul revelations' and 'still fouler concealments' of the Piccadilly Flat case, according to Christabel, summed up everything feminists should deplore about the great social evil of male immorality and the silencing of women who were denied the vote. What do we know of the Piccadilly Flat case?

In the summer of 1913, Detective-Inspector Curry and Detective-Sergeant Burmby, of Scotland Yard's recently created white slavery suppression branch, conducted a raid on a flat in Abingdon House, near London's Piccadilly tube station.[8] It was a property which they had had their eye on for some time. They were admitted by a woman called Elizabeth Telfer, more familiarly known as 'Nurse Betty' because she had qualified as a nurse and wore a nurse's uniform. In the flat were two young girls, aged seventeen and eighteen, who were found 'almost nude' in the bathroom. The flat was heavily perfumed with the scent of lilies. The police seized stashes of dodgy photos and (allegedly) even dodgier correspondence, a pocketbook and diary, a whip, a cane, a revolver and a copy of the 1912 Criminal Law Amendment Act, which specified new and harsh penalties for anyone convicted of procuring for prostitution. The main occupant of the flat, who went by the name of Queenie Gerald, was charged with living on immoral earnings and keeping a disorderly house.

Queenie Gerald was eventually fined, and was sentenced to three months' detention in Holloway prison. Nurse Telfer was summoned by the Central Midwives' Board, lost her nursing certificates and was struck off the midwives' roll.[9] But this was not enough to forestall an outcry over the case, which arose out of the belief that Gerald was guilty of procuring young girls and should have met with a much sterner penalty: it was widely rumoured that the less serious charge had been pursued by male lawyers and a government determined to protect the anonymity of an upper-class male clientele.

Drawing support from women's organisations, feminists and local churches, the protest over the case was fomented by Keir Hardie, leader of the Independent Labour Party (ILP). Hardie was an old friend of the Pankhursts and had had a love affair with Christabel's sister, Sylvia. His pamphlet *The Queenie Gerald Case: A Public Scandal, White Slavery in a Piccadilly Flat*, was published by the National Labour Press in 1913. With section headings such as 'Shielding Rich Scoundrels', Keir Hardie's pamphlet demanded the further trial of Queenie Gerald as a procuress, and the public outing of 'the filthy brood for whom she caters'. His rhetoric was colourful. Dismissing the government's claim that the evidence pointed to two or three girls at the most, all of whom were over the age of consent and clearly engaged in prostitution before their introduction to Queenie Gerald, he thundered on about the lilies, hot-scented baths, and whips and lashes 'reminiscent of Oriental orgies' which had been found in the Piccadilly flat. His tone reminiscent of Old Testament wrath, Hardie ended his pamphlet with dire imprecations about the state of an England disgraced by some 350,000 fallen women, 'all of them', he concluded somewhat bathetically 'somebody's lassies!'[10]

Papers in the Home Office and Metropolitan Police files preserved in the National Archives allow us to reconstruct something of this case. Sadly, Queenie's pocketbook and diary have disappeared, although notes say that these were to be retained by the police. There are a couple of vaguely incriminating letters. One, addressed to Queenie and signed 'Yorkshire', expresses the writer's hope that he will meet 'your auburn friend' on his next trip to London. Another, signed 'Somerset' and undated, asks simply: 'Will you get me a virgin?'[11] There is nothing in the way of hard, incriminating evidence and the Home Secretary insisted, in response to questioning in the House of Commons and elsewhere, that no evidence had actually been destroyed.[12] The officers in Scotland Yard had, after all, initiated and pursued the case: the special department to deal with white slave trafficking had only just been set up, in response to public feeling, and its officers were keen to show results.[13]

W. N. Willis, a somewhat shady, maverick figure who established the Anglo-Eastern Publishing Company and in the years before the First World War kept himself financially buoyant by publishing a series of books with salacious titles (*Why Girls Go Wrong*, *Western Men with Eastern Morals*, et cetera), expanded on the case of Queenie Gerald in his colourful *White Slaves in a Piccadilly Flat*, which appeared in 1915.[14] This was a gossipy text, with dubious status as historical evidence, but Willis was an experienced sniffer-out of vice, with many contacts in the London underworld, and some of his comments on the case are suggestive of what may well have been the truth. Gerald was no procuress, Willis asserted: she was a clever woman, careful not to break the law. (We may remember that the police found an up-to-date copy of the Criminal Law Amendment Act in her flat.) Her girls were invariably 'old hands', although they regularly pretended innocence. She paid and treated her girls well, and they were loyal to her in return. Much of what went on in the flat centred around mixed bathing and massage rather than 'immoral intercourse', Willis claimed. There were also elaborate dinner parties enlivened by *tableaux vivants*, with girls dressing up (or down) and posing as 'living statuary'. As for a diary or book of addresses of well-known clients, this was an old dodge, regularly resorted to by those in the trade to discourage police investigation. Willis thought that Keir Hardie and the suffragettes had got the wrong target, although he could appreciate that comparisons between the way that the suffragettes were treated in gaol (having a hosepipe turned on them, or being force-fed) and the way Queenie was indulged by warders in Holloway, rankled. According to insiders in the gaol, Queenie was tolerated and liked as a 'star performer', unrepentant, amusing and popular, which enabled her 'to get away with things'.[15]

Newspaper reports of Queenie's stylish appearances in court, dressed fetchingly in tight costumes with patent boots, and the Metropolitan Police files, reflecting snapshots of her career over the next decade or so, confirm the impression conveyed by Willis. The files contain several letters addressed to the police from 'The Honourable Geraldine "Queenie" Gerald Gaynor', the handwriting elegant and bold, their envelopes sealed with gobs of glossy black wax impressed with a crown and a curly letter Q.[16] Queenie Gerald was twenty-six years old in 1913. In the years that followed, her behaviour increasingly perplexed the police, leading to long descriptions of the gorgeousness of her attire (tailored black jackets, sparkly shoes, white silk stockings worked with sequins) and the luxuriance of her living conditions, with warning notes about the importance of never letting junior officers near her if they were alone.[17] But material success brought little peace of mind to Queenie, who remained vulnerable to vitriolic press attacks and an object of abuse from and persecution by moralists for many years after 1913.[18]

None of this tells us much about the white slave trade, the horrors of which so obsessed many contemporaries. To understand the history of concern about the trafficking of women and girls in Britain we need to track back to the 1880s, when campaigning journalist W. T. Stead published a sensational series of articles on 'The Maiden Tribute of Modern Babylon' in the *Pall Mall Gazette*. This story is well known.[19] Reports of English girls being lured to Continental brothels had already led to government-instigated investigation by a lawyer, Thomas Snagge. A number of concerned individuals, in particular the feminist Josephine Butler and moral reformers Alfred S. Dyer and Benjamin Waugh, pressed for more action, and in 1881 a Select Committee of the House of Lords set out to consider the law in respect of the protection of young girls 'from Artifices to Induce them to lead a Corrupt Life'.[20] The evidence on the subject was somewhat contradictory. However, the perception that the government was dragging its feet on the matter inspired Stead to dramatic action. He set out to expose the evils of the sex trade by purchasing a young girl, spiriting her away to Europe, and penning a colourful account of his actions in the *Pall Mall Gazette*.[21] The series of sensational articles which resulted was a triumph of Gothic horror-eroticism, with lashings of detail about chloroform, cries of childish terror, and the inflamed passions of old rakes gloating over torture and innocence despoiled. The episode landed both Stead and Rebecca Jarrett, a reformed sex worker who had acted as his reluctant accomplice in the affair, in gaol. But as a publicity stunt it generated all and more of the outrage that Stead had been seeking. For many reformers and feminists he had become a hero. Shortly after the publication of the 'Maiden Tribute' articles, the Criminal Law Amendment Act of 1885 raised the age of consent from thirteen to sixteen.[22] Vigilance societies, rescue homes, refuges, penitentiaries, and missions for friendless and fallen girls mushroomed all over Britain.[23]

Many commentators would see the late Victorian outcry over white slavery as a moral panic.[24] This outcry did not just occur in Britain. By the early 1900s, public anxiety about the white slave trade in North America and Europe too had swelled almost to hysteria. During the period 1899 to 1916 there were regular national and international meetings and conventions dedicated to suppression of trafficking. Through the zealous campaigning of W. A. Coote, the secretary of the National Vigilance Association, Britain played a leading part in this international movement. Twelve countries were represented at the first meeting, in London, in 1899,[25] and conventions in Paris in 1902 and 1904 called for the setting up of specialised branches of national police forces which would dedicate themselves to eliminating trafficking.[26] Britain's Metropolitan Police force had established such a department by 1912, with Inspector Curry heading a team of nine constables, and Miss MacDougall, previously a diocesan mission worker, as Lady Assistant.[27] This was the team that cracked down on Queenie Gerald in 1913. The same year saw London's Caxton Hall hosting the fifth International Conference for the Suppression of White Slave Traffic. This was attended by prelates, peers and presidents from many different countries: King George V and Queen Mary sent strong messages of personal support.[28]

The sheer volume of literature generated by all this concern over and fascination with white slavery was enormous. It included pamphlets, tracts, exposés, government and official inquiries, and an outpouring of novels and plays on both sides of the Atlantic. Many films also addressed the subject.[29] In the USA, productions such as *Traffic in Souls* (1913), *House of Bondage* (1914) and *Is Any Girl Safe?* (1916) all attracted massive audiences, often dominated by young women, presumably in search of the salacious and illicit thrills. This worried moralists, of course, already anxious about the cinema as a place where young people might hope to pick up members of the opposite sex or indulge

1.1 Innocent victim of the white slave trade pictured in *Fighting the Traffic in Young Girls; or, War on the White Slave Trade*, edited by Ernest A. Bell and published in 1910. Note the shadowy predator in the background.

in unsupervised courtship.[30] There can be no doubt that the explosion of interest in white slavery was fuelled by fascination with the sinister, the seedy and the erotic as well as by moral outrage: evangelicalism, committee building and social actions were only part of the story. *The White Slave Market*, a best-selling volume co-authored by W. N. Willis and Olive Christian Malvery (Mrs Archibald MacKirdy) in 1912 illustrates something of this mixture of motives.[31] Malvery defensively insisted that she had felt it a social duty to co-operate with Willis in exposing horrid truths about sexual exploitation. With a pious shudder, she expressed a hope that she would never have to write of such subjects again.[32] Willis, on the other hand, launched himself into the task with relish. He delighted in lurid descriptions and dodgy anecdotes bristling with racist stereotypes: haughty sensual sultans, Chinese opium dens, Malaysian pimps, and every shade of 'oriental depravity'.

Well before the raid on Queenie Gerald's flat in Piccadilly, and the meeting in Caxton Hall, the public had been baying for action against white slavery. In 1910, a fat volume edited by Ernest A. Bell brought together English and American campaigners in a series of essays entitled *Fighting the Traffic in Young Girls; or, War on the White Slave Trade*.[33] The book's cover carried an image of a terrified young maiden trapped in a cage, a shadowy, lecherous figure advancing threateningly, and a cry to action

1.2 The white slaver disguised as a helpful gentleman approaching an unwary young lady at a railway station. From Ernest A. Bell's *Fighting the Traffic in Young Girls; or, War on the White Slave Trade*, 1910.

from General Booth of the Salvation Army, 'For God's sake, Do Something!' When W. T. Stead was drowned, on the maiden voyage of the *Titanic* in 1912, many campaigners redoubled their efforts in his name. A pamphlet issued by the Ladies' National Association for the Abolition of State Regulation of Vice and for the Promotion of Social Purity in 1912 gave extremely vague details about a couple of cases of attempted abduction under the heading 'True cases which could easily be multiplied'.[34] Historian Edward Bristow noted that public hysteria had got to a point where the 5,000 girls working London's telephone exchanges were given official warnings to watch out for drugged chocolates and similar dangers.[35] Those pushing for new legislation insisted on the urgency of intervention at Christmas time, when they suggested that girls were particularly vulnerable, about on the streets doing their Christmas shopping.[36] Public pressure succeeded in bringing about a new Criminal Law Amendment Act in 1912, which tightened provisions against brothel keeping, procuring and those living on immoral earnings.[37] It gave increased powers to the police, and provided for the flogging of male procurers. There were cheers in the House of Lords when Lord Haldane expressed his approval of flogging in such cases. Some thought penalties should be even harsher. The Earl of Lytton, for instance, suggested branding offenders instead of thrashing them.[38]

While many applauded any crackdown against those they saw as 'human beasts of prey', male or female, some voices at least were raised in liberal protest. Enthusiasts for the flogging of procurers tended to gloss over the fact that those accused of procuring (as in Elizabeth Robins's novel or in the Piccadilly Flat case) were often female. A number of prominent women, most of them feminists, expressed their distaste for the penalty of flogging itself. They considered this brutal and degrading, and spoke of their unease at a new standard of inequality in punishment between women and men. Signatories to a letter of protest to this effect, forwarded to the prime minister through the Humanitarian League, included Dr Elizabeth Garrett Anderson, the labour politician Margaret Bondfield, Elizabeth Robins, Beatrice Webb, Mrs Bramwell Booth of the Salvation Army, Teresa Billington-Greig and several other prominent suffragists.[39] Rebecca West was incredulous: 'Our instincts tell us that normal healthy people do not flog other people, any more than they skin live cats in their back gardens,' she commented acerbically.[40]

Not all of this group were convinced that white slavery even existed in the form often imagined. Feminists were increasingly divided on the issue. For some, the term 'white slavery' had become coterminous with prostitution and the sexual slavery that they believed men inflicted on women. Others were uneasy about seeing the majority of men as sexually dangerous and the majority of women as victims. In June 1913, Teresa Billington-Greig published an article in the *English Review* entitled 'The Truth about White Slavery'.[41] She noted that a wave of public anger brought about by an 'epidemic of terrible rumours' was what had led to the punitive Criminal Law Amendment Act of 1912. Stories of the trapping of girls circulated everywhere. Most of these were embroidered with details of chloroformed handkerchiefs, drugged sweets, or syringes administered by strangers at railway stations. These horror stories invariably turned out, on close investigation, to be apocryphal. Everyone knew someone who had confided in someone else whose distant acquaintance had heard about the terrible case of the Hampstead hairdresser's daughter, or someone like her, who had inexplicably gone missing. Billington-Greig categorised such stories, relentlessly tried to track down evidence for what we would now call 'urban myths' of this kind, and found none. She collected and scrutinised statistics from chief constables in twelve different towns. All showed that the majority of girls and young women reported as gone missing were traced fairly quickly, more quickly than was the case with missing boys. Eleanor Carey, an experienced probation officer at Thames Police Court, confessed that she had never come across a single case of a girl being trapped or forced into prostitution.[42] In every case known to her, where a girl had been found in a brothel she had been 'a willing, though blind and misguided victim'. Many police court missionaries, wardens of women's settlements and other social workers gave the same story. Finally, Billington-Greig questioned F. S. Bullock, the Assistant Commissioner of Police responsible for Scotland Yard's White Slavery Suppression branch. Bullock replied:

> I cannot call to mind a single case of the forcible trapping of a girl or woman by drugs, false messages, or physical force during the last ten years that has been authenticated or proved. I should say such cases were very rare indeed ... The average number of cases of procuration in London is about three per annum, and none of these are really cases of trapping.[43]

All this led Billington-Greig to denounce what she dismissed as 'sedulously cultivated sexual hysterics', premised on the notion that all men were vicious while women were 'imbecilic weaklings'.[44]

F. S. Bullock thought that the level of public anxiety and the mass of scare stories gave a completely false impression of the dangers facing girls and women on the London streets. In the main he thought the panic a 'curious result' of press attention to the supposed existence of a white slave trade. The dedicated work of his special department in its first twelve months had brought no evidence of any organised trafficking in the capital.[45] Rumours of girls being waylaid by women dressed as nurses at railway stations and so forth were invariably discovered to be without foundation. This did not mean that cases of sexual exploitation were rare. Bullock himself thought that the greater freedoms afforded to girls in recent decades had brought additional risks in this respect:

> In these days of education and independence, many a girl, anxious to make her own living, but innocent of the world and its dangers, puts herself in the power of a man who cannot be called a trafficker in women, but may be and often is, a man of immoral character, and the result may be easily imagined. His proposals to an innocent girl strike terror into her heart, and such a case in the hands of a rescue worker naturally assumes the aspect of trafficking, though it is in reality an isolated case of sordid temptation and weakness.[46]

Senior police officers were increasingly uneasy about the use of the terms 'white slave trade' or 'white slave traffic', preferring 'offences against women and children'.[47]

But the term 'white slavery' had become locked into the public imagination, and would prove almost as hard to eradicate as prostitution itself. Even harder to eradicate were the fears of parents, and dark imaginings in the public mind. Girls growing up in the years before the First World War were subjected to endless warnings about the dangers of being kidnapped by white slavers. Kathleen Hale had studied at Reading University just before the war. After completing her studies she moved to London, rather nervous because her mother had 'succeeded in scaring the daylights out of me with her stories of the perils of the White Slave Traffic'. Train journeys threw her into a panic because she was convinced that 'all men, and even old women – in fact, everybody except policemen and railway guards – were potential white slave traffickers'.[48] In her biography of Vera Brittain, Deborah Gorham notes that the young Vera's relationship with her father Arthur became strained during her adolescence not least because he lived with constant fear that she might be abducted.[49] In her diary, Vera recorded that her mother had insisted on accompanying her on a visit to an aunt because 'Daddy started talking about pepperboxes, & gags, and White Slave Traffic as usual.'[50] Warned never to travel in an empty train compartment, Vera did have one scary encounter on a trip home from her select boarding school. A man, 'hairy-handed' and smelling of alcohol, entered the carriage and leered at her. When he suggested a kiss, Vera panicked, her imagination conjuring up the worst.[51] The social historian Dorothy Marshall, who also grew up in the North of England before the war, recalled an unhappy year spent at a boarding school in Blackpool where she was subjected to lurid accounts of white slavery from the other girls in the dormitory.[52] Dorothy's parents, like Vera's, instilled anxious warnings. Looking back, Dorothy considered that these early fears 'provided one strand in my make-up, it is one which I should be happy to do without'.[53]

In reality, girls travelling alone in the 1900s were much more likely to be accosted by social workers determined to protect young innocents than by pimps or predators. England's ports and railway stations were by then swarming with voluntary workers representing the many societies undertaking to safeguard lonely country girls about to enter the big city. Young girls destined for domestic service were identified as a particularly vulnerable group, and Travellers' Aid Societies, the Salvation Army, and a host of other groups stepped in to organise rotas and patrols at embarkation points and on station platforms.[54] The aim was to make sure that young workers found reputable employment, and to influence them in the way of good habits, continence, regularity and religion. Cinema foyers, bars and dance halls were also seen as key hunting grounds for procurers: the Ernest Bell publication mentioned above contained a series of graphic illustrations showing fashionably dressed villains twirling canes and moustaches and advancing on young girls in such places. The author of a warning manual for parents, *The Dangers of False Prudery* (1912), warned of 'the cinematograph, the mutascope and kindred perils', especially at funfairs and 'in ice-cream shops in Scotch towns run by Italians'.[55] Foreigners were particularly suspect: the white slavery obsessions of the 1900s fuelled a wave of xenophobia directed against Jews, Italians and Chinamen.

Those involved in campaigns against white slavery saw themselves as crusaders fighting a Holy War in the name of 'social purity'. An enormous amount of individual and collective energy went into late Victorian and early Edwardian campaigns for social (effectively a euphemism for 'sexual') purity.[56] There were societies like the National Vigilance Association, constituted in 1885 in response to Stead's 'Maiden Tribute' campaign, whose secretary, the previously mentioned W. A. Coote, devoted his life to moral reform and campaigns against the white slave trade. Coote approached his self-appointed task with Messianic zeal.[57] There were also the societies originally formed to campaign against the state regulation of prostitution, in the form of the Contagious Diseases Acts of 1864 and 1866. These acts had subjected prostitutes (but not their clients) to compulsory medical examinations for venereal disease.[58] After the repeal of the Contagious Diseases Acts in 1886, some of these societies, notably the feminist Josephine Butler's Ladies' National Association, continued their existence, broadening their scope to campaign for social purity. In addition to these, there were church-based societies for social purity such as the Anglican White Cross Society, formed by Ellice Hopkins in the 1880s to bring a higher moral standard to young men.[59] There were numerous societies aiming to protect young women. Ellice Hopkins had founded a Ladies' Association for the Care of Friendless Girls in the 1870s. The Metropolitan Association for Befriending Young Servants (MABYS) dated from 1875. Both of these had directed their efforts at the care of young girl workers in the city, aiming to keep them away from alcohol, crime and prostitution.[60]

The most successful of the societies aiming to protect young women was the Girls' Friendly Society, also dating from 1875.[61] Unlike the more forgiving MABYS, a non-sectarian organisation which, while aiming to keep young girls on the straight and narrow path of righteousness, was also involved in rescue work, the GFS stood for an uncompromising standard of purity.[62] Loss of virginity meant loss of virtue and disqualified a girl from being or becoming a member. An early attempt (in 1878–9) to soften this rule, in order to allow work with girls who repented of any 'lapse from grace', met with opposition from both the founder, Mrs Townsend, and the bishops. The society's aim was to prevent girls from 'falling'. Upper-class lady 'associates' took it upon themselves to act in a semi-maternal capacity towards unmarried, working-class girls, perceived to be in danger of being lured from virtue in factories and cities. An Anglican organisation shot through with assumptions about propriety and social deference, the GFS was astonishingly successful in the UK and even internationally, with strong links throughout the British Empire. From a base of 821 branches in 1885 it expanded to a peak of membership in 1913, with 39,926 associates and 197,493 members in England and Wales.[63]

Agnes Louisa Money, the Girls' Friendly Society's first historian, defined purity as warfare:

> Purity is *a warfare* ... and we can but strengthen and arm the young for this warfare by encouraging healthy mental activity. The love of ease, bodily and mental, the love of excitement and pleasure, the habit of having the emotions excited with no corresponding action of the other faculties, an uncontrolled imagination, a craving for escape from monotony and dullness – these are some of the dangers that lay our girls open to temptation.[64]

As well as setting up networks and relationships, meetings, lodges, residences, a circulating library and various philanthropic schemes, the GFS was responsible for a massive publishing endeavour: regular periodicals such as the monthly *Friendly Leaves*, membership journals, newsletters, tracts and improving literature of all kinds. Agnes Money explained that the aim was to combat the appeal of 'shilling shockers and penny dreadfuls', the romantic novelettes so easily available in the small shops in side streets at the time.[65] In place of the unhealthy excitement offered by these, GFS publications offered uplifting stories of moral endeavour and self-sacrifice, often illustrated with images of female saints, and with floral motifs.

White flowers, of course, carried a special symbolic charge. Snowdrops and lilies were emblems of feminine purity and heavily resorted to by Victorian sentimentalists. A separate group of organisations calling themselves Snowdrop or White Ribbon Bands flourished alongside the GFS from around 1889 to 1912, particularly among factory girls in the North and the Midlands.[66]

Miss Nunneley, promoter of the scheme and editor of the associated monthly newsletter *The Snowdrop*, explained that members promised to avoid 'wrong conversation', 'light and immodest conduct', and the reading of 'bad and foolish books'. In place of this last they were treated to heavily moralising stories with titles such as 'The Angel of the Honeysuckle', or pious poems on true womanhood by Ella Wheeler Wilcox. Reports from various localities showed that Snowdrop Bands held regular 'Blossom Nights', 'White Nights' or 'White Suppers'. Church halls would be wreathed with green and white muslin, ivy, snowdrops or white hyacinths, and the girls would sing snowdrop songs.[67] They wore ivory or enamel brooches in the shape of a snowdrop: 'the white flower of a blameless life'. Both the GFS and Snowdrop Bands adopted the practice of encouraging country members to send bunches of spring flowers to factory girls in large towns. All this flowering-plant imagery became somewhat stretched at times: *The Snowdrop* featured an obituary column under the subtitle 'Transplanted'.

The ideal of girlish innocence had been given full expression by the art critic John Ruskin in the 1860s: his *Sesame and Lilies*, first published in 1865, contained an essay on the subject of femininity, 'On Queen's Gardens', which quickly established itself as a classic statement of Victorian thinking about gender.[68] Femininity, in Ruskin's view, should be all about self-abnegation, purity and 'sweet ordering' in the home. Girls were given copies of the text, bound prettily in violet suede or green calf, on anniversaries or as school prizes. Ruskin himself had been generous in distributing copies to schoolgirls, in whose company he delighted. Ruskin's passion for youthful femininity was exemplified in a long-standing adoration of Rose la Touche, whom he first encountered when she was nine years old and proposed to (unsuccessfully) eight years later. This obsession with young girls could unsettle his aesthetic judgement: he was entranced by Kate Greenaway's prettified drawings of little girls in muslin smocks, for instance, sometimes showing an unhealthy interest in what they would look like without them.[69] In the 1880s Ruskin became a keen patron of Whitelands Teacher Training College, in London, instigating an annual May Day celebration whereby the girl students elected the 'likeablist and lovablist' of their number to serve as May Queen. The girls dressed in diaphanous frocks and garlanded each other with buttercups, dancing around a beribboned maypole.[70] Kate Greenaway designed one of the earliest dresses worn by the Whitelands May Queen. The GFS enthusiastically took up this tradition, popularising springtime displays of maidenly skipping around maypoles.

Whatever unease we may feel today about Ruskin's sexual tastes, in the late Victorian and Edwardian years the GFS, along with a host of other girl protection societies, regularly prescribed his essays as improving literature.[71] Purity workers set themselves the task of elevating rough girls into modest maidens, or 'leading giddy girls into the path of safety', as one GFS worker among factory girls in the North of England put it.[72] Many of the girls she came into contact with had been 'very rough, until the GFS tamed them', she admitted. The Reverend Carpenter, representing the Social Purity Alliance, submitted a daunting description of working girls in London:

> Let anyone go, for instance, along Commercial Road in the evening and see the awful roughness and want of modesty – the horrible loss of all that we think most tender and beautiful and pure in womanhood – among the rough girls that congregate in that road, and push their way and pass their horrid jokes.[73]

1.3 The May Day festivities at Whitelands College inspired by the art critic John Ruskin, 1889. Pen and ink drawing by an anonymous student (by kind permission of Whitelands College, University of Roehampton).

1.4 Elsie Ryall, crowned May Queen at Whitelands College in 1911 (photograph by kind permission of Whitelands College, University of Roehampton).

Any contradiction between the idea of girls as frail flowers and girls as warriors for purity tended to be overlooked. Later into the twentieth century, following the years of suffragette militancy and the impressive contribution to war work made by women between 1914 and 1918, this 'feminine frailty' idea started to wear a little thin. In 1919, for instance, the GFS mounted a full-scale 'White Crusade': a nationwide Battle for Purity. 'We are no longer a fold, but an army,' leaders declared. Although the GFS was far too conservative to lend any support to demands for women's suffrage, this new direction seemed to draw on suffrage activism, and particularly on the suffragette genius for display. The GFS leaders, following the suffragettes, mounted pageants and processions, and organised mass meetings and rallies. At a GFS celebration in the Albert Hall in 1921, for instance, battalions of girls dressed in virginal white and veiled in blue carried banners and processed, with their company forming the Sign of the Cross.[74]

Many late Victorian moralists saw girls as either innocent, or 'fallen'. The imagery was white and black. The loss of innocence – that is, of virginity – was generally regarded as a crucial turning point. Salvation Army records of girls and young women seeking shelter with the organisation from the 1880s, for instance, give case histories in the form of completed questionnaires. 'How long Fallen?' was one of the first questions.[75] Even so, the Salvation Army – as its name implied – allowed for reclamation: 'Has she given evidence of being saved?' asked a question towards the end of the record. In contrast, the GFS made no provision for repentance. Fallen girls could not become members, and members who fell were expelled. Repeated attempts to soften this hard GFS line on chastity failed. Those who pushed for change argued that the chastity rule contradicted the idea of forgiveness and failed in the spirit of Christian charity. But reformers were only successful in changing the rule as late as 1936, and even then this was in the teeth of strong opposition, and many of the old guard resigned.[76]

In Victorian culture, the fallen girl was doomed. We think of Thomas Hardy's *Tess of the D'Urbervilles*, or of pregnant housemaids drowning themselves in millponds. There are strong associations between the ideas of sexual and of social ruin: as in discussions of white slavery, the stereotypes of upper-class rake and simple country girl come easily to mind. Purity workers in the 1890s and 1900s sometimes shared these assumptions. If the loss of chastity went unpunished by ruin, then many assumed that a fallen girl herself became a danger to others, liable to contaminate their innocence with her own knowledge of the world. There was a notion that sexual knowledge corrupted once and for all: that once having experienced intercourse, a woman would lose her most precious asset, become knowing, and never regain her virtue.

There was a great deal of sexual ignorance, especially before the First World War. Sex education barely existed in any formal sense, and any idea that it should be taught in schools would have horrified most people. Some feminists thought that girls' ignorance of the facts of life increased their vulnerability. There is a hint of this, for instance, in Elizabeth Robins's novel *Where Are You Going To?* Purity workers were divided on the question. Some believed that knowledge would help forearm a girl and hence protect her virtue. Others felt exactly the opposite: that sex education would inflame curiosity, stimulate impure thoughts, and increase susceptibility to corruption. The perils of going public with 'radical ideas' on the subject of sex education were illustrated by a controversy which blew up in Derbyshire in 1913.[77] Miss Outram, responsible for an elementary school in the village of Dronfield, was teaching Scripture when her pupils asked her questions about pregnancy and childbirth. After giving the matter some careful thought she responded by reading them two stories. The first, heavily laced with references to God, touched on the matter of eggs and seeds and the beginnings of life. The second story was a stern moral warning against temptation, underscoring the importance of chastity and self-control. This was a careful enough response, one might imagine, but parents were outraged and the neighbourhood erupted in scandal. The school managers took the line that Miss Outram had corrupted childhood innocence. Some parents contended that Miss Outram had not only passed unsuitable knowledge to their daughters, but

that these girls had then gone on to exercise a corrupting influence on younger siblings. Many families withdrew their children
from the school. The episode illustrates not only the contentious-
ness of ideas about sex instruction, but also the strength of the
widespread belief that innocence actually *depended* on ignorance
of the facts of life.

Nevertheless, accounts of girls' sexual experience before marriage in this period show a much more complex picture than
purity workers often painted. Of course evidence isn't always easy
to come by. There is fragmentary evidence from refuges, homes
for 'female penitents' and shelters for 'fallen women'. These
accounts were often shaped by a sense of what was required, and
there were undoubtedly many situations in which girls needed
above all to look penitent. The Salvation Army statement books
mentioned above are a case in point: young women seeking
shelter are likely to have framed their responses according to
what they thought would yield the best result. Moreover, the
responses to the questions will have been filled in – and so
shaped by – Salvation Army workers. Answers to the question
'Cause of First Fall' show an unsurprising mixture of innocence,
regret and, only occasionally, defiance. But there is very little high
drama. 'Flirting with a lad' was a common enough response.
One suspects the reply 'Bad companions and natural depravity'
to have come from interviewer rather than applicant. Undermining the stereotype of the ravaged innocent, one poor woman
confessed that she had 'fallen' after walking out with the same
man for a full nine years.[78]

A richer source of evidence comes from an inquiry carried
out in the early years of the First World War and published
as *Downward Paths* in 1916.[79] The study was introduced by the
Anglican preacher and suffragist Maude Royden. It represented

the researches of a group of women medical and social workers
(who judged it prudent to remain anonymous), who set out to
consider the reasons why some women turned to prostitution.
About 830 case histories went into the book, which maintained an
intelligent, sympathetic and non-judgemental tone. Pre-marital
sex wasn't always shameful and disastrous, the authors pointed
out: there were parts of Britain where it was pretty much accepted as normal. Indeed, far from being passive victims of male
lust, women might even take the initiative in sex. Girls could
be just as sexually curious as boys, although the penalties for
'going astray' were worse for the female sex. Young girls living
in poverty often sought colour and adventure to perk up their
lives: 'To girls, the temptations of curiosity and of the awakening sex-instinct go often hand in hand with the possibilities of
gain, and money means so much to those who want variety,
colour, life ...'[80]

Girls' love of clothes and adornment should not be simply
condemned as moral weakness, the authors insisted – it was self-
respect that made many of them anxious to dress well.[81] Equally,
young working girls might be encouraged by attentions from
men in uniform, or gentlemen of a higher social class, because
they hoped to better themselves. Was this really such a crime?
'Going with a gentleman' might look like a safe option, and a
well-dressed man might 'throw a glamour over the transaction'
in the eyes of someone young and hopeful.[82] This was all pretty
radical, liberal stuff, and yet Royden and her co-authors went
even further. Social workers dealing with the *casualties* of prostitution saw only part of the picture, they suggested. Some women
undoubtedly did well for themselves and lived an independent
lifestyle. Others married and settled down with men who were
happy to keep them. Definitions of prostitution, and the borders

around respectable behaviour, were rarely as clear as moralists insisted. After all, Royden cautiously suggested, there was a sense in which marriage itself was a kind of economic bargain, with the wife being kept in exchange for sexual services. There were different ways in which women might profit from sex. One story in the book, for instance, referred to two enterprising girls who for a number of seasons had worked on a cruise ship running between England and America:

> They were most popular girls, the life of the ship and the pets of all the old ladies; 'women you could really make friends with', the men used to say. They would pick and choose their men, and a man might pursue them unsuccessfully during a whole voyage. By their earnings as prostitutes they supported a father and a brother who was at a University, while their family believed they were journalists. During the winter they dropped their profession, and the ship's officers would visit them as friends.[83]

Downward Paths questioned contemporary stereotypes and unsettled assumptions at every point. Maude Royden argued that panic – based on ignorance – had too often governed policy, as in the case of the 1912 Criminal Law Amendment Act. Panic about white slavery had shaped public attitudes to sex. Citing Teresa Billington-Greig's researches and similar studies, she emphasised yet again that cases of forcible abduction were extremely rare, pointing out that 'a weeping and reluctant girl is not an easily marketable asset'. Nonetheless

> Incredible and even grotesque stories were told and believed on the slenderest authority, or on no authority at all. The only demand was that they should be sufficiently frightful. Newspapers and bookstalls were deluged with articles, pamphlets

and books narrating horrors and proposing remedies as preposterous – and sometimes as horrible – as the disease.[84]

None of this was to deny that procuring existed, Royden continued, still less that girls might be drawn into prostitution through poverty and despair. But procurers had no need for chloroform or syringes, their victims had usually been rendered 'helpless enough by poverty and misfortune and apply to him [the procurer] as they might to the foreman of a relief works'. The procurer was 'less the orchard thief than the blow-fly settling on fallen fruit'. Were every procurer to be flogged to death, it was unlikely that prostitution would be exterminated.[85]

To Royden and her co-authors, the way forward was through education, social work and careful studies of the circumstances leading some girls into prostitution. Their own study is something of a landmark in understanding not just prostitution, but the sexual behaviour of young women of the day. The case histories in *Downward Paths* provide snapshots of the circumstances and options facing individual young girls in the 1900s. The girls in *Downward Paths* have agency: however difficult their circumstances, they are not just victims, and they do make choices in their lives. Their stories dispel the high drama associated with tales of 'falling' and 'ruin'. They are life histories seen not in moral terms of black and white, but in human terms, with many shades in between.

Maude Royden was equally well aware that the furore over white slavery owed a great deal to the rise of the women's movement. Women's groups dedicated to suppression of the white slave trade had mushroomed across Britain between 1900 and 1913, coinciding with the rise of militant suffragism. The image of a young girl enslaved by the predatory male could be central to feminism, especially when linked to ideas about social purity. White slavery not only served as a metaphor for the sexual oppression of women by men. In the minds and writings of many this was *the* great social evil of the day, and one which could only be remedied once women obtained the vote. 'Votes for Women' and 'Purity for Men' were twin demands in Christabel Pankhurst's manifesto. Many feminists believed that once women had the vote there would be an end, once and for all, to prostitution.

But the image of the girl as victim had an altogether wider appeal. It was reassuring to anti-suffragists, who believed in feminine frailty and who contended that women and girls were vulnerable without male protection. Arthur Lee, proponent of the 1912 parliamentary bill against 'White Slavery', had emphasised that staunch opponents of women's suffrage such as himself were under a special obligation to clamp down on 'those sinister creatures who batten upon commercialised vice, and who make a profitable business out of kidnapping, decoying and ruining ... unwilling girls'.[86] Moreover the image of the girl as innocent, and as vulnerable, had undeniable erotic charge. Stead's highly coloured account of 'The Maiden Tribute of Modern Babylon' had been shot through with near-pornographic descriptions of hardened rakes enjoying the helpless cries of panicked girl-children. A mixture of moral outrage and obsessive focus on the details of degradation has proved common in accounts of white slavery, even in more modern historical writing. Of course, publishers have not been slow to capitalise on this. In the 1960s, for instance, the paperback edition of the historian Charles Terrot's account of white slavery was presented as a shock-horror text about lust, depravity and the flesh-markets of Europe. The lurid blurb on the cover promised the reader 'Innocent girls – completely ignorant of sex – captured by trickery – abducted by force – compelled to submit to the corrupt and degraded desires of men sunk in vice and perversion ...'[87] And so forth, which presumably did no harm to the book's sales at the time.

With hindsight, then, it was no coincidence that the moral panic about white slavery coincided with the rise of the women's movement, and particularly with the militant campaign for women's suffrage. At a time when women were undoubtedly getting stronger, and becoming more assertive politically, it suited a range of interest groups, for very diverse reasons, to represent girls as frightened, as oppressed, or as victims.

2 | UNWOMANLY TYPES: NEW WOMEN, REVOLTING DAUGHTERS AND REBEL GIRLS

The British campaign for women's suffrage grew out of a new mood of self-assertion among women. This new mood was clearly evident in late Victorian society, and it was reflected in controversies over 'the woman question' and 'the new woman' in the 1890s. Part journalistic and fictional stereotype, part a reflection of social trends, the hallmark of the New Woman was that she rejected the mid-Victorian ideal of the Angel in the House. She would not be content with domesticity and self-sacrifice. She sought self-development instead.

This new era was heralded by the production of Henrik Ibsen's famous play *A Doll's House*, first performed in Britain in 1889.[1] The play's heroine, Nora, is patronised and infantilised by her husband Torvald, who treats her as a plaything. Nora's realisation that without independence and self-respect she cannot be a good wife or mother leads her to walk out on her home and family. Into the waste basket went Ruskin's prescriptions for wifely submissiveness as Nora slammed the door of the doll's house behind her and strode into the world. Feminists were inspired. The more conventional in the audience were appalled.

The controversy over the New Woman was not just about marriage: much of it focused on education and girlhood. Middle-class daughters were seen to be getting restless, which generated a lively correspondence in the periodical literature of the time. In 1894, an article entitled 'The Revolt of the Daughters' by the majestically named Blanche Alethea Crackenthorpe contended that there was a crisis in family relationships.[2] Daughters hungered after education and travel, seeking wider horizons. But the wise mother, Mrs Crackenthorpe insisted, knew the importance of protecting her daughter's innocence and reputation, and hence her chances of marriage. The article provoked responses from like-minded mothers (such as the conservative literary hostess Lady Jeune)[3] in addition to particularly spirited rebuttals from younger women and feminists, who were immediately dubbed the 'revolting daughters'. Alys Pearsall Smith (soon to become the first wife of philosopher Bertrand Russell) was hot in her defence of the daughters, who, she insisted, had a right to lives of their own. She thought that too many girls were forced to sacrifice themselves to household duty, frittering their lives away on trivialities. It was a form of mental starvation.[4] Others agreed with her. The idea of caging girls up in conservatories, like hothouse plants or pet songbirds, was senseless, declared Gertrude Hemery, another rebel daughter. Confinement made girls vulnerable rather than protecting their 'purity', she argued.[5] Another feminist, Sarah Amos, agreed but went further, emphasising the importance of social class. Whereas middle-class parents seemed obsessed by the need to protect their daughters' virtue by limiting their movements, most working-class girls went about independently by the age of fifteen or sixteen. A great deal of girls' ill-health or 'delicacy' was due to repression, she insisted. Boys, too, would be prone to 'hysteria' if their lives were hedged in by so many constraints.[6]

There is a brisk tone about the writing of these 'revolting daughters'. Their arguments are robust and unapologetic. This in itself reflects the strength of the late Victorian woman's movement. About three decades earlier, a young – and desperate – Florence Nightingale had given vent to her feelings of frustration and despair about the position of the middle-class daughter-at-home. She had similarly seen her life and the lives of girls in comparable circumstances as representing enforced passivity and intellectual starvation. Sacrificing girls on the altar of domestic duty was like crippling them, she had insisted. It was the mental equivalent of the Chinese practice of binding girls' feet.[7] Florence Nightingale had been dissuaded from publishing her essay 'Cassandra' by contemporaries (largely male) who had found it too bitter and polemical. Her arguments had clearly anticipated those expressed by the revolting daughters of the 1890s. But the feminists of the 1890s sound altogether more confident. Florence Nightingale's essay reads like a howl of pain from an isolated individual. The tone of the revolting daughters conveys awareness that they are by no means alone in their views. The women's movement had given them the voice of confidence.

At the end of the 1920s, writing what was effectively the first general history of the Victorian women's movement (*The Cause*), Ray Strachey entitled the first chapter of her book 'The Prison House of Home'. She observed that 'The first stirrings of the feminist movement began through the awakening of individual women to their own uselessness.'[8] According to Strachey, the growing realisation that many women shared similar views about the powerlessness of their social situation and what should be done about it brought 'a freemasonry of understanding'. This was the base of a feminist movement, 'the Cause'. Much had been achieved in the second half of the nineteenth century. There had been significant progress in widening opportunities for both the education and the employment of women. Political agitation had centred on married women's property rights, child custody arrangements, the fight for a single standard of sexual morality, and of course demands for the vote.

Advances in education, in particular, fostered confidence in the girls and young women of the 1890s and 1900s. This increase in confidence marked them out as a new generation, enjoying opportunities which had not been there for their mothers. Around mid-century, provision for basic schooling had been patchy. Girls' secondary education had barely existed. Private establishments (ladies' academies) were mainly in the business of grooming girls for marriage. After the Education Act of 1870, most working-class girls received some kind of elementary education, however basic. In contrast, many middle-class girls stayed at home, where they devoted themselves to helping their mothers and to family duties. Well-off families would employ a governess, but it was comparatively rare to send girls away to school.[9]

The plight of those who failed to marry could be miserable. If the family was well off, unmarried daughters might spend long hours on the kind of pursuits derided by Florence Nightingale as pointless. These included every variety of fancywork such as crochet, beading and pokerwork (the scorching of designs on velvet). Seaweed and ferns could be pressed into albums. Flowers might be fashioned from wool, coloured wax or seashells. Seashells could be glued on to boxes. Bouquets fashioned from seashells could be arranged under glass domes, *ad infinitum*. Where money was lacking, and there was a limited budget for servants, daughters could take on domestic work, although too much of this would compromise the middle-class status of the family. The occurrence in a family of too many unmarried daughters, or a father's untimely death, could precipitate real crisis. Then, a spinster daughter might be farmed out to the household of other relatives, or have to face the terrifying fact that she would have to earn her own living. Here, very few options were available to middle-class girls, apart from governessing.[10]

The often miserable fate of the down-at-heel governess was of course a standard theme of mid-Victorian literature.

The urge to widen the options available to girls who could not, or did not choose to marry was central to middle-class feminism. Improving education was crucial. One of the movement's most effective educational campaigners was Emily Davies.[11] Uncompromising in principle, Davies was an intrepid opportunist in strategy, employing all manner of tactics and relentless pressure in pursuit of her goals. It was Emily Davies who made sure that a government inquiry into the state of middle-class education in 1864 inspected girls' schools, along with boys'. It was Emily Davies who saw the importance of girls taking the same public examinations as boys, in order to prove that their brains were up to it. And at a time when the very idea of a woman's college in the universities tended to be greeted 'with shouts', it was Emily Davies who successfully navigated the foundation of Girton College, Cambridge. This was the first residential college for women, beginning its life in a small house in the village of Hitchin in 1869. Emily Davies's skill in disarming opposition became legendary. For instance, she would counter any objection that brainy women were ugly and unwomanly by seating the prettiest girls on the front benches at examination times.

Emily Davies was one of the most persistent of those working to widen educational opportunities for girls, but the movement included many effective campaigners, both women and men. Between them they employed a wide range of strategies and approaches. Two of the earliest ventures designed to improve girls' education were Queen's College (1848) and Bedford College (1849), both in London. Queen's College came about through the initiative of Frederick Denison Maurice, an academic and Christian Socialist. Bedford's founder was a wealthy widow, Mrs Elizabeth

Reid, who was keen to ensure that her college, unlike Queen's (which was controlled by men) should be governed entirely by women. Two young women in particular, Frances Mary Buss and Dorothea Beale, both former students at Queen's, went on to distinguish themselves as headmistresses of new, academically achieving girls' schools, the North London Collegiate School, and Cheltenham Ladies' College respectively. These schools (and their headmistresses) were very different. Cheltenham was exclusive. Miss Beale, very class-conscious, welcomed applications from parents who were gentlefolk but drew the line at 'daughters of trade'. Miss Buss, on the other hand, was all in favour of widening access, especially for clever girls. The two schools became in effect templates for new kinds of institution.[12]

Education for middle-class girls began to lose its genteel domestic, drawing-room atmosphere. The newer girls' schools started to look more like the institutions we recognise as schools today. There were purpose-built classrooms and corridors; rulebooks, timetables, subjects and termly reports. In some cases there were even laboratories, sports fields and halls for gym. After 1872, founders of another new venture, the Girls' Public Day School Company (originally a limited liability company, later a trust) worked to establish a network of high schools for girls throughout Britain.[13]

At the tertiary level, Josephine Butler and Anne Jemima Clough promoted university lectures for ladies in the North of England. Miss Clough, and the Cambridge academic Henry Sidgwick worked to establish Newnham College, Cambridge. Similar efforts in Oxford led to the foundation of Somerville and Lady Margaret Hall. An important milestone was passed in 1878, when the University of London became the first university in the UK to open its degrees to women. Others followed.[14] Women students were often dubbed 'undergraduettes' and housed in separate buildings and hostels. They were carefully superintended by Lady Tutors lest they should get too friendly with the men.[15]

By the 1890s, intelligent middle-class girls had many more options than had been available in the 1840s and 1850s. If their parents were supportive (and willing and able to cough up around £16 per year – around £1,000 in today's terms), they might attend a good secondary school and even qualify for college or university. Opportunities for professional training were still limited, but teaching in an efficient secondary school was a much better prospect than becoming a governess in a private home. An ambitious girl could take inspiration from recent successes and role models. Feminists rejoiced, for instance, when Agnata Frances Ramsay from Girton College achieved an outstanding first in the classical tripos at Cambridge in 1887. None of the male candidates had achieved higher than the second class in that year. Even the satirical magazine *Punch*, normally quick to poke fun at feminism, was generous. It published a cartoon showing a woman being shown into a first-class railway carriage marked 'Ladies Only'.[16] Three years later, Newnham College's Philippa Fawcett, daughter of the prominent suffragist Millicent Garrett Fawcett, achieved a brilliant success in the mathematical tripos. Her score was considerably higher than that of the man who took the prize for being top ('senior wrangler') that year. Women, however, were not eligible for the title. They were not even allowed to graduate in Cambridge until 1948. Nevertheless, successes of this kind helped to mark this restriction out as an injustice.

Girls who left home to spend time at college or university often recorded a sense of intoxication at their new-found freedom. There was the delight in arranging and decorating a room one could call one's own.[17] Letters home often brimmed with details about colour schemes, cushions, firescreens and potted plants. There was the pleasure of reading widely and having access to libraries and to other intelligent minds. There was time to exercise, to play team games or simply to explore the surrounding neighbourhood on foot or bicycle. Then there were cocoa parties, late at night, when girls could sit up talking about ideas, ideals and friendships. And there were the varied social and cultural activities associated with turn-of-the-century universities, literary and debating societies, and so forth. Before the First World War, many of these societies were single-sex, but outside the more traditional universities of Oxford and Cambridge there were more opportunities for female students to fraternise, daringly, with young men.[18] Girls at college wrote enthusiastic letters home and reported on their new-found freedoms and privileges in articles which were published in school magazines. The word got around that even for the serious-minded, college could be fun.

The career of Sophie Bryant (née Willock) illustrates some of the new possibilities for women that were brought about by educational reform.[19] Bryant was born near Dublin in 1850. Her father, a mathematician, gave her lessons as a girl but she received no formal schooling. The family then moved to London, and at the age of sixteen Sophie won a scholarship to Bedford College. She married three years later, but her husband died soon afterwards: at twenty years old, she found herself a widow. In 1875 Sophie Bryant was appointed to teach mathematics by Frances Buss, headmistress of North London Collegiate School. She proved an inspirational and supportive teacher, encouraging a steady stream of pupils to go on to study mathematics at Girton. Bryant also worked for her own degree, and in 1881 was awarded a BSc from London University. In 1884 she distinguished herself as the first woman to be awarded the university's DSc. Bryant succeeded Miss Buss as headmistress of North London Collegiate School in 1895. By then she was a well-known figure in educational circles, much respected and well-liked. One of the first women to take up cycling, she was also fond of rowing and climbing mountains. She was an ardent suffragist. In many ways Sophie Bryant was a perfect example of the New Woman.

An affectionate portrayal of the New Woman appears in George Bernard Shaw's play *Mrs Warren's Profession* (1894). Mrs Warren's daughter, Vivie, has studied at Girton: she is strong-minded, confident and self-possessed. She has a backslapping manner and a terrifyingly vigorous handshake. Shaw grounds his play in contemporary history. There are references to 'Philippa Sumners' (Philippa Fawcett), and her distinction in being placed 'ahead of the Senior Wrangler'. Vivie is shown as intellectually able and worldly to boot: she calculates whether the effort which must go into examination success is worth it from a monetary point of view. There is no sentimentality in her make-up. Eschewing personal relationships, she seeks her salvation in work. Literary and journalistic stereotypes of the New Woman tended to mock and to satirise as much as they reflected reality. 'Girton Girls' were depicted as going bicycling in masculine tweeds or slouching in armchairs, sloshing whisky and brandishing latch-keys. Women writers bore some of the responsibility for this. 'George Egerton' was the pseudonym of Mary Chavelita Dunne, whose short stories, particularly in a volume entitled *Keynotes*, became one of the literary sensations of the 1890s.[20] George Egerton's style owed much to her enthusiasm for Scandinavian writers: Ibsen, Strindberg and Knut Hamsun. Her stories set out to explore what she saw as the *terra incognita* of the female self, unadulterated by male imaginings. Her female characters are 'good chaps', they use slangy expressions and are prone to broody silences, and to going fishing. The stories were an immediate hit in Britain and America. Their awkward modishness and lack of humour made them a gift to satirists. *Punch* responded with 'She-Notes', by 'Borgia Smudgiton' (Owen Seaman), and cartoons and parodies multiplied.[21]

In 1895 the minor novelist Grant Allen hit a cultural nerve with *The Woman Who Did*.[22] The novel featured Herminia, the daughter of a clergyman, whose Cambridge education led to advanced ideas and a belief in 'free love'. When her daughter failed to understand her, the miserable Herminia swallowed prussic acid and put an end to it all. Grant Allen declared himself a feminist, but many feminists were scornful and keen to distance themselves from both his ideas and his book. Millicent Garrett Fawcett, for instance, loftily declared that free love had nothing whatsoever to do with feminism.[23] Novels and plays and journalism about the New Woman fed on themselves, with a repertoire of well-rehearsed imagery and constant reference to each other – for example, *The Woman Who Did*, *The Woman Who Didn't*, *The Woman Who Wouldn't Do*.[24] The historian exploring this literature can find herself in a hall of mirrors facing multiple distortions of reality. There were however some constants. The New Woman, even if not a Girton Girl, was likely to be highly educated and to have a mind – and a voice – of her own. For anti-feminists, this was part of the problem: in their view, womanliness required gentle submission. Vociferous critics of the New Woman genre saw its heroines as desexualised, victims of an overblown passion for learning. They condemned this literature as decadent, morbid and hysterical.[25]

By the 1890s, the gains that women had made in education had unsettled many. There was growing unease about whether education made girls unladylike. College photographs from the 1890s tend to show girls wearing stiff collars and ties over long tailored skirts. The fashion was manly and austere but practical. Few went so far as to espouse bloomers, or the bifurcated garments recommended for bicycling by advocates of Rational Dress.[26] Some college women were stylish and fashionable, taking great care over their appearance – sometimes deliberately to disarm criticism. In Newnham College, for instance, a young Mary Paley Marshall wore flowing Pre-Raphaelite gowns. In later life Mrs Marshall nostalgically recalled sitting dressmaking with classics scholar Jane Harrison. They were embroidering tennis dresses: Jane's decorated with pomegranates, Mary's with a design of Virginia creeper.[27] But women academics could also be deplorably dowdy. Student Winnie Seebohm wrote home from Newnham in the 1880s to complain about the appearance of her history tutor, Alice Gardner:

> You *should* see Miss Gardner's get-up – droopy straw hat, Shet-land shawl thrown on without any grace, and big heel-less felt slippers in which she shuffles along. Then she evidently uses no mirror for her toilet, for this morning she came down with the ends of her hair sticking straight out like a cow's tail – she drags it back tight, twists it, and sticks one hair pin through. The style of dress here is certainly *not* elegant.[28]

Alice Gardner's disdain for fashionable clothing became legendary. Lecturing in Bristol during the First World War involved her in regular train journeys. On one occasion, she sat on a railway bench, took off her hat and nodded off. Passers-by, struck by her dowdy appearance, took pity on her and chucked their spare change into the hat.[29] Some women who went to college in this period reported a climate in which too much attention to clothing and appearance was seen to indicate a lack of high-mindedness or serious purpose. But this could be misinterpreted. Both Emily Davies at Girton and Anne Jemima Clough, the first Principal of Newnham, laboured to persuade the girls in their charge to dress in a modest but feminine fashion, to stave off charges of pseudo-masculinity or eccentricity.[30]

Allegations that higher education encouraged girls to dress and deport themselves like males led to controversy about what was meant by femininity. Was it feminine to be clever or ambitious? Those Victorians who judged womanliness to depend on self-sacrifice thought not. In 1890 a two-volume English translation of the diaries of Marie Bashkirtseff, a young girl who had been living in Paris, caused a sensation in literary London.[31] The beautiful and talented Bashkirtseff had died of consumption in 1884. When she died, she was only twenty-five years old. A gifted painter and writer, Marie Bashkirtseff had kept an intimate journal since her childhood. In this she had recorded every detail of her ambitions, fears and fluctuating emotions. These confessions enthralled readers across Europe. Those who cherished a view of girlhood as all sweetness and innocence were horrified. Photographs of Bashkirtseff show her looking demure and extremely pretty, but her views were strong-minded and staunchly feminist. She wrote of her ambition, above all, to avoid the domestic fate of the ordinary woman:

> To marry and have children? Any washerwoman can do that ... What do I want? I want GLORY.[32]

The newspaper editor W. T. Stead, now widely seen as a champion of young girls' innocence and purity, was certainly unsettled.[33] Recognising Bashkirtseff's cleverness, he confessed that he found her writings 'poisoned by egotism' and altogether unwomanly. He claimed that in reading her journal, he was never quite sure whether she was posing, theatrically or melodramatically, or whether he was reading the 'genuine outpourings of a girl's heart'. He judged her undisciplined, and blamed her parents for having 'over-trained' and 'overstrained' her, for having failed to teach her self-control. Stead judged that 'Marie Bashkirtseff might have been a splendid woman if she had ever been broken in'.[34] George Bernard Shaw responded to Stead's review by taking up cudgels on behalf of Bashkirtseff, whom he saw as a kind of Ibsenite heroine.[35] Self-sacrificing women were always a drag, he insisted: Bashkirtseff was understandably rebelling against the phoney notion that womanliness depended on a capacity for self-obliteration.

Marie Bashkirtseff's writing raises basic questions about the nature of gender and femininity. 'I have nothing of the woman about me but the envelope,' she asserted, 'and that envelope is deucedly feminine. As for the rest, that's quite another affair.'[36] Was femininity merely a question of dressing up, then, nothing more than a performance?[37]

To castigate clever young women as self-deluded egotists was common enough. But late Victorian anxiety about the 'unsexing' effects of higher education extended further, into pseudo-science. From the 1870s onwards, doctors and evolutionary thinkers started to raise the possibility that higher education was damaging to women's bodies. One of the earliest to think along these lines was the sociologist Herbert Spencer, who suggested that high-pressure education might enfeeble women and render them unattractive to men.[38] In America, in 1875, Dr Edward Clarke fired a notorious broadside with the publication of *Sex in Education; or, A Fair Chance for Girls*. In this he complained that higher education was destroying girls. It was directly responsible for a whole catalogue of horrors, such as 'leucorrhoea, amenorrhoea, dysmenorrhoea, chronic and acute ovaritis, prolapsus uteri, hysteria, neuralgia and the like ...'[39] He himself, he claimed, had seen many instances of girls who were excellent scholars but who turned into pallid, hysterical women. They were tic-ridden invalids begging for opium, chloral and bromides. Sometimes their brains rotted and as adult women they were frequently sterile. Schools encouraging women to perform intellectually were encouraging girls in 'slow suicide' and threatening the continuation of the race.

Foremost in Clarke's defence in the UK was the psychologist Dr Henry Maudsley, of University College London, who aired his views in the journal *Fortnightly Review*.[40] Feminists were deluding themselves because 'They cannot choose but to be women; cannot rebel successfully against the tyranny of their organisation,' Maudsley asserted somewhat opaquely.[41] Like Clarke, Maudsley kept referring to 'the woman's apparatus', meaning her reproductive system. Girls had to rest during adolescence in order to let their 'reproductive apparatus' get started. If they insisted on study, their energies were diverted, and these bits might atrophy. Being female wasn't just a matter of dress, Maudsley pontificated, although some intellectual women with 'wasted organs' might try to disguise this with 'dressmakers' aids'.[42] This was a rather sinister insinuation. He probably meant padded bosoms.

In England several doctors fell over themselves to agree with Clarke and Maudsley. The President of the British Medical Association Dr Withers-Moore was one of them.[43] A number were specialists in gynaecology and obstetrics, such as John Thorburn, Professor of Obstetrics in Manchester, and Robert Lawson Tait, sometime president of the British Gynaecological Society. Both elaborated on Clarke's views and asserted that higher-educated women were a danger to themselves and to the race. Others, such as the Edinburgh psychiatrist T. S. Clouston, wholeheartedly agreed.[44] A great deal of scaremongering followed. Thorburn, for instance, occupied the Chair of Obstetrics in Manchester just as women were being admitted as students. When one of the first female students to register, Annie Eastwood, died tragically of tuberculosis before completing her studies, Thorburn contended publicly that her death was caused by over-education.[45]

The battle for women's medical education had been particularly hard-fought, but some gains were evident by the 1870s. The London School of Medicine for Women was founded in 1874, and after 1877, female medical students could complete their clinical training in London at the Royal Free Hospital.[46] Male doctors in Victorian times were insecure socially and professionally and there is no doubt that some felt threatened by women's determination to practise medicine. Obstetricians and gynaecologists might well have feared losing women patients who would feel easier with a female doctor. The idea that women were biologically unfit for study appealed to such men.

Women educators were forced to defend themselves. Elizabeth Garrett Anderson was the first woman doctor to qualify in Britain. She became a member of the British Medical Association in 1873. A vote to exclude any further women members ensured that she remained the only woman on the register for the following nineteen years.[47] But Elizabeth's lonely position conveyed a certain status and strategic advantage. She was able to contest Maudsley's opinions in public, for instance. Urged by her friends Emily Davies and Frances Buss, she replied to his article in the *Fortnightly Review* with brisk common sense.[48] Morbidity and hysteria were less common in educated girls than in those bored to death by a lack of meaningful occupation, she suggested. It was interesting that doctors emphasised the fragility of the middle-class girl, showing little concern for her working-class equivalents in domestic service. Girls were not necessarily enfeebled by menstruation, Garrett Anderson insisted. In any case, the burden of their intellectual work in higher education would become a lot lighter if men would stop opposing women every inch of the way.

Edward Clarke's views had dismayed women educationalists in America. In Boston, a group led by Annie G. Howes set out to collect evidence which would reassure the public that university-educated women were perfectly able to stay healthy and to mother children. Their report was published in 1885.[49] In England, this inspired Mrs Sidgwick, Vice-Principal and later Principal of Newnham College, to attempt a similar venture. Under her lead, a small group of women academics set out to investigate the health of some five hundred women who had studied in Oxford and Cambridge, using their non-student sisters or cousins as a control group.[50] The writer and poet Emily Pfeiffer was similarly encouraged by the Boston study to collect a mass of evidence and opinion on the subject of women's health, work and higher education.[51] Neither study found any evidence to suggest that women were rendered infertile or otherwise physically damaged by university work. Doctors more sympathetic to the women's cause included Queen Victoria's physician, Sir William Gull, and Professor Lionel Beale at King's College Hospital. These insisted that they saw no danger in women seeking higher education.[52] But the panic didn't easily die down.

One of the implications of this panic was that women school-teachers and headmistresses had to take particular care over the health and physical well-being of their charges. Most middle-class girls' schools – such as those run by the Girls' Public Day School

Trust (GPDST) – instituted regular medical inspections and kept detailed records of pupils' health.[53] A great deal of consideration went into thinking about the role of games, gymnastics and physical exercise in the curriculum. This careful regulation extended into higher education. Following Annie Eastwood's death in Manchester the university authorities insisted on parents of female students signing health disclaimers before entry.[54] The demand for properly qualified medical women who would serve the new girls' schools and colleges increased.[55]

Among women, there was widespread mistrust of professional men – doctors, academics and clergymen – some of whom had played an important strategic role in frustrating women's access to higher education. This mistrust combined with a growing disillusionment with male politicians to foster a new and less compromising phase in feminism after 1900. This was the era of the 'rebel women', some of whom focused their entire lives on fighting for the vote. A determination to fight with 'deeds, not words' reflected impatience with the lack of progress brought about by many years of careful argument and persuasion. The Women's Social and Political Union (WSPU) was founded in Manchester in 1903, with Emmeline Pankhurst and her daughter Christabel taking a leading role in its affairs. It marked a new departure and a new resolve.[56] In its early years the WSPU had strong ties with socialism and the Independent Labour Party (ILP). It attracted powerful support from women textile workers in the North of England. These working-class feminists had a very different background from the mostly middle-class leaders of the movement to open higher education and the professions to women. Many had started work when barely out of childhood, and for them work was often an oppressive necessity rather than a right to be fought for.[57] For such women, the fight for the vote was, at least in the first instance, a route to improving working conditions and fighting for a better standard of living rather than a ticket into higher education.

Working- and middle-class women nonetheless found themselves shoulder to shoulder, making common cause in their struggle for the vote. Between 1900 and 1914, feminism swelled into a mass movement, loud and impossible to ignore. There were spectacular demonstrations and processions – the suffrage procession mounted for the Coronation in 1911 numbered some 40,000–50,000 women and produced some stunning pageantry and street theatre. It was estimated to have been seven miles long.[58] The leaders of the Liberal government prevaricated and were evasive about plans to give women the vote. The suffragettes – unlike the more constitutionally minded suffragists, who put their faith in reason and debate – resorted to direct action. They began with heckling and disruption, and there were battles with the police in Parliament Square. They escalated their tactics, with stone throwing and attacks on property. Such tactics were met with violence and imprisonment. Denied the right to be treated as political prisoners, suffragettes in gaol went on hunger strike and were subjected to the humiliation and brutality of being strapped down and forcibly fed with tubes inserted down the nose or throat.

Many suffragettes dressed carefully, not least in order to look feminine and disarm the opposition. They were sensitive to media caricatures of feminists as harridans. Countering such representations, Emmeline Pankhust was always stylish, resembling an Edwardian society hostess in pleated silks, lace and velvets. This complemented her natural beauty. Rebecca West marvelled at Mrs Pankhurst's 'pale delicacy', and her 'pansy-shaped face' with 'a kind of velvety bloom on the expression'.[59]

2.1 Girl suffragette in Trafalgar Square, London, 1900s (photograph ©
Chusseau Flaviens/George Eastman House/Getty Images).

But militancy never looked womanly, and the less ladylike the
women's behaviour, the worse was their treatment at the hands
of the authorities. Working-class suffragists might be treated
particularly harshly. The well-connected Lady Constance Lytton,

daughter of a former Viceroy of India, disguised herself as 'Jane Wharton', a working-class seamstress, when imprisoned in Liverpool's Walton gaol for throwing stones at an MP's car in 1910. She was treated with contempt, force-fed eight times, and slapped for vomiting.[60] This was very different from the experience of her earlier imprisonments, when the authorities had been aware of her real identity.

In her book *Rebel Girls*, the historian Jill Liddington has shown how magistrates were often at a loss to comprehend the motives of working-class women activists, particularly the younger suffragettes.[61] 'Baby Suffragette' Dora Thewlis was a sixteen-year-old weaver from Huddersfield who was arrested and sent to Holloway for attempting to rush the House of Commons in 1910.[62] She had persuaded her parents to let her come to London with a contingent of local WSPU supporters. The magistrate dealing with the case suggested that Dora should be in school. He was clearly horrified that her parents had 'let her loose' on the streets of London, seeing this as an example of poor parenting. In fact Dora's mother, Eliza, also a weaver, was a strong supporter of the WSPU. She was extremely proud of Dora's independence, boasting that her daughter had proved herself a diligent reader of newspapers since the age of six or seven, and was well able to hold her own in political discussion or argument. The family were all employed in the textile industry, where it was common for young girls, like Dora, to start work in the mills as half-timers as early as ten years of age and to leave school for full-time work at twelve. This kind of background could produce an independence of mind in girls which middle-class magistrates totally failed to understand.

Suffragette militancy called for courage, whatever a woman's social background. It wasn't easy for a respectable middle-class woman to venture out with a hammer or a brick in muff or handbag, bent on damage. An intrepid Jane Brailsford once concealed an axe in a bunch of chrysanthemums.[63] Jane was described by one of her many male admirers as pale and thin, with 'a flower-like, plaintive beauty'. He added that her eyes were 'dove-like, but full of dangers'.[64] Many men were unsettled by the combination of femininity and steely resolve. To go on hunger strike, knowing about the torture of force-feeding, must have taken real guts. The government was wary of creating martyrs for the cause. But that is exactly what they did. One of the most moving elements in the Coronation suffrage procession of 1911 was the contingent of some six hundred women or their proxies who had been to gaol for their belief in women's suffrage, carrying silver-tipped arrows.[65] Suffragette leaders – particularly Emmeline Pankhurst – became, for many, both martyrs and heroines, sanctified by their devotion to the cause.

For girls growing up in the 1900s, the suffrage movement could be inspirational. Unlike the respectable matrons who had positioned themselves in opposition to the 'revolting daughters' of the 1890s, many mothers and daughters worked together in the struggle for the vote. Margaret Ker, daughter of Dr Alice Ker, the thirteenth woman to be entered on the British medical register, joined the WSPU with her mother in 1909.[66] Dr Alice Ker was sentenced to three months in Holloway after breaking shop windows in Harrods in 1912. In the same year, Margaret was sent to gaol and threatened with expulsion from Liverpool University for having set fire to a pillar box in the town.[67] For Mrs Pankhurst and her daughters Christabel, Sylvia and Adela, the battle for suffrage, though productive of much rivalry and contention, was nevertheless a family business.[68]

Women teachers were often feminists, although they had to

tread carefully and many prudently concealed their views from the educational authorities. A young Vera Brittain, at school in Surrey, recalled 'an ardent though always discreet' feminist teacher, Miss Heath Jones, who lent her students books on the women's movement and even escorted some of her senior pupils to a constitutional suffrage meeting in Tadworth Village in 1911.[69] Winifred Starbuck, interviewed for BBC Radio's *Woman's Hour* in 1958, remembered how she and her fellow pupils at a girls' private school before the First World War had been greatly inspired by the WSPU.[70] They had followed the news with excitement, and had decorated their desks with the WSPU colours of purple, green and white. Photographs and newspaper cuttings of the exploits of the Pankhursts were regularly displayed round the classroom. Their mistresses had kept very quiet, Winifred recalled, although the girls knew full well that many were sympathetic. One day the girls were scanning the lists of those who had been imprisoned for their activities only to find that one of their mistresses was among them. This teacher had gone on hunger strike and was forcibly fed. The girls were awed by her courage and sickened by the response of the authorities. They became active supporters of the movement, distributing pamphlets and attending meetings. Things came to a head when Winifred and her friends entered the sixth form. The headmistress and four other teachers were given notice to leave, clearly because of their sympathy with the suffrage campaign. The prefects canvassed their parents and organised a petition for the mistresses' reinstatement, but this was to no avail. A term of complete disorder followed. The girls rebelled and there were near riots; a number of replacement teachers left, and several girls were suspended but broke into the school at night and painted slogans on the walls. The police were called in. This sequence of events was eventually interrupted by the outbreak of war in 1914.

If girls were showing spirit and rebelliousness before 1914, there were also signs of backlash and repression. Working-class girls whose education was generally limited to a few years of elementary school rarely enjoyed the opportunities for self-development afforded to those of their more privileged middle-class sisters who attended high schools. The board school curriculum, controlled by the government, was highly gendered.[71] Girls had to do needlework and domestic subjects. Many educationalists argued that there should be much *more* emphasis on training girls for household duties, because this would remind them that their most important role was as wives and mothers. It was assumed that before they married, working-class girls were most likely to find employment as domestic servants. It was therefore deemed fitting that they should know all about blacking grates and clear-starching. Recruiting soldiers to fight in the Boer War drew attention to poor standards of health and physique among male town dwellers.[72] Many blamed working women. It was feared that standards of housewifery were declining and mothers no longer knew how to cook or feed their families. Pressure was put on the Board of Education to increase the amount of domestic economy in the schoolgirls' curriculum.[73] Women teachers of a feminist disposition sometimes contested this emphasis on domestic education, but their views made little impact at the time.[74]

The idea that intellectual education damaged a girl's chances of becoming a mother might have been expected to be wearing a bit thin by the 1900s. But the scare stories refused to go away completely. Since evidence that brainwork caused infertility was unforthcoming, opponents of women's education shifted their argument slightly. Instead, they argued that too much education tended to lessen a woman's opportunities or inclination for marriage. This resonated with prejudices about studious, unfeminine types sporting spectacles and bad complexions. Katharine Chorley, growing up in the prosperous suburb of Alderley Edge, near Manchester, in the 1900s remembered that attitudes to women's education among her neighbours were less than lukewarm:

> Even those who had heard of Girton and Newnham thought them infected resorts whose products must emerge pitted for life by the intellectual smallpox they would be bound to contract, a disfigurement that would unfit them for the marriage market.[75]

Pervasive unease about higher education for women received a potent new stimulus in the 1900s. This came from a 'theory' of female adolescence advanced in America by the writer G. Stanley Hall. Hall's snappily entitled two-volume study *Adolescence: Its Psychology, and Its Relation to Physiology, Anthropology, Sociology, Sex, Crime, Religion and Education* first appeared in America in 1904, and was widely read in Britain.[76] This book, together with Hall's other writings, echoed earlier arguments that adolescence was a particularly hazardous time for young women.[77] Hall argued that adolescence for boys was a time for adventure and exploration. Boys grew towards self-knowledge and began to acquire an adult identity. Girls, on the other hand, were incapable of acquiring self-knowledge. Their lives were ruled by 'deep unconscious instincts'. A girl's self-consciousness was only 'the reflected knowledge that others have of her.' Women never really outgrew their adolescence, and a girlish charm was integral to attractive womanliness.[78]

Hall's tone is both mawkish and creepy. The socialist politician

Margaret Cole once memorably described John Ruskin's writings as both idealising and 'slobbering over' girls.[79] Hall's prose is remarkably similar. He refers to the young girl as a 'backfisch', 'a fresh fish, just caught but unbaked, though fit and ready for the process'. She is 'wild with a charming gamey flavour'. When not implying through food imagery that he's set to gobble them up, he describes girls as 'fillies', ready for breaking in.[80]

The normal adolescent girl, according to Hall, was recognisable by her clothes consciousness, whimsicality, unconscious flirtatiousness, fads, fickleness, weepiness, giggling, coquetry, passion for secrecy, and most of all, strong distaste for study. In his view this was a self-protective instinct which should be respected by educators. Girls should be protected from too much brainwork until they had crossed 'the Rubicon of menstruation'.[81] All their energies should be conserved for this. While their periods were regularising themselves, girls should 'lie fallow', Hall insisted, and 'let Lord Nature do his magnificent work of inflorescence'.[82]

For a psychologist, Hall seems to have been remarkably unselfconscious about the drift of his imagery. But the idea of 'Lord Nature' (instead of the more commonly imagined 'Mother Nature'), going about his inflorescence was not just an unconscious slip. Women teachers, he insisted, were not to be entrusted with adolescent girls.[83] The intellectual ambitions which had qualified them for college teaching marked them out as unwomanly degenerates. They would give girls the wrong ideas, burden them with dead knowledge and turn them into pedants. Feminist teachers in particular would spoil girls for marriage and maternity. Girls should be taught refinement, dance and domesticity. Most important of all, their schools should be governed by men. At least one 'wise, large-souled, honourable, married and attractive man' should be present on the staff of every girls' school. If possible there should be several male mentors.[84] This, to Hall, was part of the natural order of things.

Hall's penchant for fluffy-minded girlishness contrasts vividly with the vehemence with which he attacked what he saw as feminine deviancy. 'Abnormal' girls were represented as vampires, a source of 'vile corruption'. Every school had a number of girl pupils who were 'little animals ... infecting boys with vice'. It wasn't difficult, he suggested, to understand why societies in the past had gone in for witch-burning: the loose woman

> becomes a veritable vampire, a curse to the race, whom primitive people in so many lands have burned or drowned with heavy weights in water or smothered in quagmires.[85]

Hall went even further. Girls 'exposed to city temptations' were responsible, he judged, for the white slave trade. Boys whom they seduced might sell their knowledge to pimps and purchasers. And white-slave agents often preyed upon girls on probation, even if sexually innocent, offering them inducements to escape surveillance.[86] This suggestion deftly wove together elements from two of the moral panics around girls in the 1900s, the idea of education as damaging to femininity, and that of the unprotected girl falling victim to sex traffickers.

Many women were revolted by Hall's writing. In America, M. Carey Thomas, President of Bryn Mawr women's college, confessed that her reaction was visceral. Addressing college alumnae in 1907, she insisted that over a lifetime's reading on the position of women she had never come across any book so degrading to women as Hall's *Adolescence*. At the time, she recalled, she had been terrified 'lest I, and every other woman with me, were doomed to live as pathological invalids in a universe merciless to women'. Since then, she and others had come to realise that 'it is not we, but the man who believes such things about us who is himself pathological, blinded by neurotic mists of sex'.[87] Hall's biographer, Dorothy Ross, provides evidence to back this up: Hall was uneasy about masculinity and conflicted about his own gender identity.[88] Projecting women at half their size seems to have allowed him to feel more of a man.

But whatever Hall's personal insecurities, his professional impact was considerable. His theories were endorsed and quoted approvingly by many psychologists, educationalists and youth workers over the next couple of decades. Women teachers were given regular warnings about the dangers of overstraining their pupils with intellectual work. Dr Janet Campbell, for instance, a medical adviser to the Board of Education, warned her colleagues not to expect too much in the way of maths from girls:

> Lessons requiring much concentration and therefore using up a great deal of brain energy, mathematics, for instance, should not be pushed. With some girls it is well to discontinue one or more subjects for a time if they begin to show signs of fatigue, and the subsequent progress will fully justify this action. Such subjects as cookery, embroidery or the handicrafts may well be introduced into the curriculum as they cause comparatively little mental strain.[89]

At a more popular level, books such as A. B. Barnard's *The Girl's Book about Herself* (1912) affected a tone of intimacy between writer and reader, warning girls against 'excessive devotion to books' and other such 'tomboyish' behaviour. Growing girls shouldn't tax their brains, Barnard scolded; they should 'put away the trigonometry and do some needlework'.[90]

More insidiously, girls who persisted in study were likely to be labelled psychologically deviant. They were seen as refusing to accept the feminine role. As the first President of the American Psychological Association, Stanley Hall encouraged both Sigmund Freud and Karl Jung to lecture in the United States and was influenced by their approach. His research students were encouraged to ponder the unconscious psychological meanings of 'rebellion' in young women. One of his favourite pupils, for instance, Phyllis Blanchard, went on to study the psychology of adolescent girlhood. She argued that self-sacrifice and masochism were the basis of 'true womanhood'. Much of the rebellion in adolescent girls would be outgrown, Blanchard suggested, as they came to terms with their limitations as females. Feminism, she averred, was nothing but a colossal 'masculine protest', a 'power goal of the neurotic'.[91]

Blanchard's work wasn't widely read, although several of the more popular writers on adolescent girlhood in the 1920s and 1930s refer to it.[92] In the years of social unrest before the First World War, there were plenty of observers who were keen to belittle suffragettes as hysterical or neurotic.[93] Or as man-hating lesbians. Blanchard's arguments would have struck a chord. All these ideas about the fragility of adolescent girlhood, and the need to wrest control of girls' education out of the hands of deviant and possibly perverted feminists, were to return after the war.

3 | BRAZEN FLAPPERS, BRIGHT YOUNG THINGS AND 'MISS MODERN'

Both the First and the Second World Wars brought dramatic change in the social position of women in Britain: they were periods of widening opportunity alongside terrible loss. The two decades between these wars were marked by great uncertainty about 'the modern girl'. Who was she? Should she be celebrated or deplored? The characteristics of the modern girl became a source of endless fascination in the press, in literature, and on the cinema screen.[1] These discussions were inevitably bound up with ideas about the desirability and meanings of social change.

It is often assumed that women 'earned' themselves the right to the vote by their patriotic behaviour in the First World War. The Women's Social and Political Union (WSPU) called a halt to militancy when war broke out in 1914, and over the next four years women's contribution to the war effort proved them competent and reliable in all manner of trades and activities formerly thought 'masculine'.[2] But getting the vote can't simply be seen as a reward for war work. It was effectively withheld from the mass of younger women who had worked in munitions and other wartime industries. The women enfranchised in 1918 were over thirty years of age. Even among this group, a property qualification meant that many unmarried, professional women living in rented accommodation found themselves excluded. It has been estimated that only about one in fifteen of the women in paid employment were entitled to vote in the 1920s. It was to take another ten years of lobbying and campaigning before women gained the right to vote on the same terms as men. In the meantime, many politicians expressed misgivings about whether girls under the age of thirty were sensible enough to be trusted with full citizenship, and discussions about the implications of 'the flapper vote' were commonplace.[3]

The word *flapper* had rich associations. It suggested a young bird flapping its wings, learning to fly. Some held it the equivalent of the German *Backfisch*, often used to denote a young adolescent girl. Others suggested that *flapper* referred to a girl's pigtail, flapping loose down her back, before she was of the age when she would be expected to put up her hair. The word might suggest tomboyishness. It almost always connoted liveliness and spirit, with suggestions of movement, dancing, jazz and frivolity. These days the word *flapper* conjures up images of long beads, cigarette holders and the charleston. But some scholars have pointed out that from the late nineteenth century the word *flapper* had been slang for a young prostitute. So in the 1920s, the term was ambiguous: it denoted a young woman sometimes innocent, sometimes anything but.[4]

A heightened anxiety over young women's sexual behaviour can be traced from the outbreak of war in 1914. With the declaration of hostilities, people took to the streets. Women were said to have become hysterical. Mothers no doubt panicked about the safety of their sons. Younger women were said to have turned into wartime nymphomaniacs.[5] Soldiers were sexy. In the previous century women who were attracted to soldiers in their regimental coats were said to have suffered from 'scarlet fever'. Now, an epidemic of 'khaki fever' was allegedly sweeping the country.[6] According to one observer, girls 'went out like cats on the tiles and shrieked madly'. This remark emanated from travel writer Mrs Alec Tweedie, who continued:

> They wanted to mate. Anything would do ... Every woman
> wanted a male creature to cling on to like a winkle. Every man
> wanted to talk to a woman and —— but few wanted to marry
> them.[7]

The turmoil associated with troops, travel and new working conditions brought opportunities. Ties of family control and supervision were loosened. Camps grew up where soldiers were in transit, and munitions factories mushroomed across the country. Girls were said to flock to the camps in order to flirt with soldiers, and some were alleged to have behaved outrageously.

It was in this context that 'the flapper' came to be seen as a social problem. Clergymen, women police officers and a variety of voluntary groups set out to intervene. Middle-class women, some of them feminists, set up 'patrol committees'. They walked round parks in the evenings, interrupting romantic assignations and turning torchlight on anyone caught canoodling on benches. Young girls might receive a stiff talking-to about respectable behaviour and national duty. Most of these flighty youngsters were not morally bad, insisted Mrs Tweedie, merely 'temperamentally unbalanced', and 'not playing the game'. Nonetheless their behaviour was seen as dangerous; they were risking not only their own reputations, but the health and safety of young men. Robert Baden-Powell, founder of the Boy Scouts, was horrified by the prospect of young men returning from the trenches to be met by 'giggling, glad-eye flappers' on the streets of London.[8]

Baden-Powell's passion for scouting hadn't always extended to the feminine side of the movement. It is said that when he turned up to inspect boy scouts at the first large official rally in London's Crystal Palace in 1909, he was acutely embarrassed to come across a party of girls in khaki shorts, calling themselves 'girl scouts' and demanding inspection alongside the boys. In Baden-Powell's worldview, 'manliness' called for a clear demarcation and distancing from anything female. Anxious to save scouting from feminine contamination, he hived the girls off to form a separate movement, the Girl Guides. The Guides were put under the tutelage of his sister, Agnes Baden-Powell, who could be trusted to encourage more ladylike behaviour. Agnes dutifully set out to feminise the tomboys. One of the first steps was to suppress the patrol names chosen by the girls themselves. Wildcats, Foxes, Wolves and Bears became Roses, Cornflowers and Lilies of the Valley. It was said that there was muttering resentment about this among the girls.[9]

Agnes's notions of acceptable femininity recalled Ruskin. Guides were subjected to homilies about the importance of home making and encouraged to crochet pillow lace.[10] Even her brother must have realised that her cloying prescriptions were outdated. A way out was at hand. In 1912 the fifty-five-year-old Robert married the brisk-mannered, twenty-three-year-old Olave St Clair Soames. They moved to Sussex, where Olave became scoutmaster of the local troop, assisted by the family's housemaid and gardener. After a reorganisation, Lady Baden-Powell became Chief Commissioner of the Girl Guides in 1916. Eighteen months later she was elevated to the title of World Chief Guide. Her work in this capacity was to stretch over the next forty years.[11]

Olave set out to deal with flapperdom. In *Training Girls as Guides* (1917) she breezily emphasised that the question of 'Our Brazen Flappers' needed urgent attention. Britain's strength depended upon its mothers and its homes, and girls were the mothers of the future. Flappers played hard and fast with freedom and

> Familiarity with freedom is apt to make a girl blasée. When she has learnt the ABC of sin it is but a step towards the first primer of vice.
>
> ... the flapper is growing brazen. She is out in the world, sometimes at a pretence of war work, but often as a mere butterfly enjoying her escape from the chrysalis of childhood, and she is meeting with temptations and dangers without having learned how to resist them. She revels in flag-days because they offer the great chance. 'Won't you buy a flag?' has taken the place of 'May I introduce myself?' And the flapper is sharp enough to see her advantages.[12]

There is a great deal in this vein. Flappers are castigated for 'aiding nature by eyebrow pencil and lip-salve, powder puff and rouge-pot, at an age when such things should not exist for her'. The charges were multiple. Flappers were precocious, they were too young to be interested in sex, or to be obsessed with young men. They were a danger to these young men, they were on the downward slope, they would grow up into rotten mothers.[13] How could this be remedied? The Girl Guide Movement set out to train girls in character and responsibilities. Guiding encouraged fresh air and backbone. Girls were encouraged to throw themselves into nature work, camping out, war-service activities, nursing and VAD work. Guides made sandbags and collected sphagnum moss for bandages. Guides enjoyed healthy competition and developed community-mindedness. Guiding would ensure the development of a new generation of healthy, clean-minded, patriotic mothers.

Khaki fever was a temporary phenomenon, but concern about flappers continued through the 1920s, merging into wider preoccupations with modernity, the party-going 'bright young

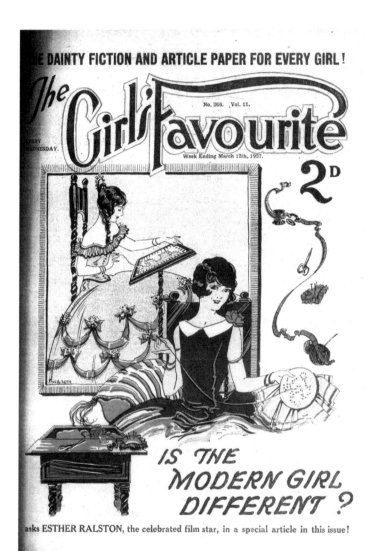

3.1 Was the modern girl reassuringly old-fashioned at heart? Cover image from *The Girl's Favourite* magazine, March 1927 (courtesy of the British Library).

3.2 Pyjama-clad, cigarette-smoking flapper. Postcard image by the French artist Achille Lucien Mauzan, produced in 1918 in Milan. The stereotype of the flapper was widely recognisable (by kind permission of Gabriel Carnévalé-Mauzan).

things' of the 1930s, and the modern girl. There were many aspects of the modern girl which attracted attention. Her hair, her dress and her demeanour, to start with. Then there were her habits (especially drinking and smoking), her tastes in leisure (dancing, cinema-going, and sunning herself in lidos), her taste in men, her sexual proclivities more generally, her feminine frivolity. Or, indeed, her *lack* of feminine frivolity. Girls with Eton-crop hairstyles and sharply tailored suits were equally cause for concern. In Britain between the world wars, just about everything thought characteristic of modern girlhood was subject to scrutiny and debate. The popular press was obsessed with the subject.[14]

The appearance of the flapper or modern girl in the 1920s was distinctive in that it was a sharp break from Victorian and Edwardian tastes. Cropped hair shocked an earlier generation for whom long tresses had been a hallmark of femininity. In the nineteenth century, a range of rituals had grown up around hair brushing and hair care, and the moment when a young girl exchanged ribbons and braids for hairpins and 'put up her hair' was still an important rite of passage, signifying grown-up womanhood. Short hair – whether 'shingled, bingled or bobbed' – was widely interpreted as looking boyish, or as an act of outright rebellion.[15] Parents might be horrified, and some girls were punished for cutting their hair. The future aviator Amy Johnson, aged eighteen, cut off her plaits and her father punished her by making her stay on for an extra year at school.[16] The artist and writer Kathleen Hale (author of *Orlando the Marmalade Cat*) recorded that she narrowly missed being expelled from university for cutting her hair during the First World War.[17] Cosmetics were another bone of contention. Many Victorian ladies associated powder and paint with the dubious morals of streetwalkers, theatre and music hall performers. But after the war, young women turned to cosmetics with enthusiasm.[18] Lip rouge, powder puffs and kohl-rimmed eyes were the hallmarks of flapperdom. The more conservative were appalled, Baden-Powell among them. As early as 1917 an article in the *Girl Guide Gazette* (entitled 'Women Slackers') had proclaimed:

> The 'Flapper', while she consumed quantities of sweets and tied her hair with astonishing bows, was amusing enough. But in her new manifestations, as she expands towards the costliest of silk stockings, smokes numberless cigarettes, and makes up with paint and powder as if to go on the stage

in a revue chorus, she stands for tendencies that the more experienced man or woman knows to be undesirable from every point of view.

Not until the next generation is born shall we know the full extent of the mischief that these restless young girls, craving to draw attention to themselves, are doing to the race.[19]

A concern for 'the future of the race' became widespread as the new, pseudo-science of eugenics gained adherence among a variety of political groups including socialists, conservatives and feminists. Baden-Powell's misgivings were echoed by Dr Murray Leslie, writing in *The Times* in 1920. His article was headlined 'The 1920 Girl: Competition for "The Elusive Male"'. The terrible loss of young men's lives during the Great War had deprived a generation of young women of any real hopes of marriage. Murray Leslie predicted a new wave of social unrest, powered by female discontent and disappointment. Standards of morality would plummet. Married men would be tempted by the easy availability of attractive, frustrated girls. This social butterfly type of girl was already much in evidence, he claimed, in the shape of 'the frivolous, scantily-clad, jazzing flapper, irresponsible and undisciplined, to whom a dance, a new hat, or a man with a car' was irresistible. These girls were a danger to young men. They would stop at nothing to snare a mate: 'Young men had dance invitations four and five deep, and our boys and young men were being spoilt before our eyes.'[20]

Flappers were portrayed somewhat inconsistently as either man-hungry or boyish, vamps or lesbians. If they weren't preying on young men, they might be preying on young women. And if they *were* hungering after men then they might be displaying an appetite for the *wrong kind* of man. Indian, Arab or Chinese men, for instance. Popular eugenics encouraged ideas about 'racial purity'. Unease about mixed-race romantic and sexual entanglements was widespread during and after the First World War.[21] Indian soldiers recovering in British hospitals were carefully watched, and their movements were confined to hospital precincts, lest they interact too much with the local population. In Brighton's Kitchener Hospital, for instance, the town was declared 'out of bounds for all natives except medical men and students'.[22] If men wanted to go for walks or to places of entertainment they had to do so under escort. Even so, there were scandals.[23] Race feuds in Cardiff in 1919 were attributed to black men associating with white girls. Local newspapers fretted over evidence that a 'low type' of British girls seemed particularly attracted to black or Indian men.[24] Chinese men were thought to exercise an irresistible allure, widely suspected to be associated with the use of drugs, particularly opium.[25]

The public imagination on this subject was fed by contemporary portrayals of Chinese men such as thriller writer Sax Rohmer's Dr Fu Manchu, or D. W. Griffith's silent movie *Broken Blossoms* (1919).[26] In Griffith's film, subtitled *The Yellow Man and the Girl*, Lillian Gish plays a twelve-year-old girl, the ethereal-looking Lucy, who stars as the ultimate victim, broken by Limehouse brutality. Kicked about by her dad ('Battling Burrows') she forms a sentimental alliance with a mysterious (and much older) poet, Cheng Huan. Their love was unsettling to contemporary audiences. Though portrayed as sexually innocent, there were strong erotic undertones of the forbidden. Viewers were titillated, charmed – and to some extent reassured – by her innocence and frailty. Lucy was certainly no flapper.

'Real-life' scandals fuelled concern that was based on fascination as well as fear. The deaths of two young women, Billie

Carleton and Freda Kempton, attracted massive newspaper coverage.[27] Both deaths were associated with drug use. Billie Carleton was a pretty twenty-two-year-old actress found dead in her bed in a suite at the Savoy hotel in 1918. She had just returned from a victory ball to celebrate the end of the war. The inquest that followed brought to light Carleton's adventurous social and sexual life, her predilection for opium and pyjama parties, and her heavy drug habit. She was nonetheless widely portrayed as a victim, as a 'broken butterfly'. Her friend Reggie de Veuille was charged and acquitted of manslaughter, but went to gaol for having supplied her with prohibited drugs. The cocaine and opium were said to have come from a Scottish woman, Ada, and her Chinese husband Lau Ping You, in Limehouse. Four years later Freda Kempton, a young dance instructress at a nightclub in central London, died after an overdose of cocaine. She had earlier spent time with a Chinese restaurant proprietor and drug dealer, 'Brilliant' Chang. There was no proof that Chang had supplied the cocaine which killed Kempton. But the newspapers nevertheless went to town with warnings about the Yellow Peril. Chang cut a handsome figure, he was suave and well-dressed, and there was no doubt that women found him attractive. This intensified reactions in the press, which tried to explain the attraction in terms of the 'strange powers of magnetism' possessed by the Chinese, or of drug-induced hypnosis. The image of Limehouse as a warren of perfumed dope dens where evil Chinamen lay in wait for innocent young girls became even more entrenched. As in discussions of white slavery before the war, many found it easier to see young women as victims, rather than to accept that they might make choices which others judged as undesirable.

If fancying non-white men was seen as undesirable in young girls, the prospect of their being seduced by other women was at least as worrying. 'Clemence Dane' was the pen name of Winifred Ashton. Her novel about life in a girls' school, *Regiment of Women*, was published in 1917.[28] Its subject unsettled those who thought their daughters safe in an all-female environment. The plot centres on the story of Alwynne Durand, a young teacher in Utterbridge Girls' School, who is befriended by the charismatic deputy head, Clare Harthill. Miss Harthill is portrayed as sophisticated and highly intelligent. She is also unscrupulous and worldly. She is shown to exercise an unhealthy influence over younger pupils and mistresses, for whom she becomes a kind of female Svengali or poisonous role model. There are hints of vampirism. One of Clare's pupils, emotionally unbalanced by her schoolgirl passion for the schoolmistress, kills herself. Alwynne is rescued in the nick of time by Roger, a straight, healthy, no-nonsense male. Winifred Ashton, who had some experience as a teacher, continued to write about what she saw as the real dangers of emotional attachments in girls' schools. These could not be simply dismissed as harmless crushes or 'pashes', she warned. Some female teachers were selfish and manipulative, and could indeed be described as 'vampire women'.[29] Coeducation, she suggested, was the only answer.

Regiment of Women hinted darkly about the dangers of same-sex attraction in women. Radclyffe Hall's landmark novel about lesbianism, *The Well of Loneliness*, was published in 1928, attracting widespread and scandalised attention, alongside legal challenges in England and America. The editor of the popular British newspaper the *Sunday Express* famously remarked that he would rather give a healthy boy or girl a phial of prussic acid than let them read the novel.[30] Before the publication of *The Well of Loneliness*, however, Winifred Ashton was not the only writer to focus on what were seen as the dangers of homosexual attachment in single-sex schools and colleges.[31] The close female friendships engendered by the suffrage movement were often viewed with suspicion. In 1921 a proposal to criminalise lesbianism (by creating a new offence of gross indecency applying to sexual acts between women) was considered by the House of Lords. It was defeated largely because it was feared that to draw attention even to the possibilities of such behaviour would besmirch the innocence of the average girl.[32]

The idea that women teachers might exercise a dangerous influence over young girls persisted. Even if they weren't sexual inverts, it was feared that they might be rampant feminists. The attitude of some male teachers didn't help. The highly sexist National Association of Schoolmasters, implacably opposed to equal pay, was relentlessly hostile to unmarried women teachers. It kept up a barrage of propaganda and was more than willing to caricature women colleagues as twisted spinsters with personality disorders.[33] Stanley Hall's insistence that men should carry authority over women if schools were to be healthy places appealed strongly to NAS types. The NAS enthusiastically supported the marriage bar, which required women to relinquish their posts if they acquired husbands. That many women teachers wanted or needed to earn, and enjoyed their work, and the fact that even if all single women teachers had wanted to marry, there weren't enough men to go round, seem not to have affected their arguments.

In 1917 a senior mistress at Bournemouth High School warned pupils that the shortage of marriageable young men after the war ended would mean that only about one in ten of them could expect to find husbands.[34] The girls would need to develop other goals in life. Nevertheless the late Victorian notion that girls' schools encouraged their pupils to develop unwomanly ambitions and damaged their femininity received another stimulus from a book published by a woman doctor, Arabella Kenealy, in 1920. This book was called *Feminism and Sex Extinction*.[35] Kenealy saw herself as a eugenic feminist, but deplored what she saw as the 'decadent and demoralizing vogue of the flapper'. Trouser-wearing and smoking young hoydens were the product of girls' schools that had lost their way, she proclaimed. Feminists had to shoulder some of the blame for this because they had insisted on competing with men. High-school girls were unsexed by an education designed for boys. A cult of competitive field games turned middle-class girls into grim-visaged hockey addicts with mannish thighs and sinewy forearms.[36] Even in the elementary schools, neglect of woman's true mission was producing 'a race of stunted, precocious, bold-eyed, cigarette-smoking, free-living working girls, who fill our streets, many tricked out like cocottes, eyes roving after men, impudence upon their tongues, their poor brains vitiated by vulgar rag-times and cinema scenes of vice and suggestiveness'.[37]

Kenealy's rhetoric cannot have appealed to everyone, but her arguments struck a chord with educationalists at government level who had indeed begun to wonder whether girls were suffering from a schooling based too much on male models. In the same year that *Feminism and Sex Extinction* was published, for instance, the Board of Education set up a committee to consider whether there should be *more* sex discrimination (they called it 'differentiation') between boys and girls in secondary schools.[38] This committee reported in 1923. It emphasised yet again the importance of not overstraining adolescent girls with exams. It contended that schooling should prepare girls and boys for adult life, and suggested that 'The broad difference between boys and girls – that the former will earn the family income and the latter will administer it, bring up the children and look after the house – is relevant as far as the majority are concerned.'[39] The committee conceded that things were changing and that more women were turning to professional careers or wage-earning than in the nineteenth century. At the same time it suggested that the movement for the emancipation of women 'has now perhaps achieved sufficient success to be no longer so potent a source of inspiration'.[40]

Feminists often felt themselves on the defensive in education between the wars. There was a backlash against women's work in some quarters as men returned from the battlefield. The London medical schools, which had reluctantly opened their doors to women students through the war years, promptly closed them again.[41] A rash of novels indicted selfish women clinging to their jobs while ex-servicemen languished, unmanned by their inability to find work.[42] The reality, especially for educated women after the war, was that jobs were in short supply. Women graduates found themselves in a particularly difficult situation, especially those who had studied science. There were stories of women with first-class degrees in science working in sardine factories during these years.[43] In the 1930s, openings in teaching – long regarded as both the safest option and something of a last resort – were drying up through an oversupply of qualified women.[44]

Working-class women, many of whose horizons had expanded during wartime, often found themselves pressed back into domestic service. Indoor domestic service still represented the largest single category of work carried out by women. It carried a low social status and had long been unpopular. Conditions of employment varied, but were commonly experienced as harsh, and with long hours, and those who 'lived in' often reported that their sleeping quarters were in chilly attics or smelly basements.

In a survey carried out before the First World War, many women had insisted that 'service is like prison'. The wearing of cap and apron was seen as a humiliating badge of servitude, and women servants sometimes complained of being treated like machines, or even 'dogs' or 'reptiles'.[45] Conditions had scarcely improved since the war ended.

In some areas girls had little choice. Winifred Foley, born in 1914, grew up in the Forest of Dean. Leaving school at fourteen, she and many of her friends looked for jobs as live-in servants in the nearby town of Cheltenham, 'Where in the 1920s everybody who wasn't a servant was a somebody; including the snooty little Pekes and Pomeranians, creatures rated much higher in their mistresses' eyes than the servants.'[46]

Foley had a number of jobs. Her account makes it clear that hardship and poor conditions were easier to bear than the loss of identity, and the stigma of having to wear cap and apron. One of her most telling experiences was as a maid in College Hall, a hostel for girls studying at University College, London in the late 1920s and early 1930s. Winifred made the mistake of talking to a friendly Canadian undergraduate, and was reprimanded. Having a conversation with a student was seen as socially assuming, 'getting above herself'. She was bitterly humiliated by this reprimand. On the verge of tears, she consoled herself by singing the 'Red Flag' and recalling her father's socialism. Then she walked out of the job.[47]

'Mary Smith', who told her story to youth worker Pearl Jephcott, during the Second World War, left school aged fifteen in 1936.[48] She found work hard to get, and resented the fact that those who interviewed her at the Junior Employment Exchange wanted to push her into domestic service. After a short stint as a shop assistant, Mary tried dressmaking, but hated it. Rather than enrol at the local 'junior instructional centre', generally known as the 'dole school', she was persuaded to try work as a housemaid with a family known to a friend. This proved a disaster. She was expected to be a general skivvy for eleven people, and found the work extremely hard. Reduced to tears time and again, Mary recorded that what hurt the most was that she was forced to eat her meals by herself, in the kitchen, while the whole family sat in the living room. After a couple of days she left and threw herself on the mercy of the dole school.

Stories like this were common, but choices were opening up. It is significant that both Winifred and Mary were able to abandon domestic service, that they found other options. After the dole school, Mary found more congenial work in a laundry, and eventually started training as a nurse, which had long been what she had really hankered after. Winifred worked as a waitress and found her own bedsitting room: she lived frugally for a while, but relished her freedom. Jobs in the service industries were becoming more plentiful with the expansion of chain and department stores. Restaurants such as Lyons' tea shops and corner houses provided meals for the growing army of white-collar workers in cities, and employment for the waitresses who worked in them. At the same time, new factories were mushrooming in the Midlands and the South of England. These began to produce electrical goods and domestic appliances on a large scale. They manufactured synthetic fibres and chemicals, or were dedicated to food canning and processing. A large proportion of those who worked on the conveyor belts and assembly lines in these new industries were young women.[49]

Through the 1920s, cinema newsreels and newspaper stories featured women entering all kinds of work and distinguishing themselves as aviators, engineers, stunt drivers and Channel swimmers. Even if times were hard, these stories acted as a tonic. It seemed that there was very little that women couldn't do, if they were only offered the opportunity. *Hutchinson's Women's Who's Who*, a bulky volume published in 1934, provides an impressive compendium of the range of work, both paid employment and voluntary public service, carried out by women. It provides lists of individual women working in medicine, schools, universities, accountancy – everything from engineering to silver fox fur breeding, angora rabbit farming, or growing violets in flower nurseries, feeding the new cosmetics industry.[50] Several organisations set out to encourage girls with careers advice, either through employment bureaux or through regular newsletters and directories. The feminist Ray Strachey chaired the Cambridge University Women's Appointments Committee in the 1930s. She also threw her energies into organising national initiatives such as the Women's Employment Federation, helping to find work for educated girls. By the mid-1930s the the middle-class-oriented *Daily Mail* was publishing articles with headings such as 'Sixty Women with Unusual Jobs'. These included women working as harbour officials, stockbrokers, aviators, farm bailiffs and piano tuners.[51]

There was no shortage of role models, since the popular press exulted in stories of 'women firsts': the first woman barrister, the first woman to swim the English Channel, to fly across the Atlantic, and so forth. This celebration of female competence was very much in evidence in portrayals of women drivers and aviators. Even schoolgirl story annuals ran features on girls learning to drive and familiarising themselves with sparking plugs and oil cans. Women doctors and teachers often purchased their own cars and were keen motorists. In novels of the time, a modish independence is conveyed through the image of a woman's hands on the wheel. In Winifred Holtby's *Poor Caroline*, for instance, the heroine Eleanor de la Roux dons a pair of leather gauntlets and drives herself to London in search of career opportunities and training. She is highly educated and a competent mechanic, as well as being ambitious for power and worldly success.[52]

Women rally drivers and aviators exuded the same qualities of intrepid femininity. After graduating from the University of Sheffield, the young Amy Johnson found herself unenthusiastic about her career prospects and frustrated in love. The thought of school teaching depressed her. She persuaded her father to pay back the grant she had accepted from the Board of Education in return for a pledge to go into teaching.[53] Amy's lover Hans refused to marry her, in spite of all her efforts at persuasion. She was stunned when she learned that he had married someone else – another graduate her own age, already pregnant with his child. Amy betook herself to London and embarked on a hectic lifestyle to numb her sorrows. She took to hanging around an airfield in Stag Lane and fell in love with the idea of flying. She also bought a car: a dark maroon two-seater Morris Cowley, borrowing money from her father to finance her purchase. She discovered that she enjoyed tinkering with engines. Amy Johnson was the first woman in Britain to be awarded a ground engineer's licence. She earned herself a place in history in 1930 when she undertook her solo flight to Australia in a Gipsy Moth biplane, affectionately named *Jason*. Amy was glamorous. She had dyed her hair blonde and was petite with a girlish figure. This, combined with her somewhat reckless courage, endeared her to many. The newspapers were full of her. A number of popular songs (including 'Amy, Wonderful Amy') celebrated her exploits. In 1932 the *Daily Mirror* reported that when young girls visiting Madame Tussaud's waxworks exhibition were asked whom they would most like to emulate when they grew up, they put Amy Johnson high on the list. (First choice was the First World War heroine Edith Cavell, then Amy, both ahead of Joan of Arc, who took third place.)[54] Flying lessons were relatively cheap in the 1920s and 1930s. It was said to be possible to obtain a pilot's licence after some eight hours of tuition. Once qualified, you could hire a plane for around £1 per hour. Even so, this was well beyond the reach of the majority. Ordinary working-class girls, inspired by Amy, took to having themselves photographed in simulated aeroplanes, a facility which became popular at funfairs or as a seaside attraction during the 1930s.[55]

Opportunities for leisure and pleasure expanded enormously between the wars. Girls with regular jobs and pay packets were major beneficiaries. They flocked to the dance halls. There were ballrooms, dance halls and dancing schools in all major cities. The Palais, the Ritz and the Locarno were household names. Hotels and even department stores offered afternoon tea dancing. Fashionable new dances and jazz rhythms with catchy names (the black bottom, the lindy hop, the boogie-woogie), generated a dizzy succession of 'crazes'. Jazz mounted in popularity, especially in bohemian circles.

Then there were the cinemas. On screen, the 'serial queen' melodramas such *The Perils of Pauline* or *The Exploits of Elaine* had proved immensely popular with munitions workers during the Great War.[56] Featuring the intrepid heroine Pearl White, these films celebrated both the dangers that threatened young women and the resourcefulness and pluck with which they overcame them. Films depicting the romantic entanglements of girls who succeeded in making spectacular marriages were usually crowd-pullers. After the Great War, cinema-going became a passion among many girls and young women who thought nothing

3.3 Amy Johnson, pioneer British aviator in the 1930s (photograph© Bob Thomas/Popperfoto/Getty Images).

3.4 Girls inspired by Amy Johnson's exploits could pose for photographs in simulated aeroplanes (postcard image from 1930s ©collection of Tom Phillips, courtesy of copyright holder).

of seeing films twice or even three times a week. The films got bolder and glossier, featuring sultry-eyed vamps, masterful sheikhs and cruel-featured Arab lovers. Female audiences swooned over Valentino, and learned a lesson or two from screen heroines with 'It' (sex appeal) who were resourceful enough to make sure they got their man. 'Cinemagazines' (short feature or news films) such as Pathé's *Eve's Film Review* catered explicitly for female audiences and reported on the latest fashions and news affecting women in a light-hearted and gossipy manner.[57] Holly-wood cinema supplied screen goddesses and glamour. Its impact on British audiences was immense. Young women's habits of consumption were changed for ever as they eagerly copied the fashions in clothing, cosmetics and hairstyles which they studied in the picture palaces. A whole new genre of film magazines, from *Girls' Cinema* to *Picturegoer* and *Film Fashionland*, provided extra sources of information about these trends.[58]

Dancing, cinema-going and a raft of new magazines target-ing young women expanded opportunities for indoor pleasures. There were new facilities for outdoor activity too. The bicycle, emblematic accessory of the new woman in the 1890s, became increasingly affordable by those on modest incomes. Cycling clubs were immensely popular among young people. Camping out in the countryside had particular appeal. Girls growing up between the wars often recorded memories of bonfires and sleep-ing in the great outdoors as a time of happiness and freedom. The range of physical activities thought appropriate for girls expanded, as women took up rowing, athletics or gymnastics. Some joined the Women's League of Health and Beauty, founded in 1930, which held that 'movement is life' and encouraged syn-chronised exercises in the open air.[59] Swimming and sunbathing became common pastimes. The knitted – and later ruched and elasticised – bathing costumes of the inter-war period looked daringly revealing to contemporaries. Lounging about on the beaches, or on the sun-decks of the new open-air lidos which were built across Britain in the 1930s, provided new opportunities for flirtation. It wasn't long before the press stoked up contro-versy about the seemliness of mixed bathing among the young.[60]

Indeed, all these new forms of leisure provoked anxiety in

some quarters. There were those who found the idea of mixed bathing improper and deplored the fashion for bodily display. Others followed the Arabella Kenealy line and argued that competitive sport damaged femininity. Reading University's Vice Chancellor, W. M. Childs, had fretted himself silly about whether rowing and sculling were safe sports for women undergraduates. His successor Franklin Sibly inherited his concern. Women students had to produce medical certificates and written permission from parents before they were allowed to go on the river, and racing against male crews was strictly forbidden.[61]

Cinema-going aroused all kinds of concern. Cinemas were dark places. Romance on the screen might give people ideas and what was to stop them getting up to no good in the back row? Even the posters advertising film showings were considered 'lurid and distasteful'. Young girls were sometimes considered to put themselves in moral danger simply by going to the pictures. Mary Allen of the Women's Police Service contended that young audiences were 'aroused to breathless excitement' in their seats. 'They shout with fear and terror and dance about in their places.' There was a danger of young people becoming 'over-sexed', she thought.[62] The National Council of Public Morals had set out to investigate the influence of cinema on the young in 1916–17, and fears of this kind were much in evidence.[63] The concerns were amplified over the next couple of decades. Cinemas themselves became bigger and more luxurious, with deep-pile carpets and exotic fittings. They were places where people could dream, and escape temporarily from the hardships of everyday life. Moralists worried that Hollywood glamour would lure girls astray. Seduced by their desire for luxury, they might become restless gold-diggers, painted hussies, scornful of homely virtues.

The flapper herself was often defined as 'pleasure-seeking', hankering after sweets, cocktails and new sensations. Young women were emerging as an important group of consumers in the economy of the 1920s and 1930s. Their spending power was increasing. The demand for cosmetics, inexpensive clothes, rayon stockings and underwear shaped the growth of a range of new industries. The film historian Jenny Hammerton has shown how images of girls enjoying fashionable new products were a regular feature of *Eve's Film Review*. In one sequence, for instance, a young woman resplendent in a feathery negligée reclines on her bed, reading magazines, eating chocolates and smoking cigarettes at the same time. Her indulgence in these multiple pleasures is made easier by a 'novelty magazine holder' and a gimmicky little gadget which both dispenses – and lights – cigarettes at the touch of a button. The mood was playful, and tongue-in-cheek: girls were shown as having fun.[64] But some social observers fretted over the easy availability of new pleasures. Negative descriptions of working-class girls often described them as hungry for cheap amusements. Indeed, the very idea of girls seeking pleasure seems to have discomfited many people. Their imaginations often pictured a swift descent from 'easy pleasures' to 'easy virtue'. Moreover, the fact that cheap, mass-produced clothing and cosmetics enabled working-class girls to look good unsettled hierarchies. Novelists such as J. B. Priestley and George Orwell picked up on the idea of factory girls looking like actresses as one of the most startling developments of the period.[65]

These anxieties certainly impacted on contemporary attitudes to sexuality. It wasn't just columnists in the *Daily Mail* who were likely to hint at a connection between confectionery and immorality. The academic psychologist Cyril Burt, reporting on 'The Causes of Sex Delinquency in Girls' in 1926, insisted that

3.5 Factory girls in Walthamstow, north London, mid-1930s, modelling carnival hats. Many young women preferred factory work to domestic service. Factory work could provide more space for spirited independence and camaraderie (photograph © Fox Photos/Stringer/Getty Images).

some of the youngest girl delinquents on his lists 'have become habitual little courtesans for the sake of sweets or the money with which to buy them'.[66] Girls' desire for new products and pleasures was suspect in a moral sense. This might feed into an undercurrent of social disapproval of women who looked too glamorous, or appeared to have too much worldly success, who might be seen as being 'no better than they ought to be'.

Some of this pursed-lip social disapproval was evident in the trial of Edith Thompson in 1923. Edith Thompson was a highly intelligent, attractive and successful businesswoman. Bored with her husband Percy, she had been having an affair with Freddy Bywaters, a sailor and shipping steward. Freddy was eight and a half years younger than Edith, who was twenty-eight. The pair exchanged passionate letters about life, literature and their love, and fantasised about how they might be together. Percy was the obstacle. One night Edith and Percy were returning from the theatre when Freddy intercepted them. He got into an angry row with Percy and stabbed him. Percy died from the wounds. There was no evidence that Edith was other than horrified and confused by the attack. Bywaters shouldered all the blame, insisting that she was completely innocent. But the letters – where Edith had fantasised about ways in which she might be rid of Percy – were seen as condemning her. The pair were jointly charged and tried for murder. Both were found guilty and hanged. Many authorities have since concluded that Edith was effectively hanged for nothing more than having *fantasised* about the death of her husband, or indeed, for the 'crime' of adultery.[67] What was clearly evident in this sad and horrifying case was that the massive outpouring of public sympathy which followed the announcement of the death penalty was all for Freddy, not for Edith. Freddy was seen as a decent, loyal young man who had been led astray by a designing and worldly woman.[68] As the contents of the romantic correspondence between the pair became public, attitudes to Edith had hardened. Her lifestyle and appearance were scrutinised and found less than 'respectable'. Her love of dancing, her flirtatiousness, her pleasure in new hats and expensive perfumes were all seen as suspect. Even her own brother-in-law denounced her as 'a flighty, forward flirt, pleasure-loving ... loud and vulgar'.[69] Edith had no children. This gave the press the opportunity to portray her as an unnatural or selfish woman. Others saw in her a warning of the moral dangers of cheap literature and the appetite for mass consumption. In a neat reversal of earlier anxieties about women's education, one writer in the *Daily News* asserted that what girls needed was *more*, not less schooling. Edith, he claimed, had been 'educated to a point', but not enough to restrain her wayward imagination. She had left school at fifteen:

> Then, when what she needed was God and William Shakespeare, she was given cheap sweets and Gloria de Vere ... The Thompson case is a symbol of what happens to a State which attains to a certain degree of material prosperity, but lacks a genuine passion for art and religion.[70]

Sexual relationships were still often fraught with danger for girls. In 1921 the sad case of Edith Roberts, 'the Hinckley girl-mother' attracted controversy and outrage among feminists. Edith lived in Leicester and was described as 'a factory hand' in the hosiery trade. Aged twenty-one, she looked about fourteen. She was a shy and quiet girl. Her father, a foreman dyer, said of her: 'no father in the world ever had a better daughter'. Edith was indicted for having murdered her newly born female child. The baby was said to have been suffocated with a camisole. Edith's baby had been born while she was in bed with her sister Lily. She had been too frightened and too ashamed to own up to the pregnancy, and had told herself that the baby had never drawn breath. She was clearly traumatised and probably in denial. Found guilty, she fainted while the judge was summing up. According to the press reports, she had to be held up, apologising, crying and moaning as the judge donned his black cap and pronounced upon her the death sentence (though with a recommendation to mercy).[71] There was an outcry in Leicester, with feminists and other protesters outraged by the fact that there had been no women on the jury, and by the double standard of morality demonstrated in the case. The father's responsibility had been ignored completely.

Edith Roberts's case was contentious enough to lead to a change in the law. The 1922 Infanticide Act allowed for cases of this kind to be judged manslaughter rather than murder, because of disturbance to the 'balance of the mind' at the time. Edith was sent to Walton gaol in Liverpool, where she was described as quiet and gentle, 'of a refined and reserved disposition', and as 'a good devout church-woman'. Pressure for her release continued, and she was eventually discharged in June 1922.[72]

Unmarried mothers were frequently driven to desperation by their situation. In Brighton, in 1931, Eva Garwood, 'a picture palace assistant', was convicted of strangling her newborn son and dumping his body in a local churchyard.[73] Because of the 1922 Act, she was convicted of infanticide and not subjected to having the death penalty pronounced on her. Coroners' records and records of forensic investigations (such as those of the famous pathologist Sir Bernard Spilsbury) show that it was not uncommon to find the remains of newborn infants stuffed up chimneys or buried under floorboards.[74] It was even more common for women to attempt abortions, either hazarding the procedure themselves or subjecting themselves to dangerous interventions from amateurs or backstreet abortionists. It is difficult to find out how many such abortions were successful, but coroners' records make it clear that many young women died trying to rid themselves of their unwanted pregnancies.

Stories of young women's vulnerability were not hard to find. The literature of the period abounds with images of 'odd women'; sad unmarried types, housemaids in basements, shopgirls and waitresses lonely for romance. Indeed the novels of George Gissing, Arnold Bennett, George Orwell, Patrick Hamilton and Graham Greene are replete with vignettes of such women.[75] They are depicted as easy prey for unscrupulous male fortune hunters or wide boys. Rose, in Graham Greene's *Brighton Rock* (1938), is putty in the hands of the scheming Pinkie. These are fictional characters, of course, but they resonated with aspects of contemporary reality, and were also a reflection of individual writers' outlook and views about the world they lived in. They were in themselves comments on social change. Arnold Bennett, for instance, like George Gissing, was markedly uneasy about social change. In *Our Women*, published in 1920, he contended that it was a good thing that women should now expect to earn their own living. Women had been too parasitic on men in the past. Middle-class women with nothing to do had faffed around playing the part of 'that odious creature', 'Lady Bountiful'. Nevertheless, he pontificated, women needed charm and domestic skills if they were to please men. Modern young women were in danger of losing these. Their education, he thought, should teach them to be home-builders, and maybe there should be Chairs at Girton in 'womanly subjects' such as 'coiffure'? A woman without a man was unhappy, Bennett contended: she was incomplete and vulnerable.[76]

Sad stories were not uncommon, but they were not the whole picture, either. Young women were often much more resourceful than their fictional prototypes, even when faced with men of the most unscrupulous and predatory type. Hayley Morris was a wealthy broker who owned a mansion and estate at Pippingford Park, near Ashdown Forest in Sussex. He had an appetite for young girls. With the help of his 'housekeeper' (whom he later married), a twenty-two-year-old woman called Madeleine Roberts, and another young woman, also under his spell and living in London, he regularly advertised for domestic staff. Young women 'of refined birth' were wanted, according to one of these adverts (placed in 1925), 'to look after large dogs in the country'.[77] The wages were generous: a pound a week and all expenses found. Those who arrived at Pippingford soon found themselves propositioned by Hayley. Some complied, or were scared into complying; others got away. Kathleen Weston, a nineteen-year-old, telephoned for help, then walked out. The police were alerted and picked her up in a lane. A full inquiry followed. Hayley Morris was indicted – on twenty-two counts – for conspiring to procure young girls for immoral purposes.

It transpired that Morris had also been in the habit of cruising around Brighton in his Rolls-Royce, trying to pick up girls. Two witnesses testified that he had taken them dancing at the Metropole Hotel and 'flashed his money about', lavish with chocolates and drinks. They weren't taken in. Seventeen girls were traced and interviewed. Three had been under sixteen when they first encountered Morris. Miss MacDougall, 'Lady Assistant to the Police', was on hand with support and reassurance, lest any girls feel uneasy about testifying. The Metropolitan Police handled the case with tact and efficiency.[78] Inspector Savage, in charge of the case, was commended for his excellent work. There is a letter on file from one of the girls involved, thanking Mr Savage 'for his very great kindness' to her and to her mother during 'the most Beastly experience we have ever gone through'.

Hayley Morris went to gaol for three years. Madeleine Roberts served nine months for acting as his accomplice. This horrible case illustrates dangers that could face girls who were engaged for indoor domestic service, especially in isolated households. During the trial it emerged that Morris had tried to lean upon the telephonist working at the Nutley exchange, near Pippingford, to put through only those calls made 'in gentlemen's voices'. But his instruction was ignored as unacceptable. The telephone and the motor car were important resources in this context, making it easier for young women in danger to raise the alarm and to get away.

Morris made sure that none of the girls he pursued got pregnant. Stocks of quinine pessaries and douches were found on his premises. Knowledge about birth control, and aids to contraception, both became more easily available between the wars. Where women themselves made free decisions about their use, they could be life-changing. Marie Stopes's phenomenally best-selling works *Married Love* and *Wise Parenthood* (1918) were landmarks in popular education.[79] Her first birth control clinic opened in north London in 1921. Stopes emphasised that her advice was for married couples only. Nevertheless, her relish for controversy ensured massive publicity. At a time when unmarried mothers were often stigmatised and shamed as social failures or delinquents, many women were terrified of engaging in any kind of sexual relationship outside marriage. The availability of more reliable forms of birth control began to lift some of this fear.

As a young woman the future writer Elspeth Huxley left her home in Africa in 1925 to embark on a degree course in agriculture at Reading University. She was interested in sex, although, she later wrote, 'we were all nervous about starting babies, and if things got as far as that, more inhibited than girls later became about checking up before-hand that our partner had a french letter'.[80] Elspeth was frank about her own fumblings with sexual partners – during walks on the towpath to the village of Sonning, or lying among boats in the dusk after Henley Regatta. One went as far as one could, while avoiding going the 'whole hog'. But it wasn't always just about prudence: there was also a shortage of opportunities. 'It was not religion or morality that kept most of us relatively chaste, but lack of facilities,' she insisted.[81]

Young women of 'advanced views' were beginning to experiment. This was clearly the case in intellectual and artistic circles, especially in London. Victorian prejudices about it being acceptable for men to sow wild oats before marriage, but not women, were everywhere being challenged – especially in an environment where marriageable men were in short supply. Even before the First World War there had been rumblings of a new kind of thinking. The popularity of a play by Walter Houghton called *Hindle Wakes*, first performed at the Aldwych in 1912, illustrates this.[82] The play centres on the story of a mill girl, Fanny Hawthorn, who has a fling with her boss's son over a holiday trip to Llandudno. Her parents discover this, and all hell follows. Fanny's mother determines opportunistically that Alan, the factory owner's son, must marry her daughter. But Alan is engaged to another girl, from a wealthy background: it is clear that the night with Fanny was 'just a bit of fun'. The two families meet to decide how to put things right. Alan's father reluctantly decides that his son should do the honourable thing and marry the girl he has slept with. But any chance of this botch-up solution coming about disappears when Fanny, an intelligent and independent-minded girl, speaks out for herself. She refuses, point blank, to be pushed into marriage with Alan. Fanny has come to see Alan as a bit of a wimp. She admits that going to bed with him was no more than a bit of fun for her too. *Hindle Wakes* enjoyed a long run in London and was filmed four times over the next thirty years – twice as a silent film, in 1918 and 1927, with sound in 1931, and again in 1952. It was also to be televised in 1976. Its message was clearly particularly potent and relevant for audiences between the wars.

In bohemian and literary circles all kinds of experiments were going on. 'Sapphism' and male homosexuality (the latter illegal) were perfectly acceptable to many. The 'Bright Young

3.6 'Miss Modern' resplendent in her cutting-edge swimsuit. Cover image, *Miss Modern*, August 1934 (© IPC Media 2012; courtesy of the British Library).

Things' sometimes flirted with drugs as well as downing cocktails; their escapades and wild partying became the stuff of press exposures and comic novels.[83] A more telling guide to what was going on in this milieu in the 1930s can be found in Nerina Shute's autobiography *We Mixed Our Drinks*.[84] Shute at nineteen was a typist, bored by her work and ambitious to try journalism. She aspired to be bohemian rather than ladylike. With her friends, she cultivated an image of sophistication and outrageousness, but confessed that this often functioned as a cover for insecurity. Sexual confidence was particularly hard to acquire. She recalled 'the sheer awkwardness of being a modern girl and at the same time, a virgin'.[85] Shute wrote for *Film Weekly* and secured a contract with the *Sunday Graphic* for a regular diary series written by 'an ultra-modern girl'. She was encouraged to shock. In place of valentines, she wrote, young women were now discussing contraceptives. Equipped with a volume of Marie Stopes, she determinedly set about losing her own virginity, and later experimented with bisexuality. She bleached her hair blonde. Carefully made-up, she dressed to look like a film star, or glamour girl, walking along Bond Street with a gardenia in her buttonhole and a small white poodle tucked under her arm.

Shute worked for a while as a publicity manager for the American cosmetics firm Max Factor. She was fascinated by the potential of cosmetics to alter appearance, marvelling that 'she was changed by make-up and peroxide and expensive suits into a modern person who caught the eye'.[86] But she was never easy about this deliberate creating of illusion, later abandoning the attempt to look like a glamour girl.

Shute's memoir probes beneath the surface of what it meant to be labelled 'a modern girl'. A magazine which targeted young women, the first issue of which appeared in October 1930, provides more insights. The magazine, published by George Newnes, was called *Miss Modern*. It ran for ten years, ceasing publication after the outbreak of the Second World War in 1940. *Miss Modern* was a highly attractive publication which addressed girls as independent-minded, competent young women, with a regular wage packet, and an interest in relationships and style. 'At last I have found a paper that doesn't waste half of its space on housekeeping and baby affairs,' wrote one reader appreciatively.[87] The paper was up-to-the-minute in its advice on fashion, with film star Madeleine Carroll writing a regular column on beauty and cosmetics. It carried adverts for soluble sanitary towels, alongside knitting patterns for bathing costumes and knitted dressing gowns with feather trimmings. There were patterns for sewing every kind of garment, from office frocks to satin beach pyjamas. Much of this must have been beyond the means of the majority, but they could still dream. The girl on a tight budget was provided with helpful hints such as how to make jewellery out of split peas, or by stringing nutmegs into necklaces and painting them gold. There were endless debates about the modern girl. It was assumed that the majority of young women still hoped to marry. But adverts for personal insurance and pension schemes encouraged girls to look after themselves if they didn't. There were fewer torrid romance stories in *Miss Modern* than in some of the contemporary magazines produced for young women. In 1938 a story called 'Flowering Desert' warned that

> No woman who awakens the desire of an Arab sheikh can ever feel secure – for love in the desert is passion unleashed, more bitter than sweet, more humiliating than rapturous.[88]

'What are you marrying *for*?' asked an article in the same issue, advising readers to consider their goals. Was it love/security/children/loyalty/shared interests or companionship they were after? Women needed to be clear about what they wanted. It was no good sulking later because a newly acquired husband turned out to be 'a plodder' in the business world.[89] Miss Modern might dream of romance, and find pleasure in imagining a more luxurious way of living. But she was encouraged to keep her feet on the ground – and her eye on the road – nonetheless.

4 | GOOD-TIME GIRLS, BABY DOLLS AND TEENAGE BRIDES

In the mid-1930s the Home Office did what it could to head off a minor moral panic about girls. There had been a spate of headlines in the British newspapers deploring 'Immoral Little Girls', 'Shameless Little Hussies' and so forth. A 1934 issue of the *Daily Express* inveighed against 'Girls under 16 Who Tempt Men', adding 'They have neither morals nor manners, says a Judge.'[1] The judge in question was Mr Travers Humphreys, who had presided over a case against a sixteen-year-old errand boy at Wiltshire Assizes. The boy had been charged with sexual offences against a thirteen-year-old girl. Mr Justice Humphreys was in no doubt that the girl was the more sexually experienced of the pair and that she had 'led the boy on'. He considered it iniquitous that the boy should be criminalised while the girl was let off scot-free, and he wrote to the Home Secretary to explain his position.[2] The newspapers used the case to sound off about moral depravity in young girls. Then the Archbishop of Canterbury decided to get involved, writing to the Home Office about whether he should bring up the issue in the House of Lords.[3]

Officials in the Home Office were tactful. Travers Humphreys was gently reminded that the recent Children and Young Persons Act of 1933 allowed local authorities to send girls who were considered in need of care and protection to 'Approved Schools'. The girl in question in the 1934 case had in fact been sent to Walcot Home for Girls in Bath.[4] The Archbishop of Canterbury received a full and careful reply to his letter. The Home Office conceded that girls under seventeen who were 'out of parental control and beginning to lead a loose life' posed a problem for the authorities since they often found it hard to settle in approved schools. They frequently ran away from these institutions and it was difficult to know what to do with them. The letter suggested that the archbishop might consider calling a small conference to consider some of these matters, rather than simply fanning the flames of more scandal and publicity.[5]

The Archbishop of Canterbury convened his symposium on 'Lax Conduct Amongst Girls' at Lambeth Palace in April 1935. Dr A. H. Morris, architect of the 1933 Children and Young Persons Act, attended on behalf of the Home Office. Representatives from the Salvation Army, the Church Army and various youth associations were also there. There was a great deal of vague talk about whether sex education and the availability of contraceptives should be seen as a problem, or as a solution. The archbishop thought that something might be done by stopping the needless advertising of contraceptives. One or two people thought that the age of consent to sexual intercourse should be raised to eighteen. The meeting petered out inconclusively, which was just what the Home Office had predicted.[6]

More liberal attitudes to female sexuality were seen as causing new problems. Gladys Mary Hall's study of prostitution in the 1930s emphasised the enormous changes in attitudes to sexual morality which had taken place since the Great War. The book's introduction conceded ruefully that 'Between the old bogies of Victorian prudery and the new bogies of sexual promiscuity it is not easy to see and think clearly.'[7] Hall defined prostitution to include 'paid and unpaid forms of sex promiscuity'. She maintained that professional prostitution was in decline. This was because women were becoming much more adventurous about sex. It was becoming part of courtship. Many young women were ready to go to bed with their boyfriends in exchange for gifts, meals out, or a motor-run.[8] Men much preferred this arrangement. Professional prostitutes, Hall concluded, were being replaced by amateurs.[9]

Hall's way of looking at this subject, like that of so many of her contemporaries, made the relationships between young women, consumption and pleasure suspicious in a *moral* sense. There was little evidence, Hall insisted, to show that poverty was driving women into prostitution. However, there was ample evidence to show that they slept with men to obtain luxuries. Young women hankered after fashion, particularly 'dress, drink, dainties and gay times'. Hall cited the psychologist Cyril Burt's work on female delinquency, in which (as we saw in the previous chapter) he claimed that very young girls often became 'habitual little courtesans' for the sake of sweets.[10]

The 'joy-ride girls', the flappers bent on weekend pleasure, were transmuted in the public imagination into the 'good-time girl'.[11] The good-time girl was 'no better than she ought to be'. She had probably had her head turned by watching too many Hollywood movies. She was likely to wear cosmetics and cheap perfume, and to dream of owning a fur coat. With the outbreak of war in 1939 the kind of anxieties around girls' behaviour with servicemen which had been evident during the previous world war resurfaced. Posters warned of peroxide-blonde harpies preying on soldiers for favours. There was widespread concern about 'venereal disease' (VD) reaching epidemic proportions in the armed forces. When American servicemen arrived in Britain, anxieties intensified and acquired another dimension.[12] Would English girls throw themselves at well-fed and healthy-bodied American GIs with good teeth? Would they trade their virtue for nylons and chewing gum? And what about *black* American servicemen? Fears of miscegenation – 'the spectre of half-caste babies' – were again close to the surface.[13]

Across the country in the 1940s, local newspapers, probation records and juvenile court proceedings show a high level of concern about girls consorting with servicemen. In Brighton, for instance, Mrs Cooke, a woman probation officer, wrote to the Home Office Children's Department over her worries.[14] She maintained that girls under seventeen were regularly hanging about with soldiers, and refusing to attend VD clinics. Echoing Gladys Hall, Mrs Cooke insisted that enthusiastic amateurs were putting professional prostitutes out of business. She complained that local councillors were reluctant to address the problem because they did not want to detract from Brighton's reputation as an 'unfettered holiday town'.

These various fears were all brought into sharp focus in 1944, in connection with the widely reported horrors of what became known as the 'Cleft Chin' murder case. This was the sorry tale of two individuals, one a seventeen-year-old girl named Elizabeth Marina Jones but styling herself 'Georgina Grayson', the other a Swedish-born American GI named Karl Hulten.[15] The pair went on a six-day spree of cold-blooded, hit-and-run crime and violence in London and South-East England which led some to liken them to an English Bonnie and Clyde phenomenon, although the Hulten–Jones collaboration was nasty, brutish and short. It certainly lacked any romance. George Orwell, who wrote about this 'pitiful and sordid' case in his essay 'Decline of the English Murder', was somewhat at a loss to explain why it should have become the 'cause célèbre' of the war years and predicted that it would soon be forgotten.[16] He judged that it lacked the haunting, memorable qualities of the 'old domestic poisoning dramas' or Jack the Ripper stories which lived on in the public imagination.

Elizabeth Jones met Karl Hulten in a café near Hammersmith tube station in October 1944. She introduced herself as a dancer, Georgina Grayson. He posed as a lieutenant called Ricky Allen. He was actually a private who had deserted. Back home, he had both a wife and a baby daughter. Elizabeth had a troubled history. Her parents had despaired of her as a child and she had run away first from home (in Neath, Glamorganshire) and then from the approved school in Cheshire to which she had been sent by a juvenile court. At sixteen she married a family friend, mainly to gain independence from any further supervision. Almost immediately she fought with, and left, her husband and ran off to London. Her husband being on active service, Elizabeth benefited from an army separation allowance of 32 shillings per week. In London she supplemented this by working for brief spells as a tearoom waitress, cinema usherette and barmaid. She then tried to establish herself as a striptease artist and dancer. This proved harder than she had expected. However, she seems to have built up a network of contacts among American service-men, and to have made reasonable money by 'hostessing'. She allegedly kept a scrapbook, with plentiful details.

The couple appear to have tried to impress each other with their recklessness and bravado. Hulten boasted of connections with a Chicago mob. Elizabeth professed an appetite for danger, fantasising about becoming a gangster's 'gun-moll'. They took to the road that evening in Hulten's (stolen) heavy truck. Their first victim was a girl cyclist, whom they deliberately pushed off the road, robbed and left in a ditch. The following day they attempted to hold up and rob a taxi driver, but were frustrated by the sudden appearance of an armed American officer. Their next move was to pick up a nineteen-year-old girl. She had missed her train, and they offered her a lift to Reading. Hulten stopped the truck at Egham, claiming a fault with the back axle. The girl got out of the truck with Jones to try to see what was going on. Hulten hit her over the head with a steel bar. Jones and Hulten then robbed the girl of her possessions and lobbed her into a river. Amazingly, she survived to tell the story. The following night, Hulten and Jones, still short of money, decided to target another taxi driver. Their victim this time was George Heath, driving along Hammersmith Broadway. Heath, married with two young sons, was a good-looking man of distinctive appearance: he had a pronounced cleft chin. Hailed by Elizabeth, Heath stopped his car and the pair got in. When they reached the Great West Road, sometime after midnight, Hulten asked Heath to pull in. As Heath was opening the rear door to enable his passengers to get out, he received a bullet through his back from Hulten's automatic. He was shoved into the front passenger seat, and as Hulten drove on, Elizabeth went through the dying man's pockets stripping him of anything they might sell. They dumped Heath's body in a ditch and drove back to Hammersmith.

The next day, the pair celebrated. They treated themselves to a day at the races, a meal out, and the cinema. There seems to have been an easy familiarity between the two, but no sexual intimacy. Hulten later confessed that a rash on Jones's body had made him wonder whether she was diseased. He commented that the American Army medical authorities had warned men against such things. Neither appeared remorseful after killing Heath. Rather, their recklessness increased. Jones expressed a whim for a fur coat. So they drove to the West End and hovered near a side entrance to the Berkeley Hotel. They watched women emerge until one appeared, resplendent in white ermine, which caught Elizabeth's eye. Hulten leapt out and tried to strip the coat from the woman's back. A policeman appeared at this point, so they made a quick getaway. The couple parted soon after. Within days, police found Heath's body, and then his car. They closed in on Hulten. Elizabeth Jones began to panic, talked to third parties, and was soon herself arrested and charged.

The trial drew crowds and attracted massive attention in the press. Hulten appeared nonchalant and unrepentant in court and doodled sketches of cars and aeroplanes on a pad throughout the proceedings. He blamed Elizabeth, Elizabeth blamed Hulten. Both were found guilty and sentenced to death, although in the case of Elizabeth there was a recommendation to mercy. Elizabeth sobbed convulsively as the verdicts were announced, and she left the court shrieking accusations at Hulten as 'a brute'. Both parties appealed. Hulten's appeal was dismissed.[17] Elizabeth Jones was given a last-minute reprieve.

There was a public outcry at this. Most of the objectors thought that the verdict should have been the same for both parties. Large numbers of protestors – including many women – thought that Jones should hang. Indeed graffiti to this effect, accompanied by crude drawings of a figure dangling from a scaffold, were chalked on to walls in her Glamorganshire home town. Factory girls in some parts of Britain threatened strikes over the judgment. Support for Elizabeth was muted, although interestingly she received several offers of marriage. Hulten was hanged on his twenty-third birthday in March 1945.

What Orwell had found so squalid about the Cleft Chin murder was its pointlessness; there was no feeling in it. This was no crime of passion but a callous affair reflecting 'the anonymous life of the dance-halls and the false values of the American film'.[18] But this was precisely what caught the public imagination.

Elizabeth Jones brought into focus widespread but diffuse contemporary fears about the good-time girl. Alwyn Raymond, a journalist who wrote a popular account of the case, represented Elizabeth in just these terms. She is described as a striptease artist who had been booed off the floor, but had discovered the lucrative potential of American servicemen.

> From this discovery can be dated the life of dancing, drinking and comparative luxury that she counted as success. In a few weeks, she had thrown away all her old clothes. Now it was silk stockings, high heels, American perfume, flashy jewellery and all the things that she thought made her 'glamorous'. And she took upon herself what she called a 'stage name' – Georgina Grayson.[19]

The Cleft Chin murder inspired a number of accounts and fictions. A. J. La Bern's popular novel *Night Darkens the Streets*, first published in 1947, was inspired by the case.[20] The story is that of Gwen Rawlings, a working-class girl from Pimlico. Gwen is described as gorgeous but empty-headed, easily seduced by the glamour of American film stars. There is a rather contemptuous, even sneering tone about her portrayal as a 'back-street blonde' with too much lipstick and 'a gaudy soul':

> Out of the wilderness of Pimlico came Gwen Rawlings, an ignoramus with starry eyes, a well-developed body and an undeveloped mind. She had no inherent vice, only a greed for the sweet things in life ...[21]

Gwen runs away from home, rents a room and secures a job in a nightclub. She poses as a sophisticate, but is soon out of her depth and taken advantage of: the city is shown as darkly menacing for girls. An affair with a jazz musician offers her a short period of happiness. This is soon interrupted as she finds herself falsely implicated in theft and unable to defend herself in the juvenile court. She is sent away for 'moral protection' in an approved school. Stripped of her feminine clothes and subjected to an austere regime, she becomes hysterical. Far from becoming penitent, she is corrupted further by the influence of other delinquent girls. Humiliation gives way to plotting and rebellion. Gwen runs away and hitches a lift to London. After a series of escapades she finds herself consorting with a set of dodgy, undesirable types in Brighton. One night she and her friends set out to drive to London for the races – they are all drunk. Gwen is at the wheel, swigging from a whisky bottle, when the car hits and kills a policeman. Desperately fleeing from all this, she takes up with a couple of American servicemen who have recently deserted. Like Hulten and Jones, they turn to robbery and violence. Gwen's story ends with her being tried for murder and found guilty – with a recommendation to mercy.

In May 1947 the popular paper *Picture Post* drew attention to a forthcoming film, based on the La Bern story but entitled *Good Time Girl*.[22] The film was produced by Sidney Box for Gainsborough, an offshoot of the Rank Organisation. *Picture Post*'s article was headed 'Fight in a Reformatory', and consisted mainly of photographs of girls running amok: climbing over desks, kicking, slapping and biting each other, and tearing each other's hair out. These photographs (by Bert Hardy) carried captions such as 'Good-time girls become the tough-time girls' and 'The kind of scene that teachers have bad dreams about'. The feature unleashed a storm of controversy.[23] A strongly worded complaint to the Home Secretary suggested that the film presented an appalling picture of what went on in approved schools: it was deemed near-libellous and detrimental to the government's

4.1 Girls in an reformatory run amok. Scene from the controversial film *Good Time Girl* (1948) (photograph © Bert Hardy/Picture Post/Getty Images).

interests. The film was judged to be harmful to the interests of Elizabeth Jones (a former inmate of the approved school in Sale, Cheshire, and by May 1947 serving time in Aylesbury borstal). Equally, it was considered damaging to her parents.[24] There were calls to Chuter Ede, as Home Secretary, to take action. Correspondence in the National Archives shows that the Home Office made contact with Gainsborough Pictures and explained these concerns. Chuter Ede had lunch with Mr Rank. However, the British Board of Film Censors did not consider that there was a case for censorship. Sir Sidney Harris, chair of the BBFC, maintained that 'censorship cannot be used for the purpose of preventing misrepresentations'.[25]

There was an attempt to reach some kind of accommodation. The Home Office wanted Gainsborough to portray the approved school in the film in a more sympathetic light. A letter to Mr Rank voiced a number of concerns, such as the harsh depiction of authority, and the out-of-date uniforms worn by the girls 'which might have been seen many years ago in a reformatory' but were argued to have no resemblance to the clothes worn in the schools of the 1940s.[26] Some changes were made in response to these Home Office concerns. For instance, a short scene was inserted in which the school's headmistress comments on the difficulties of securing the right kind of teachers committed to working with difficult girls. But these changes failed to reassure many government officials, who thought the scenes in the film showing what went on in an approved school were so well acted and convincing that they might provoke great disquiet.[27]

The film told the story of Gwen Rawlings (played by Jean Kent) in the form of a morality tale, related by a female probation officer (Flora Robson) to a young girl (Lyla Lawrence, played by Diana Dors). Unhappy at home, Lyla was just beginning to go off the rails: 'Why shouldn't I have a good time?' she asks petulantly. By the end of the film, the sad story of Gwen's descent into damnation has convinced her to reform. Finally released in the spring of 1948, *Good Time Girl* met with a mixed reception.[28] Some felt that it glamorised vice. The *Daily Mail*'s critic thundered against the film as 'sordid', 'vicious' and 'loathsome'. The reviewer in the *Sunday Dispatch* alleged that it had made him vomit. Women's groups in Newcastle protested vehemently, insisting that 'Girls should not see this film,' and asking, 'Is it our desire to debauch our young people altogether, or do we really wish foreigners to think that this is the British way of life?'[29] The *Evening Standard* was more phlegmatic: 'Bad girl makes worse film,' announced its opinion column.[30] 'The film has a MORAL,' announced the *Evening Standard*:

> Today's sermon tells us what happens to little girls who like dancing and jewellery and run away from their brutal daddies who beat them – as if you didn't know.

Dilys Powell in the *Sunday Times* was one of the few who

considered the film a morality tale rather than an incitement to debauchery. But even she wondered whether its depiction of the workings of the juvenile courts was overly pessimistic.[31] Comparatively few of the reviewers seem to have engaged with questions about the kind of treatment meted out to girls in approved schools, even though both *Night Darkens the Streets* and *Good Time Girl* were critical of current practice. It was the government's reputation in this respect that had worried the Home Office.

Approved schools for girls attracted a disproportionate amount of public interest. This was probably not unconnected with the subject's potential to stimulate erotic imaginings and the regular production of second-rate films and bad novels.[32] Markedly fewer girls than boys came before the juvenile courts.[33] Girls were more likely than boys to be classified as delinquent for moral and sexual, rather than criminal, behaviour. Lilian Barker, Governor of Aylesbury Girls' Borstal in the 1920s, judged that most of the girls in her care got into trouble because they were 'over-sexed'. 'Sex to my mind ought to be put in the same category as stealing and lying,' she asserted, adding somewhat scarily: 'It has to be got out of them somehow.'[34]

Dame Lilian acquired a reputation for humane prison governance. But some reform schools (later approved schools) could be frightening places. Knowle Hill, originally a reformatory school for girls in Kenilworth, Warwickshire, housed up to fifty girls. There had been riots among the inmates in 1923: the school was said to be entirely out of control and the police were called in.[35] An officer reportedly was badly bitten by one of the girls. Punishments were harsh. Some girls were whipped with the tawse on their hands or buttocks. Others were forced to swallow castor oil – a traditional punishment which produced cramp-like stomach pains. A few girls alleged that they were threatened with injections by the school doctor, which they were told would be painful and make them sick. The Home Office had been forced to intervene by visiting the school and carrying out an inquiry. Much of the girls' testimony was denied. Notes on the case suggest that the injections may have contained apomorphine, sometimes used in cases of hysteria.[36] The issue of corporal punishment was controversial: two female inspectors had strongly objected in the Knowle Hill case. But while discouraging the practice, the Home Office was reluctant to ban it altogether. An internal memorandum in 1923 submitted that the task of controlling difficult girls – especially when hysterical – could be formidable.[37] The punishment book from Knowle Hill shows that canings and slappings continued into the 1950s.[38] A boy from the local grammar school, who visited as part of an exchange in 1970, never forgot his sight of the 'padded cell' at Knowle Hill, a small lockable room with heavy padding on walls, floor and door.[39] There were, no doubt, institutions run on enlightened and compassionate principles, but others found it hard to shed the punitive traditions of the reformatory.

The good-time girl had become a folk-devil. Stereotypes of her appeared in surprising places, sometimes under the guise of 'objective' social research. In 1946, for instance, the *British Medical Journal* published an article on 'The Unstable Adolescent Girl' which had originally appeared as an appendix to a report of the Committee of Psychiatry and the Law, and had gained the approval of both the British Medical Association and the Magistrates' Association.[40] This urged attention to what it defined as a serious social problem, one which it contended had become worse since the end of the Second World War: that of 'the good-time girl', 'unamenable to discipline and control'. These unstable girls often showed 'precocious physical development, especially in the breast and hips'. They were cunning, and targeted good-looking men with money.

> They spend a great deal of time on making up their faces and adorning themselves, though they often do not trouble to wash and are sluttish about their undergarments. Their favourite reading matter consists of the weekly journals dealing with the love life of film stars, and they live in a fantasy world of erotic glamour. Frequently they are a good deal more intelligent and sophisticated than their parents, whom they outwit and despise.[41]

This report has echoes of Cyril Burt, who had characterised girl delinquents as sometimes highly intelligent but 'oversexed': reckless adventuresses with no sense of shame.[42] According to the *British Medical Journal* writers, such girls did not settle well in remand homes or approved schools, and needed medical and psychiatric treatment. These wayward girls, they submitted, were out of control.[43]

Criticism of young girls' appearance, their hairstyles, make-up and mode of dress is common in post-1945 accounts of wayward girls. H. D. Willcock's report on juvenile delinquency, for instance, published in 1949, contained observations such as 'the girls are all extremely heavily made up, with extra thick lipstick applied carelessly', and 'Their faces were heavily and inexpertly made up, one [girl] sported a pair of long ear-rings.'[44] Writing about girls' problems, and problem girls, is shot through with prejudice stemming from assumptions about class, aesthetics, taste and morality. With references to breasts and underwear, and accusations of sluttishness and nymphomania, these descriptions are also eroticised. This is apparent in the representations; it is also clear from the way in which they were read, both at the time and subsequently. An internet trawl for 'reform school girl' yields predictable results. And nearly a century later, accounts of the riots and of the punishments meted out to the hapless girls at Knowle Hill are detailed on semi-pornographic websites.[45]

The post-war moral panic over good-time girls was fuelled by unease over the belief that they were earning 'easy money'. Women who struck up relationships with men from upper- or upper-middle-class backgrounds often came in for particular vilification. They were resented as being 'on the make'. Ruth Ellis, tried and hanged for shooting her abusive lover David Blakely in the mid-fifties, suffered from the class hostility of those who condemned her social ambition along with her sexual behaviour as a good-time girl.[46] Like Gladys Mary Hall in the 1930s, most investigators maintained that girls traded sex for luxury, not out of necessity. Scotland Yard's Detective-Inspector Robert Fabian, whose colourful tales inspired a popular BBC television series, *Fabian of the Yard* (1954–6), insisted that he knew what made a girl become a prostitute. It was 'sheer laziness, and vanity'. These girls were as hard as nails, he asserted. His own hardened, man-of-the-world tone blended with an American-crime-writerish misogyny:

> A whore is a bad apple. There is a big brown bruise on her soul, of self-indulgence and selfishness. I do not think that there exists in London any such person as an honest prostitute. They taint any flesh they touch.[47]

But the pipe-smoking Fabian also set out to reassure. The Metropolitan Police made it their business to look out for runaway girls and wayward daughters, he contended. A big van ('the Children's Waggon') did its rounds every evening, collecting young girls who had gone missing or escaped from remand homes, in order to deliver them to safety.[48] Fabian's writing bristles with double standards, demonising good-time girls, indulgent towards the men who would consort with them.

But one group of men was singled out for particular opprobrium. Immigrants – particularly of Maltese and Sicilian origin – were seen as particularly responsible for the burgeoning of vice in post-war London. The popular press whipped up a great deal of scandal about the Messina brothers, a focus of police attention since the 1930s, who were finally forced out of Britain in the 1950s.[49] But it is difficult to know how representative the Messina enterprises were. Most of the women in the Messina network seem also to have been immigrants, often with Maltese or Italian connections, a fact which undermines any stereotypes claiming that the Messinas preyed on English girls who had run away from home.[50]

In 1958 the film *Passport to Shame* claimed to expose the evil of girls trapped into prostitution by pimps with Italian-sounding names. The film began with a spoken introduction by Robert Fabian warning of 'the terrible methods used to trap innocent girls into prostitution'.[51] The film trotted out all the clichés of 1900s white slavery: drugged cigarettes, blondes writhing on beds, a girl caged in by a grille of iron bars. A young Diana Dors added filmic interest, trussed up in a basque and suspenders. In the 1950s, lurid stories of London vice and criminality filled the pages of the *People* and the *News of the World*.[52] Any evidence of white girls consorting with immigrant or 'coloured' men continued to provoke horror, and often predictably stereotyped reactions, in the press.

The real situation could be very different. Just before the end of the Second World War, for instance, social investigator Phyllis Young investigated conditions in the Stepney area. She found that local cafés served as rendezvous for meetings between coloured male immigrants, often seamen, and white girls.[53] Reversing common stereotypes of girls as victims, Phyllis Young described how these girls were often opportunistic, bent on seeking a livelihood. She suggested that they found 'the coloured man an easy prey'. Other girls were genuinely attracted to foreigners, finding them more passionate, or charming, than the 'average Englishman'. Mixed marriages were becoming more common.[54] Edith Ramsay, who battled for many years as a community worker in the East End, noted that runaway girls often met with a warm welcome in the 'counter-society' of the café world. In her opinion, forced prostitution was rare. But the high wages obtainable in the sex trade were to her a worrying incentive.[55] After the war, Inspector Fabian's confident assertion that London was the vice capital of the world, full of foreign pimps on the prowl for innocent girls, unsettled parents further.[56]

Nevertheless, most girls lived lives very distant from all this. The delinquent adolescent female, the reform-school girl who loomed so large in the popular imagination after the war, was something of a rarity. Between five and eight times as many boys as girls came before the courts, charged with indictable offences in the 1950s.[57] Around six times as many boys as girls were admitted to approved schools between 1952 and 1957.[58] There were fewer approved schools for girls than for boys in Britain (39 for girls, 88 for boys) because they simply were not needed. In 1958, for instance, only 766 girls in the whole of England were sent to approved schools.[59]

One journalist who was well aware of the extent to which moral panic had distorted the picture of youthful femininity was *Picture Post*'s reporter Hilde Marchant. In January 1951, *Picture Post* published a feature written by Marchant and entitled

4.2 Betty Burden, a young hairdresser in Birmingham in 1951, helping her mother with the weekly wash. *Picture Post* journalist Hilde Marchant wanted to reassure readers that girls were family-minded and sensible, unlikely to be swept off their feet by teenage culture (photograph © Bert Hardy/Picture Post/Getty Images).

'Millions Like Her' which described the life of Betty Burden, a young working-class girl in Birmingham.[60] Betty's life was described as typical of Britain's young girls. She was introduced as 'The real thing – not the imagined creature the sociologists theorise about, novelists write about, and moralists deplore.' Betty lived with her family in what could only be described as a slum: back-to-back housing in an area scarred by industrial waste and bomb damage. But behind the squalid interior the inside of the house was gleaming. Her family was close-knit and caring. Betty worked as a children's hairdresser in a Birmingham department store. She had a boyfriend and enjoyed dancing. She didn't smoke, rarely drank alcohol, and dressed modestly and neatly. A great deal of her time was devoted to helping her mother with housework, Sunday dinner and the weekly family wash. The feature was illustrated with a series of photographs by Bert Hardy celebrating Betty's love of her family, her modest aspirations and her unimpeachable respectability. Both text and captions make it clear that Betty and young girls like her were the hope of post-war Britain.

The research organisation Mass Observation carried out a survey of 'teen-age girls' in London in 1949 which painted a similar picture.[61] Two hundred girls were interviewed. Most were reported as fairly happy and satisfied with their lives. Their leisure activities focused around cinema, dancing and going shopping. Most got on well with their families and felt no great urge to leave home. Friends were important, and going out with boyfriends was particularly so after the age of around fifteen. The majority of the girls looked forward to getting married and having children. The writer of the report judged that this was less to do with romance than with the desire for independence and a home of their own. Other surveys drawing on larger samples came to similar conclusions. Leslie Wilkins's study of some 450 adolescent girls in 1955 showed that most girls wanted to be married by the time they reached their mid-twenties.[62] Thelma Veness's study of another six hundred girls, a few years later, showed that 90 per cent expected to marry and saw home making as their vocation, although over half of these expected to combine work with marriage at some point.[63] A home of one's own was a particularly important component of many girls' dreams for a better future. Getting married was seen as the first step to securing a home. Somewhat disconcertingly, researchers found that many girls' expectations of husbands petered out once the latter had provided them with a home and children.[64] When asked to imagine their lives as adult women, large numbers of girls fantasised about their husbands dropping dead in middle age, leaving them with a new freedom.

4.3 Young women working on an assembly line in a clothing factory in Leicester, 1948. Many girls were keen to leave school as soon as possible and looked forward to early marriage (photograph © Picture Post/Hulton Archive/Getty Images).

Most girls' lives were shaped by the fact that their schooling ended in very early adolescence: at fourteen, most commonly, in the war years. The school leaving age was not raised to fifteen until 1947. Secondly there was the trend to early marriage. This had been evident before the Second World War, but became more marked afterwards. In 1921 only about 15 per cent of brides had been under twenty-one years of age. By 1965 this proportion had risen to 40 per cent.[65] Early marriage was more common among working-class girls. Formal education was often experienced as a somewhat unreal interlude in their lives, and they might be impatient to leave school and start earning. The older elementary schools were often bleak and unattractive places, and it was not always easy to see the point of lessons. But some middle-class girls could be equally keen to leave school as soon as possible. They often resented having to wear uniform and being treated as children. Early school leaving and marriage at a young age meant that jobs could be seen as short-term, stop-gap experiences. The mathematician Kathleen Ollerenshaw, writing about girls' education in post-1945 Britain, commented that it was increasingly the fashion 'for a girl to step from the school choir to the church altar, and to discard her prefect's badge for a wedding ring'.[66]

The slaughter of young men during the First World War had made it impossible in the years that followed for many young women to find husbands. This encouraged some to take education – and career opportunities – seriously. Things looked different after 1945. Following the Second World War, young women's chances of marrying were excellent. Women teachers feared that the rush to marry young would undermine their pupils' commitment to scholastic achievement. Parents entering daughters as pupils in some of the more academic girls' secondary schools were sometimes required to sign a pledge to keep their daughter at school at least until her sixteenth birthday. These signed commitments cannot have been legally binding, but headmistresses nevertheless hoped to exert moral pressure.

The girls' schools of the 1950s became battlegrounds. There had probably always been a tendency for women teachers to see girls' interest in boys as a distraction from intellectual pursuits. In the 1950s this led to regular conflict over uniform regulations, for instance, or girls' interest in cosmetics.[67] Issues around institutional regulations and personal autonomy became particularly vexed in a context where there was so much ambiguity around being grown up. Girls who were legally able to marry at sixteen (albeit only if their parents consented) didn't always warm to the idea of regulation underwear. What business was it of teachers

4.4 Schoolgirls in a domestic science class show off their cake-making skills(early 1960s) (© Fred Morley/Hulton/Getty Images).

to insist on the colour of bras and pants? Skirmishes over nail varnish and skirt length became endemic.

The desire of some women teachers to keep girls in a state of sexual hibernation (or denial) for as long as possible was undermined by pervasive cultural trends. Nabokov's *Lolita* was published (in Paris) in 1955, although the book was banned in the USA and the UK until 1958.[68] In *Lolita*, the novel's narrator, Humbert Humbert, becomes sexually obsessed with and then abducts a twelve-year-old girl. He threatens her with reform school if she tries to run away and leave him. *Baby Doll*, the controversial film with a screenplay by Tennessee Williams, was released in 1956. It starred Carroll Baker in the role of its lubricious, thumb-sucking heroine, married at seventeen but planning to hold on to her virginity until her twentieth birthday. The sexualisation of young girls in the 1950s was hardly new, but it provoked new tensions.

Most literary representations of 'the nymphet' came from men.[69] But women's fashions also took a disconcertingly regressive turn. There were 'baby doll' nightdresses and pyjamas. And even Paris began to show a leaning towards little-girl dresses and coats. Grown women started to wear Alice bands with girlish bows perched on the top of their heads.[70] In her essay *Brigitte Bardot and the Lolita Syndrome*, written in 1959, the French feminist Simone de Beauvoir expressed ambivalence. The child-woman might be a new force of nature, free from conventional feminine artifice, she judged. Her appeal was based on both challenging and reinforcing desire and confidence in men.[71]

Among educationalists, the question of what – and how – girls should be taught yet again became increasingly vexed. Did they need more sex education, or less? More might offer protection, but equally, might put ideas into their heads. If the majority of girls left school at the earliest opportunity and got married as soon as they could after that, conservatives insisted, shouldn't their education show more emphasis on courtship and married life? There was a growing tendency to divide girls into two categories: the 'normal' majority, who looked forward to lives centring on marriage and family life, and a deviant minority of intellectual girls who likely as not wore spectacles and would end up as spinsters. John Newsom (later Sir John) was County Education Officer for Hertfordshire when he published his controversial polemic *The Education of Girls* in 1948.[72] He suggested that girls' schools, run by bookish women teachers, had got their mission wrong. Girls needed fewer books and should be taught more cookery so that they could cosset their future husbands. Men cared very little for erudition in women, Newsom pontificated, but they did enjoy a good dinner. Experience had taught him, he added snidely, that those who disagreed with this view were 'normally deficient in the quality of womanliness and the particular physical and mental attributes of their sex'.[73] In other words, intellectual women could be justifiably dismissed as freaks and made poor role models.

These ideas made an impact. Government reports on education such as the Crowther Report, *Fifteen to Eighteen* (1959), and Newsom's own report on the education of children of average and less than average ability, *Half Our Future* (1963), made constant reference to the need to adjust girls' education to the needs of young brides. The curriculum, Crowther urged, should reflect girls' interest in dress, personal appearance, and human relationships.[74] And they needed lessons in housewifery. The writers of the Newsom Report admitted that some girls found domestic science a waste of time because they already had their fill of housework at home. But these girls, it was ventured, had even *more* need of domestic training – so that they could learn to appreciate just how fulfilling home making could be.[75] Views like this cut little ice in the more academic girls' schools, where many teachers maintained an aloof detachment from domestic subjects.[76] Needlework and cookery sometimes had a token presence in the curriculum, but it was tacitly understood that these were low-status subjects only to be taken seriously by the less academic girls.

Germaine Greer's celebrated feminist polemic *The Female Eunuch* was first published in 1970. It contained a memorable image of the schoolgirl: 'Sitting in her absurd version of masculine uniform, making sponge fingers with inky hands, she must really feel like the punching bag of civilisation.'[77] The description is vivid because conflicting social expectations for women were indeed fought out in the classroom, and girls found themselves caught in the crossfire. Grammar-school girls might be seen by

Newsom and his supporters as in danger of becoming defeminised, but in less academic institutions (or the lower streams of grammar schools) the concern was often the reverse. Here girls' behaviour might be seen as troublesome because they were *too* interested in their appearance, boys and sex. Caroline Brown, whose book *Lost Girls* was an account of her experience of teaching difficult girls in a remand home in the 1950s, remembered that art lessons often came to grief because the girls would steal the materials. Depressed by institutional garb and desperate to look feminine, they would improvise with art materials as makeshift cosmetics. Paintbrushes were snipped into false eyelashes, and red paint was used as rouge or lipstick.[78] Too feminine or not feminine enough? It was hard to get it right.

Autobiographical and personal stories bear this out. Girls' experience of schooling in the 1950s was strongly shaped by social class, but conflicts over femininity were nonetheless present at every level. Emma Tennant was the privileged daughter of a wealthy family (her father was the second Baron Glenconner) with estates in Scotland and the West Indies, grand houses and servants. She was a pupil at St Paul's Girls' School in London, a school with an excellent reputation. She insisted on leaving at fifteen. Like many of her class, Emma expected to marry soon after 'coming out' and a season as a debutante. This was what happened. She married at nineteen and soon became a mother, but the marriage proved ephemeral and she was left rudderless. Emma came to regret her lack of learning and embarked on ambitious if not always successful schemes for self-education.[79]

Tennant's semi-autobiographical account of this period in her life is entitled *Girlitude*: her conception of girlhood alludes to servitude in the sense of feeling imprisoned and defined by others, in spite of her wealthy background. Journalist Jill

Tweedie's middle-class background, though comfortable, was less elevated than Emma Tennant's. Jill was educated in south London at Croydon High School for Girls. A clever girl, she stayed at school long enough to pass her School Certificate at sixteen, but at that point her parents suggested that she should go on to a finishing school in Switzerland. The idea was for her to acquire feminine graces. Jill's teachers shook their heads disapprovingly and suggested she consider university instead. Her domineering father – with whom she had a charged and difficult relationship – poured scorn on this idea. There was no more talk of university.[80] Off she went to an expensive establishment in Switzerland where the girls were 'polished', talked to each other about sex, and learned the art of *repassage* (ironing).[81]

Lynn Barber, another journalist, has written an account of her girlhood and education at Lady Eleanor Holles School in London in the 1950s.[82] Barber's background was different from Tweedie's and Tennant's in that her parents had raised themselves into the professional middle class through a fervent belief in education and social betterment. Lynn was born, bred and trained to achieve, and confidently expected to go to university. However, as a teenager she found herself sucked into a relationship with an older man who subsequently proposed to her. Initially attracted by his worldliness and sophistication, she was unsure about the situation and confidently expected her parents to object. She was shell-shocked when they didn't.[83] Not only did they approve of the idea of their daughter's engagement but they immediately backtracked on their ideas of Lynn going to Oxford, suggesting that marriage was much more important for her future. The bubble of illusion popped when Lynn's fiancé turned out to be a crook and a conman who was all set to embark on bigamy – he already had a wife and children. With some effort, Lynn was steered back on course for A levels and university. What is interesting about this story is that it shows the fragility of expectations around education and career success for daughters in even a bookish and professional middle-class family in the 1950s.

Most girls learned that their education mattered less than that of their brothers. It was the old story: daughters were expected to marry and men didn't like women to be too clever. Even in the more academic schools of the 1950s, girls were often steered into sitting for two rather than three A levels, since that would get them into teacher training college if not university. After all, teaching was probably what they'd end up doing if they didn't get husbands. Better still, in the eyes of many parents, was secretarial college. Even girl graduates often followed up their degrees with a stint in a secretarial college. Hopefully they might marry the boss. There wasn't much else. Hardly surprisingly, many intelligent girls in the 1950s experienced femininity as a form of belittlement. Jill Tweedie (a tall girl) remembered that

> You had to become the Incredible Shrinking Woman. You had to make yourself smaller than them [men] in every way possible: small ego, small brain, small voice, small talk.[84]

The educational writer Jane Miller grew up a tomboy and went to Bedales, a coeducational and 'progressive' school. She learned early that boys 'were simply and obviously better than girls', and she acquired 'a contempt for anything girlish' in consequence.[85] Jane's bookish and artistic background supplied complex messages about gender. She had strong-minded aunts, for instance, who also disdained feminine frippery. Jane recorded a poignant memory of going to a family party 'wearing modest court shoes, with what were known as Louis heels, and raspberry-pink lipstick

– all this in order to try out what felt like a new and transvestite femininity'.[86] The aunts, Jane remembered, 'honked and spluttered' with laughter. Femininity itself could be experienced as a form of humiliation, a 'passport to shame'.

The 1950s, then, were not altogether a good time to be a girl. Things were beginning to change, however. The (Butler) Education Act of 1944 had introduced secondary schooling for all in England and Wales. The school leaving age was raised from fourteen to fifteen from 1947. The Butler Act later became notorious for enshrining a 'tripartite' system of education, which was effectively class-based. Children were divided into brainy types, those who were good with their hands, and a lumpen, 'less able' majority. The eleven-plus examination was there to weed them out and to grade them, like eggs. But the Act broke new ground for bright working-class children and for girls. Indeed, girls did so well in the eleven-plus examinations in the 1950s that some local authorities began to discriminate in favour of boys, lest the girls take over the grammar schools.

A grammar-school education could be a lifeline for a clever working-class girl. The writer and poet Maureen Duffy was born in 1933 and was brought up in difficult and impoverished circumstances. School was hugely important, in spite of conflicting messages and the strains and competing emotional claims of home. She learned to be guarded about herself and her sexuality, later coming out as a lesbian. Maureen Duffy noted in her autobiographical novel *That's How It Was* (1962) that 'the great enemy to advancement for working-class girls' in the 1950s was to become pregnant.[87]

The literary scholar Lorna Sage was born ten years later than Duffy in 1943. In her brilliantly insightful autobiography *Bad Blood* (2000), she describes growing up in Hanmer, Flintshire in the 1950s.[88] Lorna's social background defied easy description. Her grandfather was an Anglican clergyman, a difficult man with dodgy morals. Lorna's father was in the haulage business and her parents lived in a council house. Lorna tells us that her father only stopped hitting her as she entered her teens, a point at which spanking acquired sexual overtones. Sex and disappointment seethed beneath the surface of family life.[89] Lorna's grandfather lusted after her friends. Her uncle Bill made leery passes at his niece, seeing her as 'the poor man's Brigitte Bardot'. Access to books and a sound education at Whitchurch High School nurtured Lorna's imagination and provided her with a rich intellectual and imaginary life. At the same time, she and her best friend Gail were lured by the sounds of a new teenage culture. Brushing their hair into ponytails, they experimented with black eyeliner and white lipstick. They 'crackled with emotional static', brooding over the allure of Elvis-type bad boys.[90]

There were clever girls, and there were ordinary girls. Whitchurch High, like so many of the girls' grammar schools of the time, suggested a choice: 'You were supposed to choose between boys and books,' Lorna remembered. Girls were seen as 'the enemies of promise; a trap for boys', although as she ruefully observed later, 'with hindsight you can see that the opposite was the case'.[91] At sixteen she met a clever boy, Vic Sage, and the pair became close. Their physical intimacy seemed natural enough. However, without even being aware of having 'gone all the way', Lorna found herself pregnant.

There was consternation – and shame – all around. But the outcome confounds any assumptions about the 1950s as a completely hopeless decade for girls. Lorna's and Vic's parents eventually came round. The teachers at Whitchurch High also rallied, and Miss Roberts, her English teacher, was non-judgemental and supportive. The young people married and continued with their A levels. Getting into university was more of a challenge, for Lorna if not for Vic. Eighteen-year-old mothers were not seen as ideal applicants. County Education Officers would routinely stop girls' grants if they married or became pregnant. But the University of Durham eventually accepted both Lorna and Vic, and Lorna's parents looked after baby Sharon during termtime. Both Lorna and Vic went on to build successful careers in academia.

The 1950s was a decade characterised by troubled beginnings for girls. The widening of educational opportunities was slowly raising aspirations. This in itself increased the frustration and conflict that would eventually drive social change. Young women who made it to university in the years after 1945 certainly expressed frustration. Autobiographies and novels of the time exude it. Clever girls cooped up in the women's colleges of Oxford and Cambridge often felt excluded, relegated to living on the margins of an extended, male-public-school kind of world. Margaret Forster's first novel, *Dames' Delight* (1964), wittily caricatures the world of the women's college.[92] It depicts ageing, scholarly spinster dons focused on understanding the intricacies of medieval strip-farming and totally failing to communicate with younger students who are obsessed with sex and living in the shadow of the atom bomb. In Andrea Newman's novel *A Share of the World*, also published in 1964, women students in London similarly agonise over sex and relationships and show uneasy commitment to academic work.[93] Outside secretarial work or teaching, jobs for women seemed scarce. None of the women graduates in these novels has a clue what she will do after graduation.

These novels about women students can be seen as analogous to the 'angry young man' literature written by men in the 1950s.

There are obvious parallels between *Dames' Delight* and *Lucky Jim*, for instance, although Kingsley Amis's novel was published ten years earlier, in 1954. The sense of blockage, of being stuck in a cul-de-sac of unhelpful social expectations, is pervasive in both texts. But in women's novels and plays of the 1950s and early 1960s there is a stronger sense of marginality and exclusion. In 'angry young man' literature written by men, male working-class outsiders seek revenge on – or access to – power and social privilege by seducing middle-class girls. Two key texts written by women in this period are arguably more radical in that in each case their central protagonist looks outside the pale of respectable society altogether for some kind of hope or salvation. Nineteen-year-old Shelagh Delaney's play *A Taste of Honey*, first performed in 1958, showed a teenage girl, Jo, finding solace in relationships first with a 'coloured' sailor and later with a homosexual, Geoff, whose care and attention help her manage through the turmoil of coping with an illegitimate pregnancy.[94] Lynne Reid Banks's *The L-Shaped Room*, first published in 1960, dealt with similar themes.[95] The novel's heroine, Jane, is a middle-class, unmarried girl who has been thrown out of her father's house on account of her pregnancy. She takes a bedsit in a seedy lodging house in Fulham. A gay black neighbour, John, and a Jewish lover, Toby, provide support. A spinster aunt, Addy, turns into something of a fairy godmother, leaving Jane a bequest which provides her with another dimension of independence. There is an implicit critique of patriarchy. Jane's male doctor, like her father, is judgemental and controlling, but also capable of benevolence. The novel ends with reconciliation. Jane's father, after a bout of misery and alcoholism, wants her back. Jane, her independence and autonomy now secured, returns on her own terms.

A Taste of Honey was adapted into a hugely successful film, starring Rita Tushingham, in 1961. Lynne Reid Banks's novel proved an instant (and lasting) best-seller. A film version of *The L-Shaped Room*, with Leslie Caron as Jane, appeared in 1962 and created a strong impact. Both Shelagh Delaney and Lynne Reid Banks had succeeded in telling stories about girls which challenged conventional morality. These were stories from the young woman's point of view. In the past, unmarried mothers had often been silenced through accusations and shame. Now, questions about teenage sexuality and how society should deal with unmarried pregnancy began to be asked more openly. Neither 'respectable society' nor patriarchy looked as if it had all the answers.

5 | COMING OF AGE IN THE 1960S: BEAT GIRLS AND DOLLY BIRDS

Beat Girl, a British film directed by Edmond T. Gréville in 1959, heralded the 1960s with a dire warning to fathers. An early poster for the film featured a wild-haired girl in saucy black underwear and a rah-rah skirt. The girl fingered her bra strap while a rather unhealthy-looking young man in the foreground strummed his guitar strings. The poster announced threateningly: 'mad about "beat" and living for kicks, this [girl] could be your *teenage* daughter!'[1]

Beat Girl starred Gillian Hills as Jennifer, a Brigitte Bardot-style, sulky 'sex kitten'. A sixteen-year-old art student, Jennifer goes increasingly off the rails and is a trial to her middle-class architect father Paul Linden. Linden, coming across with suave masculine reasonableness, was played by David Farrar. There were performances from the pop musician Adam Faith, Oliver Reed and Christopher Lee. Lee played a creepy strip-joint operator. Noëlle Adam played the part of Jennifer's French stepmother, Nichole, disconcertingly close to Jennifer in age and appearance – tousled hair, tight gingham – if not in attitude. Jenny excels in awfulness, a true daughter from hell. She sneers at Nichole and sneaks out of the house at night to jive in a basement coffee bar. The Off Beat coffee bar in Soho happens to be close to a strip club, Les Girls. From a chance encounter it emerges that loyal new wife Nichole had something of a dodgy past, before redeeming herself by falling in love with Jennifer's father. This knowledge supplies Jenny with opportunities for further persecuting Nichole, this

5.1 Poster advertising the film *Beat Girl* (1959): a miscreant daughter strums her bra strap in tune with young pop singer Adam Faith's guitar (© GAB Archive/Getty Images).

time with blackmail. At the same time, she herself weighs up career prospects as a stripper in 'the vice trade'. In the meantime she amuses herself with wild parties in her father's house, and episodes of dangerous driving with the gang.

Against all odds, it works out just fine in the end. An old friend of Nichole's stabs and kills the creepy, oleaginous owner of the strip joint. Jenny has hysterics but quickly comes to her senses and realises she's had a lucky escape. In the final scene Paul, Nichole and Jenny walk away from sleazy Soho, vice and squalor, hugging each other and ready to play happy families properly, this time round.

Beat Girl bridges the concerns of the 1950s and the 1960s. It has themes in common with 1950s 'sexploitation' movies such as *Passport to Shame*, which professedly aimed to stir up public concern about 'vice' while revelling in its on-screen possibilities. There are plenty of prurient moments in *Beat Girl* too: few opportunities were lost to show buttock-squirming strippers or Jennifer in baby-doll pyjamas. The idea of a well-meaning, middle-class father tested by a daughter's craze for popular music was not new. It had received an earlier, and much more anodyne treatment, in the 1955 British screwball comedy *As Long As They're Happy*.[2] In this earlier film, directed by J. Lee Thompson, stockbroker John Bentley, living in suburban Wimbledon, finds his life disrupted by his daughters' passions for the wrong type of men. The youngest swoons over American crooner Bobby Denver (modelled on Johnny Ray). A crisis arises when all the women in Bentley's household, including his wife and his maidservant, are seduced by Denver's crooning and his masculine charms. The paterfamilias gets his own back by flirting with a floozie (Diana Dors). Nevertheless, order is eventually, and reassuringly, restored.

But *Beat Girl* showed patriarchal authority besieged by something rather more challenging. Paul Linden is shown trying to put Jennifer in her place by telling her that in spite of her cosmetics ('all that muck on your face') she is 'just a little girl'. This is clearly wishful thinking on his part. Jennifer is all woman. And her friends in the Off Beat coffee bar, articulate about what they see as the older generation's limitations and failings, aren't in the mood to be treated as children either. *Beat Girl* is memorable for its heavy-handed rendering of teenage slang – 'square', 'fade-out', 'daddy-O' and so forth – trowelled on to emphasise a whopping new generation gap.

Beat Girl managed to press a lot of alarm buttons before coming to its rather unconvincingly reassuring conclusion. There was a great deal of concern about young people slipping off the bandwagon of respectability. Some post-war films focusing on juvenile delinquency had shown girls as passive victims of male hooligans. In *Cosh Boy* (1953), for instance, a young Joan Collins plays the part of the hapless Rene, exploited by a loutish young Roy Walsh.[3] Made pregnant, she attempts suicide. All comes well in the end, though. Rene is saved from drowning and Roy gets a good thrashing. Unlike Rene, Jennifer in *Beat Girl* is no mere plot device: she is cantankerous, lippy, and out of control.

Representations of young people jiving, or hypnotised by jazz in coffee bars and basement cellars, were fast becoming a way of drawing attention to the problems of youth. After the Second World War, clubs of all kinds mushroomed in British towns and cities. These venues were often very small. A modest terrace house might have separate clubs on each floor. This was the case, for instance, at 4 Queen's Square, Brighton: premises which were associated with a notorious murder case in the early 1960s. There were three clubs at 4 Queen's Square in the late 1950s. The basement housed the Whiskey-A-Go-Go coffee bar, the ground floor the Calypso Club, while the Blue Gardenia Club occupied the first floor.[4] London and large towns like Manchester and Birmingham saw a huge rise in the numbers of clubs.[5] In the

London borough of Stepney, for instance, it was reported that whereas in 1954 there had only been eighteen registered clubs, by 1960 there were ninety-two.[6] In a debate in the House of Lords about the difficulties of licensing and controlling these venues, it was claimed that none of the ninety-odd clubs in Stepney was respectable.[7]

As meeting places for young people, these clubs gave parents and magistrates headaches. Many of these places were no doubt harmless enough. They were often very crowded though, which raised questions of safety. In addition, the atmosphere was often dark and laden with cigarette smoke. There were reports of 'Indian hemp', and suspicions, or even observations, of 'heavy petting'. In places like Stepney, Notting Hill and Manchester, the clubs allowed young people from different social backgrounds and of varied ethnic origins to mix freely. The authorities suspected the worst.

Contemporary cinema added to their misgivings. Appearing in the same year as *Beat Girl* (1959), the film *Sapphire* similarly raised issues around girls, clubs and danger.[8] *Sapphire* focused on the fictional case of a girl of that name who was murdered. Her body had been found on Hampstead Heath. We learn little about this girl except that she liked dancing in clubs, and wore sexy underwear. The film features memorable footage of young people, black and white, dancing wildly in the 'Tulip Club'. In the aftermath of the Notting Hill riots of 1958, the subject of race relations was highly topical. Although the film sets out to contest 'colour prejudice', it nevertheless seems mired in it. Detectives investigating Sapphire's murder watch a young woman dancing with a trance-like expression on her face, and are told that she dances like this because she is a 'lilyskin': white-skinned, but with black blood. It emerges that Sapphire was of mixed race. The glamorous underwear – a red taffeta petticoat under a demure skirt – is supposed to suggest this. 'That's the black under the white all right,' comments the policeman. The hypnotic response to beat music indicates that all is not what it seems. 'You can always tell, once they hear the beat of the bongo,' someone observes helpfully. Whatever its intentions, the film suggests the hidden danger of miscegenation.

In the East End of London, social worker Edith Ramsay and an impassioned local cleric, the Reverend Williamson, campaigned against the mushrooming of local clubs, which they saw as closely bound up with the rise of prostitution in Stepney. Ramsay, dubbed 'the Florence Nightingale of the brothels', lived in Stepney and had many friends and strong relationships in the locality.[9] She also had easy access to the network of clubs and cafés in Commercial Road and Cable Street. In the mid-1950s, Ramsay argued, prostitutes (known locally as 'pavement waitresses') could be found along the roadside, but the impact of the Street Offences Act of 1959 was to drive them off the streets and into the clubs and cafés.[10] The proximity of the London docks ensured that these all-night cafés were patronised by a richly varied clientele of West Indians, Somalis, 'Jugo-Slavs', Sikhs and Maltese, as well as the locals. One of Edith Ramsay's main concerns was that the cafés and clubs offered a warm welcome to vulnerable young girls – both local girls and runaways from home and from approved schools elsewhere in the country – who were tempted into prostitution through the very high wages obtainable.[11]

The wartime study of conditions among the immigrant population in Stepney by Phyllis Young (mentioned in Chapter 4) illustrates the background to these concerns.[12] This report offered a very different perspective. Young found that during the Second

World War Stepney proved a magnet for large numbers of young white women aged between sixteen and thirty-five, from all over the country, but particularly from bombed-out Coventry and Hull. Some of these young women, Young explained, adopted a predatory attitude to unattached foreigners. There were large numbers of lonely and vulnerable ex-seamen and immigrants haunting the cafés. British girls often found the foreign and darker-skinned men particularly attractive. Young's account differs dramatically from the complaints of Reverend Williamson, who urged the London County Council to crack down on 'foreign pimps and club-owners'. He accused immigrants of 'living on our poor girls who are weak in mind and character'.[13]

The moral panic over clubs in Stepney was highly revealing of contemporary anxieties and prejudices. For the Reverend Williamson, clubs were centres of vice to be thundered at. He denounced them as centres of everything he deplored: unchecked immigration, girls 'oozing money' on account of their 'elastic moral standards', contraceptives, and jukeboxes, which he clearly saw as the work of the devil. Ramsay was rather more measured in her attacks, except when it came to homosexuals. Remarking on the different categories of 'pouffes', whom she alleged flocked to the clubs in Stepney, she concluded that their presence undoubtedly added to a 'prevailing sense of evil'.[14] Investigating the clubs, both Williamson and Ramsay produced colourful descriptions of club-goers and atmosphere which were eagerly reproduced in the press. Relaying goings-on in the Shamrock Club, for instance, Williamson reported a girl 'in scanty clothes' 'waggling her bottom' to jukebox music and then stripping down to her G-string.[15] About fifteen men were said to have been watching this performance. Visiting the St Louis, Batty Street and Play Box clubs, Ramsay described 'young, grubby and shabbily dressed girls ... embracing coloured men', and a 'curious atmosphere of frenzy and indecency' as couples engaged in 'expert Rock and Roll'.[16]

A campaign to extend magistrates' and police powers to crack down on and control the clubs gained the support of Labour peers Lord Stonham and Baroness Ravensdale in the House of Lords. Introducing the subject in the Lords in 1960, Lord Stonham took the line that 'Vice has "never had it so good" as in this country'.[17] He saw clubs as debauching the young: as centres of vice, drugs, striptease and squalor. Baroness Ravensdale, much respected for her work with young people in London, spoke in the Lords about how she had been treated to a tour of the clubs in Stepney, escorted by Miss Ramsay. She would not name the establishments in question, Irene Ravensdale announced dramatically, because she did not 'want to be slashed or to have vitriol thrown into my face'.[18] The baroness proceeded to regale the House with descriptions of jukeboxes and teenage girls in G-strings. She also attacked the clientele of the lunchtime strip shows popular in the clubs. These audiences consisted mainly of 'ordinary City types, with black coats and striped trousers'. '[B]egging your Lordships' pardon', she continued, these men 'stride religiously into "Peeporama", and they take a pal so that they can put it on an expense account. They are aged between 30 and 55. Why do they go in? They go in to giggle and goggle and leer at these miserable strip-tease girls.'[19] Striptease was big business, she continued ruefully, before swerving off into another paragraph of revelations and rhetoric. 'Doomed girls' were smoking in doorways, touting themselves and coining money; they would 'charge a "fiver" for a long spell and £1 for a quick bash'.[20] The baroness's journey around the clubs had left her in no doubt that they all had 'the blackest record':

The prostitutes were tragic and squalid and the men with whom I spoke and chatted mainly coloured. I have no doubt that they were all experts in vice, dope-selling and drug-peddling. One coloured man even offered me a dance to a 'juke box', and when I said that I was too old for the 'Cha-Cha' he said that he would put on a slow fox-trot for me.[21]

Some of these 'experts in vice' had manners. Baroness Ravensdale admitted that her host had been hospitable, even solicitously so. He 'had the touching decency to say to Miss Ramsay and me as we left that he hoped his companions had caused us no inconvenience, as some of them were pretty drunk. There is a chivalry even among these thugs and gangsters.' Hardly surprisingly, however, it was the shock-horror stuff that made it into the newspapers. The good manners, chivalry and the concern for young girls – for all of which Ramsay and Ravensdale found ample evidence in the clubs of Stepney – made for far less colourful copy. It was all too easy to stir up public outrage about what Baroness Ravensdale described with spirit (and in a sequence of mixed metaphors) as a 'running sore', 'a great evil crossword puzzle that links up vice with drugs, nudist shows and striptease' in the clubs.[22] Other pillars of the establishment leapt to her defence, quick to seize the moral high ground. For the Bishop of Carlisle, for instance, the clubs were places 'of evil in a gross and beastly form', where wicked men lured young women into becoming 'the victims and slaves of vice'.[23]

The idea of London as a 'festering sore', harbouring networks, 'crossword puzzles' or cobwebs of vice was unsettling, and of course it was taken up with gusto in the Sunday newspapers.[24] One of the main concerns of the Wolfenden Report on Homosexuality and Prostitution, published in 1957, was with 'public order and decency'. Comparatively liberal on homosexual acts (which Wolfenden recommended decriminalising if in private, and between consenting adults), the committee had taken a harsher line on prostitution.[25] A double standard (fines for female prostitutes soliciting in public places, their male clients not regarded as nuisances) remained undisturbed. The Street Offences Act of 1959, mentioned earlier, was specifically designed to push prostitution from the streets. According to Edith Ramsay and other observers, however, this not only succeeded in driving prostitutes into clubs and cafés, but also encouraged a proliferation of 'call girls', operating to some extent underground.[26] The idea of vice hidden in basement cellars and private clubs was no less unsettling than the idea of vice on the streets. On top of this, anxieties about immigrants and the foreign ownership of many of the clubs (such as the Maltese club and café proprietors in east London) added to concerns. And were girls always the *victims* of vice? The gentlemen discussing the clubs in the House of Lords liked to portray them as such, but there was evidence that becoming a call girl was an attractive career option that brought lucrative prospects.[27]

It was against this rich background of unease that the Profumo affair erupted in the early 1960s. John Profumo, Secretary of State for War in Harold Macmillan's Conservative government, had a short affair with attractive young model and showgirl Christine Keeler. Scandal blew up when it was rumoured that Keeler had at the same time been sleeping with Yevgeny Ivanov, a senior attaché at the Soviet embassy in London. This had threatening implications for national security in the era of the Cold War. Profumo himself made things worse, first by lying to Parliament, then admitting that he had lied and resigning.

There were all manner of ramifications. Christine Keeler's

relationships with two West Indian lovers, Johnny Edgecombe and the jazz musician Aloysius 'Lucky' Gordon, led to episodes of jealousy and violence which received plenty of coverage in the press. It was these events, the arrests, and the subsequent trial of Johnny Edgecombe, which originally brought Profumo's relationship with Keeler into the public domain. Keeler and another young woman, Marilyn (Mandy) Rice-Davies were both friends and to some extent protégées of Stephen Ward. Ward, a society osteopath (whose patients had included Winston Churchill, Ava Gardner and Gandhi), was a complex figure with both aristocratic connections and interests in London's underworld. He was to prove the most obvious victim of the affair. Charged with living off the immoral earnings of Keeler and Rice-Davies, Ward committed suicide.[28]

Many aspects of the affair shocked the public. Most obviously, it exposed the muddy morals of persons in what was then known as the Establishment. The image of London as a city of vice was also reinforced. It now appeared that there were murky networks linking Notting Hill jazz musicians, West Indian immigrants, drugs and sex with aristocrats and politicians. Lively reports of call girls playing around in privileged haunts such as Lord Astor's property in Cliveden disturbed and assuredly titillated the readers of the weekend papers.[29]

No small part of the discomfiture of some of those caught up in the affair stemmed from the parts played by Christine Keeler and Mandy Rice-Davies. Their behaviour confounded conventional categories. Neither could easily be dismissed as wholly innocent or as wholly wicked, and both insisted on telling their own stories. Both Keeler and Rice-Davies strenuously contested descriptions of themselves as call girls or prostitutes. Rice-Davies objected that 'I have been branded a cheap prostitute. That is not

5.2 Mandy Rice-Davies unperturbed about the public impact of her revelations (© Express/ Stringer/Getty Images).

so. I am an expensive courtesan, if you like, but never a prostitute.'[30] Keeler's determination to solicit media attention and to speak up for herself it seems took John Profumo by surprise. He had underestimated her, assuming her to be uneducated and only interested in make-up and hairstyles.[31] Both girls had come to London at the age of fifteen, independently, to seek their fortunes. Keeler's background was working class: she had been brought up in a converted railway carriage in Buckinghamshire. She was twenty-one when the scandal broke in 1963. Rice-Davies's family was more middle class: she had grown up in Shirley, outside Birmingham. Both had done stints of modelling and worked as 'showgirls' in Murray's Cabaret Club in Soho. Both girls were extremely resourceful. Keeler was tough-minded: she had survived a number of personal setbacks. Rice-Davies was shrewd, sexy and quick-witted. Under questioning at the trial of Stephen Ward, the prosecuting counsel challenged Rice-Davies by insisting that Lord Astor denied ever having met her, let alone having an affair with her. 'Well, he would, wouldn't he?' replied Rice-Davies sweetly, a retort which was immortalised in the *Oxford Dictionary of Quotations*.

Both Keeler and Rice-Davies showed a flair for publicity and a keen eye for profiting from 'exposures'. Keeler tried to sell her story to the highest newspaper bidder. Rice-Davies published *The Mandy Report*. She warned her readers gleefully that she was about to tell 'a wicked, wicked story':

> the sorry tale of a young girl, barely more than a child, baited with mink and diamonds until trapped in a web of complete moral depravity ...[32]

This silken promise of a goodnight story may well have caused some of her acquaintances to writhe sleeplessly, uneasy in their beds and consciences. Mandy would reveal the truth at last, she promised, spilling the beans 'about the millionaires who buy women as casually as they order champagne', and about 'the snake-pit masquerading under the title of High Society'. Then there were the details of the sex parties, which she claimed had shocked both her and her friend Christine, as far 'too "kinky" for us'. The press didn't know how to deal with these girls. As has often been the case in more recent scandals and kiss-and-tell stories, such as Monica Lewinsky's relationship with President Bill Clinton, it was difficult to decide who was the exploiter and who was the victim. The historian Frank Mort has shown how Christine Keeler and Mandy Rice-Davies were variously represented as naïve ingénues, modest young women, sexual victims or wanton seductresses.[33] The *Sunday Mirror* denounced both girls as shameless tarts, and Rice-Davies as a 'pert slut'.[34] But both were capable of standing up for themselves, and refused to be silenced.

The Profumo affair effectively undermined the credibility of Macmillan's government. It discredited the male establishment, and suggested that young women from working-class backgrounds might not always be amenable to patriarchal control. Girls were getting somewhat uppity, it seemed. And the wages of sin (as columnist Marjorie Proops observed in the *Sunday Mirror*) might be anything but deadly.[35] It was getting hard to tell the difference between 'whores' and 'liberated' – or enterprising – young women-about-town.

The colourful adventures of Christine and Mandy in the vice haunts of the metropolis may have appalled and enthralled observers in the rest of Britain, but the experience of most fifteen- to twenty-year-old girls was obviously very different. Anxiety over the influence of clubs, coffee bars and basement jazz, however, spread. The historian Louise Jackson has shown how Manchester City Police mounted an attack on what they saw as the 'Coffee Club Menace' in the early 1960s.[36] In Manchester, clubs such as the Jungfrau in Cathedral Street, Beat City, the Cavern Club or the Twisted Wheel were important meeting places for young people. They were 'members only' clubs, which meant they were outside the licensing laws and that the police had no automatic right to enter them. There was concern over drugs, especially cannabis and 'purple hearts' (Drinamyl). Like the clubs in Stepney, these places were suspected of being a magnet for girls who had run away from difficult family situations, or from approved schools. These girls were regarded as being 'in moral danger'.

The press published lurid stories. In 1964 the *Daily Mail* reported that Manchester's Heaven and Hell club, with its dark,

gothic interior, was associated with the 'dangerous teenage immorality lurking in the basements of Britain's big cities'. The
News of the World trumped this a year later by reviving stories
of white slavery, this time centring on Manchester's coffee bars
and beat clubs.[37] Two pretty young girls who had been 'dossing'
in the clubs were said to have been abducted and delivered for
auction among Pakistani men in Bradford. This pressed all the
old alarm bells about race, immigration and sexual danger, even
though it turned out that the girls in question were both over
seventeen and that the real story was very different.[38]

In Manchester, police raids on the clubs brought a relatively
small number of minor prosecutions. Most of the young people
attending these venues were simply there to have a good time. But
suspicions persisted. Part of the reason was simply unease about
youth culture. The year 1964 was one which brought outbreaks
of violence between Mods and Rockers on the south coast of
England, particularly in the seaside resorts of Clacton, Margate
and Brighton. In Brighton, the council had been concerned since
the late 1950s about overcrowding, criminal networks and stolen
goods in relation to the town's myriad clubs and coffee bars.
What went on at the Mogambo, or the Whiskey-A-Go-Go, certainly
worried parents, although to this day people record on local
websites their happy memories of teenage dances in such places.[39]

In Stepney, the Reverend Williamson had denounced jukeboxes as 'pagan altars'.[40] They had become the symbols of a new
teenage culture. In 1945 there were fewer than 100 jukeboxes in
Britain, by 1958 it has been estimated that there were probably
over 15,000.[41] Jukeboxes purveyed the new rock 'n' roll in clubs
and cafés all over the country and were interpreted by even
the most law-abiding teenagers as something of a challenge to
convention. Lorna Sage, growing up in the rural environs of

5.3 Trendy teenagers enjoying the sounds at Brad's Club, London, early 1960s (© Terry Fincher/Stringer/Getty Images).

Whitchurch, Shropshire, records the impact of Bill Haley and his Comets.[42] She became a teenager just as music separated the generations and young people became 'a tribe apart'. Lorna remembered a delight in Jerry Lee Lewis, Elvis Presley and the bad boys of rock 'n' roll; their heavy sensuality, the 'insidious bump and grind'. On a family trip to Southport, she and her friend Gail rushed from one jukebox to another, intent on drowning out the music of Pat Boone with Elvis's 'All Shook Up' at maximum volume. They were shrieking with glee at this, 'like the Bacchae who dismembered Orpheus'.[43] The behaviour was harmless enough, but probably not quite what was expected of young ladies at Whitchurch High School.

Class, like ethnicity, was an important consideration. In the mid-1950s, Karel Reisz and Tony Richardson's short documentary film *Momma Don't Allow* featured young people jiving in a north London jazz club.[44] The working-class youngsters (especially the

5.4 The lure of the juke-box (© Evening Standard/ Getty Images).

Teddy boys) are fashionably dressed, confident and relaxed, until a middle-class contingent arrives and class tensions threaten disruption. Rock 'n' roll, like youth culture generally in the early 1960s, was seen as emanating from the working class. Jazz clubs, coffee bars and beat cellars attracted a mixed clientele, and many parents, particularly of daughters, were uneasy about this. Sociologist Brian Jackson, investigating communities in Huddersfield in the mid-1960s, found that teenage girls attending the local grammar school were uneasy about going into coffee bars, let alone jazz clubs.[45] They saw them as attracting 'Teddy boy' types, or girls who hadn't been well brought up. But outside the bigger towns and cities, the majority of teenagers probably enjoyed rock 'n' roll in parentally approved environments: youth clubs in church halls, at sixth-form dances, or even (given the growing importance of television sets and portable record players) in the family home.

A short film feature issued by British Pathé early in 1963 must have warmed the hearts of many a middle-class father of teenage girls. Entitled *Beatnik Beauty*, this film was set in Mayfair and introduced its audience to Stephanie Beaumont, a 'beatnik' who strides purposefully into the frame dragging on a cigarette.[46] She looks stylish and cutting-edge in her leather jacket, biker boots and denim jeans. Notwithstanding this cool 'don't mess with me' image, Stephanie is about to be both messed with and transformed. A smooth male voice-over describes the process of prettifying and taming. Stephanie is hauled into a Mayfair salon by two white-coated lady beauticians with hair backcombed and smoothed into a semblance of Mr Whippy sundaes. She is strapped into a chair, and her own hair is treated to an 'egg rinse', her face plastered with 'anti-wrinkle' unguents. She is clapped into rollers and face masks. Finally she emerges, lacquered and encased in gold brocade and lamé. The commentator burbles delight at her ladylike elegance; at her transformation from beatnik into Cinderella. To a contemporary viewer she looks prissy and defeated, like Greer's Female Eunuch incarnate.

The style revolution of the early 1960s could scarcely be ignored by contemporaries: it had obvious links to the widening gap between generations. The historian Sheila Rowbotham remembered how in east London, comparatively young working-class women 'still sported elaborate beehive hair-dos' as they pushed prams on shopping trips.

> But the teenage girls' hair was now straight and they wore the dark-coloured three-quarter length leather jackets made in the local East End sweatshops.[47]

Style-reading wasn't straightforward, though. Well into the early 1960s, candyfloss hairdos could signify a taste for old-fashioned adult glamour, as well as rebellion. Female musicians such as Dusty Springfield or the American girl group the Ronettes exemplified this. But the newer fashions for whitish lips, black-rimmed eyes and a boyish body in jeans or miniskirt tended to put conservatives on their guard.

The social observer Peter Laurie, writing about youth in the 1960s, insisted that 'The real dynamo behind the teenage revolution is the anonymous adolescent girl from twelve to sixteen, nameless but irresistible.'[48] Laurie's book on *The Teenage Revolution*, published in 1965, carried a frontispiece photo of a fifteen-year-old girl with pale lips and a fashionable 'urchin-cut' hairstyle. The author wasn't sure what to make of her, but she certainly made him feel uneasy:

Look at this face ....

These Mod lips are almost painted out. Her body is straight and resistant as a plank. Her eyes, hedged by spiky lines, are watchful, alert, not to be taken in. Whatever she is going to be, she is not going to be a woman in the traditional sense. At least, not for the moment ...

To me she seems the face of the teenage revolution.[49]

Laurie compared this girl's appearance with the way most women had looked in the 1940s. Back then, he reminisced, girls looked like ripe fruit ready for the plucking – unlike this stroppy teenager who looked as if she didn't give a toss. We are told that the girl was photographed on her way to a pop concert in Slough. Laurie pelts her with insinuations. She is accused of being disdainful, of taking the welfare state for granted, of looking uncompromising, even menacing. She didn't look like a potential mother ('you cannot imagine her pushing a pram; she makes sure you cannot'). Worst of all, he didn't fancy her at all:

5.5 Police struggle to contain young girls outside Buckingham Palace, as the Beatles are honoured with MBE awards in 1965 (© Central Press/Stringer/ Getty Images).

> She despises a lot of things ... It is difficult to imagine finding her sexually attractive. In fact, she makes sure that she is not.[50]

What crimes! There can be little doubt that Laurie would have approved of his nameless girl being subjected to the *Beatnik Beauty* treatment that had turned Stephanie Beaumont into a Stepford Wife. But his casual assumption of male objectivity together with his personal sexual judgements, in what sets out to be a serious sociological text, make troubling reading today. They remind us of the ease with which young girls could be represented as folk devils. We know nothing at all about this fifteen-year-old girl except that Laurie didn't take to her, and that his interpretation of her appearance triggered all his nervous anxieties about contemporary social change.

In the early 1960s, pop concerts joined jazz, jukeboxes and rock 'n' roll on the list of things widely seen as responsible for leading girls off the rails. Swooning over crooners proved just the beginning. Falling in love with Paul Anka, Tommy Steele or Elvis was a common enough state among girls at the end of the 1950s. But 'Beatlemania' was something on a different scale. The Beatles' path to fame began with club performances in Liverpool and Hamburg from 1960. Their first recorded single, 'Love Me Do', was released in 1962, the album *Please Please Me* in the following year. From then on there was no stopping the Fab Four, either in terms of their commercial success or their success in winning the hearts of the majority of teenage girls in the UK and indeed in many other parts of the world.

Much of the adulation was harmless enough, and of the schoolgirl-crush variety. When the Beatles flew back to Britain from New York in February, 1964, for instance, girls from London's East Ham were ready with a welcome banner crafted from massed daffodils, and a home-made cake, iced in their image.[51] It was the sheer *size* of the welcome committee that turned the event into something troublesome. Some five or six thousand girls descended on the airport. Some were allegedly only twelve or thirteen years of age, and had hitch-hiked from home without telling their parents. In addition to managing the crowds, the police found themselves searching for lost daughters alongside distraught parents, in what soon began to look like a massive refugee camp. Scenes like this were to become common, both at airports and anywhere where tickets for the group's performances went on sale. In 1965, when the Beatles went to Buckingham Palace to collect their MBE awards from the Queen, fans took their lives in their hands by scaling the spiked gates. The police had difficulty holding the swarming girls back. Photographs of the skirmishes show the police dishevelled, helmets on the skew, while the girls flail around like maenads.[52]

Henry Price, Tory MP for West Lewisham, owned himself worried about the 'hypnotic' effect of the Beatles on the young. They were behaving, he thought, like the hot-gospellers of a new religion. Fans looked like addicts: 'Their eyes become glazed, their mouths gape, their hands wobble loosely and their legs wobble just as loosely at the knees.'[53] This, Price concluded solemnly, is known as 'being sent'. One could only hope that they would grow out of it. Some critics were much more harsh. Paul Johnson, warning of 'The Menace of Beatlism' in the left-of-centre *New Statesman*, retailed the clichés of class prejudice and a disturbing misogyny. Girl fans revealed a 'bottomless chasm of vacuity', he wrote, their faces

> Bloated with cheap confectionery and smeared with chain-store make-up, the open, sagging mouths and glazed eyes, the hands mindlessly drumming in time to the music, the broken stiletto heels, the shoddy, stereotyped, 'with-it' clothes.[54]

Psychologists pondered the appeal of the four lads. Dr Frederick Cameron suggested that their appeal could be explained by their boyishness. They didn't come over as adult males. They weren't threatening in any way, and they appealed to their fans like 'cuddlesome pets': safe, and somewhat ambiguous sexually.[55]

Schoolgirl passions were evident in Bill Adler's volume *Love Letters to the Beatles*, published in 1964. This was full of 'I'll never love anyone else' stuff. 'Daer Paul' [sic] wrote Amy Roberts, for instance, 'I have fainted for you six times.'[56] Others begged their idols for relics, hair clippings, or even a bristle from a toothbrush. One girl growing up in the 1960s recalled the rituals of worship:

> Girls would sit in class and write 'Paul, Paul, Paul' a thousand times in an exercise book, and every article of their clothing or their school satchels would have 'I love John' or 'I love Ringo' across it.[57]

In Wrexham, north Wales in 1963, girls smuggled bottles of port and rum into school at lunchtime in order to celebrate John Lennon's birthday. 'Fifteen Tiddly Schoolgirls on the Mat', announced the *Daily Mirror* gleefully.[58] Even in sedate Cheltenham, home to the famous Ladies' College, girls were acting crazily at Beatles concerts, bombarding the stage with little notes beseeching the boys to telephone them and claim them as their sweethearts.[59]

There are cultural historians who have emphasised female passivity as the basis of 'fandom', pointing out that many girls enjoyed pop music in the company of one or two best friends, probably in their own bedrooms. Inexpensive portable record players made this possible: in the early 1960s a Dansette record player was a hugely popular birthday or Christmas present for a teenage girl. But Beatlemania was of course not just a passive condition; despite Dr Cameron's assertions it was also an expression of desire. The American feminist and social scientist Barbara Ehrenreich has argued convincingly that Beatlemania constituted 'a huge outbreak of teenage female libido' which might legitimately be regarded as an opening salvo in the sexual revolution.[60] Just as many observers in the 1920s had looked on female outpourings of grief over the death of film star Rudolph Valentino with total incomprehension, adulation for the Beatles confounded those adults who failed to understand their long-haired, androgynous appeal. Girls found the Beatles sexy. And teenage girls' open expressions of desire were a challenge in a society keen to protect sexual innocence in the young. At the same time, as Ehrenreich and her co-authors emphasised, such overt abandonment constituted rebellion against the rules that defined female sexuality as something 'to be bartered for an engagement ring'.[61]

Helen Gurley Brown's international bestseller *Sex and the Single Girl*, first published in the USA in 1962, has also been seized on by many social commentators as a harbinger of the sexual revolution.[62] The book sold two million copies within three weeks. It has always attracted a mixed response from feminists. Some have recoiled from the ways in which its author encouraged women to market themselves to men, and to use sex as a vehicle for social advancement. Others have recognised the radicalism, in the early 1960s, of urging women to discard guilt about 'premarital sex' and openly challenge the double standard. Helen Gurley Brown exhorted women not to fade into 'mouseburgers'. Up until the 1960s, books on office etiquette had advised women to look demure and to behave meekly, turning themselves into willing subordinates who silently anticipated their bosses' every need. *Sex and the Single Girl* would have none of this. Instead, Gurley Brown saw women as taking a much more assertive role in office politics and acquiring confidence in their own sexuality. The book has often drawn comparison with the popular American television series of the 1990s *Sex and the City*. Helen Gurley Brown made being young, single and working in the city sound like fun.[63] But this vision was far more radical in the 1960s than it was in the 1990s; the pressures on girls to marry young were so much greater in the earlier period. It wasn't uncommon for girls to despair, thinking themselves 'on the shelf' if they reached the age of twenty-five before mating, they hoped, for life. Gurley Brown pooh-poohed this as nonsense, insisting that there was no rush to find Mr Right. Girls should take their time to look around and to try men out so as to be sure of getting the right partner.

That this was a message that appealed to many was evident from the book's success and also from the success of the magazine *Cosmopolitan*, which Brown went on to revamp and edit from 1965. *Cosmopolitan* targeted young women and prided itself on its sexual openness; a UK edition was launched in 1972 and the magazine went from strength to strength. 'Cosmo girl' became shorthand, internationally, for the young, independent city types who were seen to constitute a core readership.[64]

How independent were these girls? There were indeed signs of a new independence among young women in the 1960s. They were the first generation to grow up taking secondary education for granted. Jobs were available, and they were (independently) relatively affluent and well-fed. Teenage spending patterns were the subject of a great deal of contemporary comment by social observers (notably by the sociologist Mark Abrams)[65] and also in the popular press. 'Call them Spendagers!', quipped the *Daily Mirror* in 1963, affecting astonishment at what a nineteen-year-old shorthand typist spent on looking 'with it'.[66] More girls were leaving home to live in bedsits. Journalist Katharine Whitehorn's *Cooking in a Bedsitter* was first published in 1961. Five years earlier she had been photographed by Bert Hardy for an article in *Picture Post* on loneliness in the city.[67] In one photograph she was shown pensive, sitting in front of a gas fire in what was obviously a cramped bedsitting-room. There was a milk bottle on the table and her smalls were drying on a clothes-horse beside her. Readers were clearly supposed to see her as lonely and miserable. By the 1960s, however, living away from home had acquired a certain

5.6 The young journalist Katharine Whitehorn photographed for *Picture Post* alone in a bedsit warming her toes by the gas fire (1956) (© Bert Hardy/Getty Images).

glamour. There was fun in contrivance: making coffee in a jug, or what could be rustled up on a single gas ring. Working in the city, living in digs or lodgings, could spell freedom. Similarly, studying at university, living in a hall of residence or student hostel, opened up spaces for sexual experimentation away from the supervision of parents.

The image of the 'dolly bird' in 'Swinging London' became emblematic of Britain in the 1960s. Girls began to dress differently from their mothers, in Quant-inspired dolly-dresses, high boots and miniskirts. The writer and publisher Alexandra Pringle described the 'Chelsea girl' of the sixties as having 'confidence, and it seemed, no parents'.[68] New kinds of magazines appeared, catering for these younger women: *Honey* in 1960, followed by *Petticoat* and *Flair*.

5.7 Miniskirted dolly birds shopping in a boutique on London's fashionable King's Road, 1960s (© Evening Standard/Hulton Archive/Getty Images).

Sex and the Single Girl was widely read in Britain before the contraceptive pill became generally available. Girls still went in fear of unwanted pregnancies and the social shame that continued to be associated with single motherhood. Nevertheless, studies of teenage sexual behaviour pointed out that in spite of these fears, more young people were experimenting with pre-marital sex, whether 'heavy petting' or 'going the whole way'. G. M. Carstairs, a professor of psychiatry and regular commentator on teenage sexual behaviour, estimated that 11 per cent of sixteen-year-old boys and 6 per cent of sixteen-year-old girls had some experience of pre-marital sex.[69] Among eighteen-year-olds, the proportion rose to 30 per cent of boys and 16 per cent of girls. Carstairs took his figures from Michael Schofield's study *The Sexual Behaviour of Young People*, carried out in the early 1960s. Such studies showed widespread acceptance of the idea of pre-marital sex among the young, even though a double standard persisted in that many still professed to believe that a girl should be a virgin as she went to the altar.[70]

Schofield emphasised the 'tremendous prominence of marriage as an immediate goal in the lives of many teenage girls'.[71] In the first half of the 1960s, the age of marriage was still falling, especially among working-class girls. This was a period of transition. The rise of 'permissiveness' – a newly tolerant and relaxed attitude to sexual mores – brought difficult adjustments. Girls might find themselves in a quandary about sexual behaviour, not sure how to square risk with reward, how to embrace experience without falling victim to double standards and the often unforgiving strictures of traditional morality.

The cultural emphasis on the sexuality of young girls which had been apparent in 1950s representations of Lolitas, Baby Dolls and nymphets showed little sign of abating. Interest in sex and the single girl easily extended to an interest in sex and the schoolgirl. This interest was sometimes literary, sometimes social-scientific, sometimes prurient. James Barlow's novel *Term of Trial* (1961) focuses on the story of a down-at-heel schoolmaster, one of whose young female pupils falls in love with him. She tries to seduce him. When he refuses to sleep with her she is peeved and accuses him of having attempted to assault her sexually. His career goes down the tubes as a result. This tale of masculine vulnerability in the face of schoolgirl precocity was turned into a film, starring Laurence Olivier, Sarah Miles and Simone Signoret, in the following year.[72]

If anything, the 1960s accentuated the association of schoolgirls with soft porn. Cartoon artist Ronald Searle's hugely popular portrayals of schoolgirls at St Trinian's school dated from the 1940s.[73] Searle's original drawings featured daemonic, calculating little monsters and subversives. The various film versions inspired by his original vision (1954, 1957, 1960, 1966 and later 1980, 2007, 2009 and 2012) show increasingly sexualised images of the schoolgirls.[74] During the 1960s their skirts get shorter and their gymslips tighter with noticeably bulging bodices. (In the later versions we get stocking tops and cleavage.) The film *The Yellow Teddy Bears* (1963), alternatively titled *Gutter Girls*, took this further with a tale of schoolgirl promiscuity in the fictitious Peterbridge Grammar School, where girls signified and celebrated the loss of their virginity by wearing yellow brooches in the shape of teddy bears.[75] One of the girls, Linda, fears she is pregnant as a result of a fling with the school's window cleaner, Kinky, a would-be pop singer. Much more amusing, but scandalous at the time, was *The Passion Flower Hotel*, a novel by 'Rosalind Erskine', first published in 1962.[76] This featured girls discussing breasts, men's preferences for tarty types, and *Lolita* over packet soup in the history library at a posh girls' boarding school. As narrated by the resourceful Sarah Callender, the girls demonstrate their entrepreneurship and interest in widening the curriculum by forming 'The Syndicate', a venture designed to foster sexual experimentation with pupils at a neighbouring boys' school. Like the boys, the girls admit to a healthy degree of sexual curiosity. Some prove skilful at striptease and adept in the construction of louche stage personalities ('Miss Gaby de la Gallantine' and 'Princess Puma'). In general, individuals of both sexes prove rather too self-conscious to get up to very much. *The Passion Flower Hotel* became an immediate best-seller. It was, of course, written by a man. 'Rosalind Erskine' was in fact Roger Erskine Longrigg, educated at Bryanston and Magdalen College, Oxford, a graduate in modern history and the son of a brigadier.[77]

Given the pervasiveness of 1960s representations of teenage sexuality, it is not surprising to find that girls were often unsure about how to relate to boyfriends. In their investigations, Schofield and his colleagues were concerned to find that unmarried girls were often reluctant to use contraceptives. They preferred to leave the responsibility to male partners. But they weren't generally insistent on their boyfriends using contraceptives either. Why was this? It was partly because such calculation was felt to look brazen and hence 'unfeminine': girls liked to look 'innocent' and didn't want to create the impression that they were experienced, or too ready for sexual experience, in case it gave the wrong signals.[78] There was a great deal of shyness and reticence. Equally, many girls feared that if they approached family doctors for advice on birth control, they would be interrogated about their morals instead. This was indeed often the case, even well into the following decade. The writer Janice Galloway described in the second volume of her autobiography, *All Made Up*, how she and her fiancé approached a doctor for contraceptive advice in the late 1970s only to be treated to a lecture on the importance of abstinence. Janice became pregnant, and had to endure an abortion, not long afterwards.[79] Doctors in university health centres often took a liberal line on contraception. Even so, there were many 'casualties'. In 1969, Anthony Ryle, of Sussex University's health service, argued that unplanned pregnancies were the source of a large proportion of student casualties, estimating that around 10 per cent of women students became pregnant during their three years as undergraduates.[80] Studies of female students at the University of Aberdeen in the early 1970s showed that a disturbingly high proportion of female students with active sex lives took no precautions whatsoever against unwanted pregnancy.[81]

So, were young women the casualties of permissiveness or its beneficiaries? It is certainly possible to argue that girls benefited less than boys from the softening of conventional standards of morality in the 1960s. But ultimately they gained a great deal. Sexually active young women in the 1950s had lived in constant fear of pregnancy. A whole clutch of novels and autobiographical accounts of the period have attested to this. The novelist Penelope Lively, reflecting on her student years in Oxford in the 1950s, described how the fear had inhibited contemporaries:

> in those pre-Pill days grim tales of clandestine abortion haunted us all. There was much scared and private counting of days and watching of the calendar. Each of us knew, or knew of some girl to whom it had actually happened: that awful realization, the nausea, the panic. This was no climate of sexual liberation – it is strange now to think that the sixties were only ten years off.[82]

As the sixties progressed, student demands for more easily available contraceptive advice grew more vocal.[83] Discussions about unwanted pregnancy became much more open. Pressure for reform of the law on abortion also mounted nationally.[84] The Abortion Law Reform Association had existed since 1936. In a landmark case, two years later, gynaecologist Aleck Bourne had tested the then legal ruling that abortion could only be justified if the life of the mother was in danger by terminating the pregnancy of a highly distressed fourteen-year-old who had been gang-raped by a group of British soldiers. Bourne was tried and acquitted, thereby establishing a precedent for abortion in cases where a woman's physical and mental health was considered to be at risk. Reliable statistics on abortion in this period are difficult to come by. However, in most post-1945 discussions of the subject there was agreement that whereas middle-class women might find access to 'legal' and hygienic abortion, albeit at a price, working-class women had to rely on self-help, or 'back-street' practitioners. The toll of suicides, botched abortions and septicaemia was alarming. Home Office statistics suggested that annually, thirty to fifty women were dying as a result.[85] In 1967 the Liberal MP David Steele introduced a private member's bill which succeeded in getting abortion law reform through parliament: several previous attempts had failed. The 1967 Abortion Act made abortion legal, under certain conditions and with the signatures of two doctors, up to twenty-eight weeks of pregnancy.

By the end of the sixties, then, young women had more control over their own fertility than ever before in history. The pill was widely adopted as the preferred contraceptive choice for young, unmarried women as well as wives. Abortion was no longer inextricably associated with illicit transactions involving fistfuls of pound notes and seedy rooms in backstreets. These choices were by no means universally available, of course: much depended on social class, education, and where one lived. But the number of women benefiting from such changes has led historians such as Hera Cook to conclude that we should think in terms of a sexual revolution.[86] From the end of the 1960s, sexuality became increasingly separated from reproduction. Girls could experiment, sexually, without the constant fear of pregnancy. This undermined fatalism, and gave much more scope for personal development and career planning. In the universities before the end of the sixties, female students had tended to be looked upon as a class apart. They were seen as needing special supervision and disciplinary arrangements lest they get pregnant and cause trouble for the authorities as well as themselves.[87] These fears began to recede from the early 1970s on.

If young women were coming to enjoy a greater sense of independence and control over their lives, this was in part also a result of more general trends. There was a great deal of discussion in the 1960s about the age at which young people could be considered adults. Teenagers were maturing physically at earlier ages: girls were reported as reaching puberty on average at thirteen and boys at fifteen years of age. They were better-educated and better-off than teenagers in previous generations. They were increasingly independent and inclined to get stroppy when treated as children. And yet the law of the land, in England (though not in Scotland), defined young people under the age of twenty-one very precisely as 'infants'.[88]

This law was causing trouble in a number of areas. The trend to early marriages was exacerbating the situation. With the consent of their parents, young people could marry once they had reached sixteen years of age. Without parental consent, they had to wait until they had reached twenty-one. As 'infants', young men who married before the age of twenty-one could not enter into contracts. This meant that they might be husbands and fathers, but could not enter into hire-purchase agreements or take out mortgages.

More women than men were marrying before they reached the age of majority. All too frequently this was leading to conflict with parents, who either thought their daughter too young to know her own mind, or who themselves disapproved of her choice of partner. In such cases, parents were increasingly referring the situation to the courts. The aim was to make an unbiddable daughter a ward of court in order to prevent her from marrying or from running away to Gretna Green, just over the border into Scotland, which had long been the resort of runaway lovers.[89] Scottish law had traditionally allowed boys to marry at fourteen, girls at twelve years of age. Since 1929, both parties had to be at least sixteen, but could still marry without their parents' consent.

Elopements from England (and from Europe) were given regular coverage in the press. Between 1945 and the mid-1960s, applications for wardship had risen to such a level that the courts claimed to be overwhelmed by the demand. Lawyers complained that the system was unenforceable and unworkable. The High Court judge Sir Jocelyn Simon contended that

> A not untypical situation is where the parents come to the court saying that their daughter is out of control and associating with some thoroughly undesirable man; at the suit of the parents the court makes an order forbidding the association: the next thing that happens is that the parents appear before the court saying that their daughter is now pregnant and joining in a prayer that their prospective son-in-law should not be sent to prison.[90]

Another area of social life where there were problems relating to the existing law on adulthood was higher education. The universities had long accepted something of the responsibility of standing *in loco parentis* in relation to undergraduates. In practice, university authorities' sense of moral guardianship and protection was extended more fully to girls than to male undergraduates. Women students were often obliged to live in halls, hostels or 'approved' lodgings. They were subject to rigorous 'gate-hours' and markedly more supervision than their male peers.[91] Disciplinary arrangements could be strict, and female students regularly grumbled that they were treated like schoolgirls. Widespread student dissatisfaction among both sexes in the 1960s often led to outright revolt against what was experienced as 'paternalism'. Students insisted that they should be treated as adults. The demand was by no means new in itself, although the extent of student protest in the 1960s was distinctive.

The setting up of a committee to consider and to report to Parliament on the 'age of majority' was instigated by the Lord High Chancellor, Gerald Gardiner, in 1965. As a student at Oxford after the First World War, Lord Gardiner had learned something about students coming into conflict with university authorities. In the 1920s he had been disciplined for supporting a student of Somerville, Dilys Powell. The future film critic had been in trouble for climbing into college after hours.[92] There had been even more trouble when Gardiner chivalrously helped her to publish a cogent indictment of the infantilising rules and restrictions in the women's colleges of the day. Gardiner had left Oxford with an undistinguished (fourth-class) degree in jurisprudence. He was to prove himself an outstandingly effective champion of liberal causes.

Under the chair of Mr Justice Latey, the Parliamentary Committee on the Age of Majority set out to consider whether the law needed changing. It consulted widely, and concluded that it did. To begin with there was little clarity or consistency. A whole hotchpotch of different laws, customs and regulations had grown up, some of them over centuries, about when the young should be considered grown up. There were glaring inconsistencies, for instance, in when one might vote, marry, die for one's country, or buy tobacco or liquor. That twenty-one had established itself, in the main, as the age at which young people were considered adults the committee regarded as historical accident. Before the Norman Conquest, the young were deemed adult at fifteen. By the time of Magna Carta, however, young men weren't thought ready for knightly service until the age of twenty-one. This was allegedly because armour was extremely heavy and it took strength to lift a lance or sword while wearing it.[93] The committee maintained that modern conditions demanded different rules. Its report, penned by Katharine Whitehorn, adopted a distinctively jaunty, iconoclastic tone. Young people were growing up faster and demanding respect. Their elders didn't always know better. Above all, the trend to early marriage looked set in and unlikely to change. The majority of the committee thought that young people should be allowed to make their own decisions about marriage at eighteen.

This did not mean that the members of the committee thought youthful marriage a good thing. They were ruefully aware that early marriages often ended in divorce. However they were influenced by the judiciary, by social organisations and even by the agony aunts presiding over the problem pages of popular newspapers.[94] The general view was that the existing situation, requiring parental consent and so often leading to conflict and wardship preceedings, was unworkable. The committee concluded:

> We, like many of our witnesses, think that young marriages are especially vulnerable, and not to be encouraged, but the fact that they are on the increase shows that the requirement of consent does no more than play Canute to the rising tide of young marriage.[95]

The Latey Committee recommended that the overall age of majority, covering full legal capacity, contracts and marriage should be reduced from twenty-one to eighteen. This recommendation was effected by the Family Law Reform Act in 1969. The most immediate impact was felt by the greetings card industry. The traditional twenty-first birthday card, with its silver-paper-covered 'key to the door', was no more. Eighteen never had quite the same ring to it.

Not everyone was happy about the change. Wealthy parents

worried that their eighteen-year-old sons and daughters would come into their inheritances too soon for their own good and might become vulnerable to sexual opportunists and gold-diggers.[96] But there had always been the possibility of carefully drawn up trust funds to guard against this.

The 1969 Act had a strong impact on higher education. Students were now adults and could not be expected to submit to 'moral tutelage' and the kinds of surveillance over their private lives which had caused so much trouble in the past. Since these systems of moral surveillance had fallen so much more heavily on girls, they were particular beneficiaries. Stories of having to move beds into corridors when visited by male guests, of having to climb into hostels after hours, or of hiding men in cupboards while the domestic bursar (housekeeper) snooped around, receded into legend. Moral tutors who had veered towards nervous breakdown trying to police gate-hours and dress codes must have felt a profound sense of relief.

Young women, then, gained a great deal of autonomy as a result of the social changes of the 1960s. Personal stories attest to a new expansiveness and a widening of horizons. It became less exceptional to travel alone, in America or Europe, as a kind of 'gap year' or simply to get away from home. There is a certain irony in the fact that just as the Latey Committee was arguing that society had to adjust to the tide of teenage marriage, this tide began to turn. As opportunities opened up and sexual behaviour changed, the idea of falling in love with, and committing for life to, a first sexual partner became seen as questionable. Was it prudent to be so carried away by romance? Girls' magazines began to discuss the pros and cons of 'trial marriage', or just living together with boyfriends for a time to see how things worked out. In *Honey*, the young singer and career woman Cilla

Black mused on the ways in which the 1960s had altered her outlook on life:

> When I was at school I thought that if I was not married by the time I was eighteen I'd kill myself.
>
> Now I think I'd be mad to marry before I'm thirty-five.
>
> Money changes a girl's attitude to romance, I can tell you.[97]

Looking back on the 1960s, the writer and feminist Sara Maitland judged that most of all, they had been 'transforming times, the beginning of the transforming time for almost all women in Britain'.[98] Linda Grant, a pupil at an academic girls' school in Liverpool in the 1960s, recalled that during that decade she had led something of a double life: 'During the day I scrambled to keep up with my notes on the English Civil War. At night, in my PVC mac and mod mini-dress I sneaked down to a pub where I hung out with people who drank pints and said they were poets.'[99] Much of this was concealed from her parents. The confidence which sustained her through all this was a sign of the times. In retrospect, Linda concluded that although she had experienced the sixties as 'a series of shocks', 'It was apparent that the entire country was behind me in rejecting my parents' values. It was a superb vote of confidence in a teenage girl.'[100]

6 | TAKING LIBERTIES: PANIC OVER PERMISSIVENESS AND WOMEN'S LIBERATION

Almost inevitably, some people feared that the challenges to traditional authority and the rise of more tolerant, 'permissive' attitudes to sexual behaviour in the 1960s had gone too far. Liberty, they proclaimed, was in danger of becoming licence. Young people were in danger of losing their moral compasses. It was suggested that young women, particularly, might need less freedom and more protection, if they were not to come to grief. Those who deplored what they saw as the increasing addiction of the young to sex, drugs and rock 'n' roll could point to well-publicised stories of excess and misbehaviour. These stories carried a particular charge when girls were involved.

Marianne Faithfull's career in the media first took off when she established herself as a singer of lilting folk-songs at the age of seventeen. Convent-educated, she had grown up in Reading, with colourful forebears. Her mother claimed aristocratic roots as a baroness of Viennese origin, whose great-uncle had been Leopold von Sacher-Masoch, author of the erotic novel *Venus in Furs*, and progenitor of the word *masochism*. Marianne Faithfull's looks were as alluring as her ancestry: a blonde with bee-stung lips, she suggested a cross between an angel and a milkmaid. The Rolling Stones manager Andrew Loog Oldham, seeing her for the first time, famously reported that he had seen 'an angel with big tits'. As she was still a teenager, the tremulous tones of Marianne Faithfull's first hit, 'As Tears Go By', had their counterpart in a winsome diffidence: in press interviews

6.1 A young Marianne Faithfull looking innocent, 1967 (© Stanley Sherman/Getty Images).

she confessed to worry over her A levels and uncertain ambitions about whether to apply to university.[1] But after the birth of a son and the collapse of her marriage to John Dunbar, Marianne's halo of innocence became somewhat tarnished. Her relationship with Mick Jagger of the Rolling Stones brought notoriety, punctuated by a series of incidents involving drugs and nervous exhaustion. By 1970 the *Daily Mirror* commented that her love life was 'almost as public as the weather forecast'.[2] After a drugs raid on Keith Richards's house in West Wittering, Sussex, in 1967, the press had a field day. Police officers were said to have been treated to the sight of Marianne, a modern apotheosis of Venus in Furs, naked and nonchalant under a fur bedspread. Represented as having been coolly unperturbed, she later described the experience as having been difficult and very damaging.[3]

Speculation about the details of Faithfull's love life was wild. A story about (unspecified) sexual practices involving a Mars bar circulated widely. This was too risky for most journalists to write about. Consistently denied by those implicated, the rumour nonetheless achieved the status of an urban myth and has proved ineradicable. The press developed a complex relationship with Marianne, who tended to give mixed messages in interviews. 'I really do want to be good,' she told Don Short of the *Daily Mirror* early in 1969, lamenting that she felt helpless in the grip of events which had entangled her. In the previous year she had continued to take drugs, conceived a child with Jagger, horrified critics of permissiveness by refusing to consider marriage in spite of this pregnancy, and gone on to miscarry a baby daughter. 'I am still happily sinning away with Mick,' she was quoted as having reported.[4]

Marianne Faithfull's role as a leather-clad sex symbol in Jack Cardiff's 1968 film *Girl on a Motorcycle* (alternatively titled *Naked under Leather*) didn't appeal to everyone. When she was not speeding along country lanes (minus a crash helmet) the film featured Marianne and her lover (played by Alain Delon) in a series of psychedelically rendered erotic clinches, or as reviewer Dick Richards in the *Daily Mirror* put it, writhing around 'like octopuses in an acute state of coloured DTs'.[5]

Richards was impressed by Faithfull's performance as a lusty young girl who 'clamours for attention as an amoral sexually greedy wanton young hussy'. But it was too easy to assume that the role was in character, and Marianne's boast that she had slept with three of the members of the Rolling Stones before deciding that the group's lead singer was her best bet didn't exactly help her reputation.[6] In retrospect, she saw herself as having been a victim of double standards which glamorised sexual adventure and experimentation with drugs in young men, while condemning women who behaved similarly as sluts and bad mothers.[7] There was undoubtedly some truth in this. Faithfull's open interest in sex, and her willingness to condone sexual relationships and pregnancy outside marriage, would attract little attention today, but appeared scandalous in the 1960s. At that time, as the *Daily Mirror*'s agony aunt Marjorie Proops pointed out, there was widespread belief that a refusal to marry suited men more than women.[8] Confident young men might see marriage as a prison, but for young women it often represented a much-needed security. Moreover, given that there was still something of a stigma attached to illegitimacy, was a refusal to marry fair to the children? After her break-up with Mick Jagger, Marianne Faithfull's drug addiction got out of hand, she lost custody of her son and was reduced to living on the streets of Soho. For some, she was a walking lesson in the dangers of permissiveness. 'I'm Miss Anti-Family Values,' she confessed some years later.[9]

The tone of press reports on Marianne Faithfull's personal trials was often generous: journalists saluted her courage in battling addiction, and male reporters continued to be disarmed by her looks, frailty and vulnerability. Young women's perceived misdemeanours did not always elicit this degree of tolerance and sympathy. Contributors to *The Times* regularly fretted over whether the 'free and easy' attitudes to morality which they saw around them were encouraging licentiousness.[10] Muriel Box's film *Too Young to Love*, based on the American play *Pick-up Girl* and released in 1960, had been an early stimulus to the debate over parents' responsibility for daughters.[11] The film featured a fifteen-year-old girl who, left alone too much, lapsed into sex delinquency. Adverts capitalised on the film's erotic charge, of course: 'Love-hungry girls on the loose!' proclaimed the lobby cards. Nevertheless, the message was taken seriously. Teenage girls needed a firm hand, argued psychologist Dr Elizabeth Radford in 1963; too much money and too much freedom and they would almost always go to the dogs.[12] In 1966, another psychologist, Phyllis Hostler, reported 'hair-raising stories of necking and petting parties in quite ordinary homes'. Boys were badgering girls into sex, she asserted, and parents needed to stand firm and keep an eye on things.[13] In the early 1970s, Ivor Mills, a professor of medicine at the University of Cambridge, took up the same theme, asserting that his own research showed that more than 90 per cent of the teenage girls who had sexual intercourse had it in the parental home while their parents were not looking.[14] Parents needed to watch out, he argued: they had become altogether too tolerant.

Of course, not all parents were in a position to watch their daughters' every move. A growing number of girls were escaping parental surveillance by going away to university. After 1969, as recounted in Chapter 6, eighteen-year-olds became classed as adults, and university authorities were no longer deemed to be in loco parentis. But this didn't put paid to anxieties and scandals over permissiveness: if anything, the new freedoms brought a new wave of fretting. Simon Regan, a muckraking journalist with the News of the World, set out to exploit this in 1968, in a series of articles designated as 'shock surveys' of what went on in universities. Hard-working taxpayers were supporting student protests, political disturbances and sit-ins, he asserted.[15] Plus sexual promiscuity.[16] The past five years had seen a sexual revolution in Britain's universities, Regan continued. Sociologists had shown that 'percentage-wise, there are fewer virgins in universities than in any other section of society'. Promiscuity was rampant on campus, he alleged, and so was drug taking.

The political unrest in higher education in the late 1960s met with little sympathy from those who considered students to be long-haired layabouts with dubious morals. In 1971, a nineteen-year-old female student was expelled from Margaret Macmillan College of Education in Bradford after admitting that her boyfriend had been living with her, in her college room, for some weeks. 'A Girl with a Man in Her Cupboard' ran the headline.[17] The case went to appeal, where Lord Denning ruled in favour of the authorities, finding that the student had flagrantly broken the college rules. The case generated a great deal of controversy.[18] Some expressed satisfaction with Lord Denning's judgment, asking why the girl's boyfriend should have thought it acceptable to live in the girl's room at taxpayers' expense, and insisting that student grants should not be used to subsidise 'immorality'. Student teachers, it was argued, needed to show respect for the kind of rules that they would later be responsible for enforcing. Rather fewer voices were raised in protest, although the *Guardian* published one letter suggesting that the girl had been victimised and that her morals were her own business. Did people want educational qualifications reduced to a 'Mrs Whitehouse Certificate of Godliness and Cleanliness'? this writer asked.[19]

By 1971, Mrs Mary Whitehouse had become the figure in Britain most associated in the public mind with the backlash against permissiveness. A schoolteacher and evangelical Christian, she had been active from the mid-1960s in a campaign to 'clean up TV', founding the National Viewers' and Listeners' Association in 1965. In 1971, Whitehouse co-operated with a number of other campaigning individuals and groups to organise the Nationwide Festival of Light, which aimed to show that the vast majority of respectable British citizens – 'ordinary responsible people' – thought that the permissive society had gone too far.[20] Also involved were Lord Longford, at the time conducting a personal campaign against pornography, the journalist Malcolm Muggeridge and the young Christian pop singer Cliff Richard. A mass rally in Trafalgar Square on 25 September 1971 attracted an estimated 25,000 people, keen to demonstrate against obscenity and pornography. Beacons were lit across Britain to signify opposition to what campaigners identified as moral breakdown, and there was an attempt to evangelise among young people.

It is difficult to establish how much impact the Festival of Light had.[21] The organisation it brought into being soon faded from the public view, although it continued to exist, alongside smaller campaign groups which were also founded in the early 1970s with similar objectives, such as The Responsible Society, headed by Valerie Riches.[22] Mary Whitehouse was to remain the scourge of permissiveness (and of the BBC) for another couple of decades.

At root, critics of permissiveness shared concerns around what they perceived as moral decay brought about by misguided progressives, pornography and pressure groups such as the Abortion Law Reform Association. Beyond these, they tended to express disquiet over a catalogue of contemporary social phenomena, ranging from swearing on television, through nudity on stage, to the way young people dressed and wore their hair. Long hair on young men was suspect, as was too much exposure of flesh by young women, whether via midriff or miniskirt. Some of the most vocal opponents of the permissive society had grown up in what they thought of as an era of clear-cut gender distinctions. Single-sex schooling was considered normal, especially for the middle classes, and boys went on to do National Service, which was thought to make men of them. A short-back-and-sides haircut indicated a well-disciplined personality. Those who had imbibed these values were often disconcerted by the 1960s fashion for 'unisex'. To them, young men floating around in Mr Freedom velvets and florals or girls in sharply cut trouser suits were anathema. As a result, there were many attempts at sartorial policing in the late 1960s and early 1970s. Girls in offices and law courts in the 1960s were often banned from wearing skirts above the knee, for instance. The year 1971 saw the famous London *Oz* trials. Three editors (Richard Neville, Felix Dennis and Jim Anderson) of the satirical underground magazine *Oz* were charged with obscenity and conspiring to corrupt public morals after the publication of a special 'Schoolkids' issue in 1970.[23] There was something carnivalesque about the proceedings, which frequently descended into farce. Neville, Dennis and Anderson dressed up as schoolgirls during the committal hearing. But once the trial was over and the young men were taken to prison, they were punished by having their hair forcibly cut off: a harsh expression of authority getting its own back.

The more focused concerns of those who deplored permissiveness included sex education, promiscuity, contraception, abortion and pornography. These were all subjects which generated controversy over the position and protection of young women. In the minds of the moral right, girls tended to appear as either victims or sluts. They were chaste or they were promiscuous. They needed supervision and protection and should not be left alone. The average, sexually curious young girl simply did not appear in their imaginings. The spectres of schoolgirl mothers, or feckless young hussies bent on one-night stands and expecting abortion on demand when they got into trouble, loomed large. So did fears of sexually transmitted disease among young girls.

'More girls in London have VD,' announced *The Times* medical correspondent in 1970.[24] He reported that the proportion of teenage girls attending the venereal disease department at Guy's Hospital had quadrupled over the previous fifteen years, whereas the level of teenage boys' attendance had remained stable or even declined over the same period. This change was attributed by the authors of the study to the 'emancipation' of women. Although both the actual figures and the proportions in studies of this kind were small, critics on the moral right tended to exploit them as evidence of social decline. Those who sought to reassure and to encourage young people to come forward for testing to ensure sexual health were in danger of sideswipes from Mary Whitehouse and her ilk, who accused them of treating VD 'as no more serious than the common cold'.[25] Researcher Michael Schofield emphasised that conservatives were prone to exaggerate the dangers of contracting venereal diseases in the 1970s as a way of frightening young people out of sex. He cited Germaine Greer's dry observation that this was rather like trying to persuade people not to eat as a precaution against food poisoning.[26]

It was partly concern over unwanted pregnancies and venereal disease among teenagers that led the British Medical Association and other public health organisations and groups to lobby the government to improve sex education in schools. Schofield lent his support. His 1965 study *The Sexual Behaviour of Young People* had found little evidence of promiscuity among teenagers.[27] What he *had* found was an alarming state of sexual ignorance, and he urged that the schools needed to do something to remedy this. But the whole issue of sex education in the early 1970s became entangled in the conservative backlash to the permissive society.[28] The subject became a political nightmare. Mary Whitehouse and moral-evangelists who saw themselves as standing for family values, such as Valerie Riches and The Responsible Society, insisted that control over children's sex education was a parental right.[29] They maintained that schools had no authority to usurp this. Their bête noire was a body of 'trendy teachers' whom they condemned as wishy-washy liberals undermining family values. Shock headlines in the popular press of the 'Sex Lessons for Tiny Tots' variety only exacerbated this explosive situation, which detonated in 1971 over Martin Cole's sex education film *Growing Up*.[30]

Dr Martin Cole (inevitably dubbed by the tabloids 'Sex King Cole'), was a lecturer at Aston University in Birmingham. His controversial views on sex therapy and abortion rendered him suspect in the eyes of moral conservatives even before he unveiled his film. *Growing Up* was intended for use in schools. Some 550 viewers were present at its screening in London's Conway Hall in 1971. Scandal erupted because the film showed short scenes of masturbation and sexual intercourse, with a reassuring-sounding commentary suggesting that these activities were normal. The film's frankness enraged many, including large numbers of people who hadn't actually seen the film. Secretary of State for Education Margaret Thatcher expressed her distaste and Lord Longford described it as pornographic. There was particular outrage over the suggestion that girls engaged in masturbation. Jennifer Muscutt, the young woman seen to touch herself (briefly, and little more) in the film was a teacher in Birmingham. She was immediately suspended from her post.[31]

The anti-permissive lobby objected to sex education not least out of a conviction that it would encourage young people to experiment. Their vociferousness brought results. In July 1971, for instance, the Family Planning Association felt obliged to cancel discussions on sex education aimed at young people which had been planned to take place at London's Festival Hall. Attractions were to include pop groups and the release of 'ten thousand gas-filled balloons discreetly donated by the London Rubber Company'. According to an article in *The Times*, the event had been welcomed by teachers and youth leaders, but the organisers got cold feet when confronted by hostile publicity in the tabloids and warnings that discussions might attract 'too many girls under the age of consent' ('Yobbos, teeny-boppers and Lolitas', according to one report).[32]

Sex education for girls was a particular minefield because conservatives wanted to preserve chastity and innocence. Most of the sex education books used in schools underplayed girls' interest in sex and suggested that they were more interested in love and romance.[33] Boys were represented as driven by adolescent hormones; male sexuality was shown as urgent and difficult to control. Girls' sex drive, on the other hand, was supposed to be mild and diffuse. It was often suggested that it remained dormant until aroused by actual experience of intercourse (when it might suddenly become worryingly voracious). In addition to this, a girl was supposed to take responsibility for a boy's continence, by not egging him on or letting him get carried away. Mary Hoffman, an educational journalist who despaired of this prejudice in the 1970s, poured scorn on typical descriptions of adolescent girls' sexuality. Pauline Perry, for instance, in *Your Guide to the Opposite Sex* instructed her (boy) reader with the following:

> You should not for a moment think that girls have no sexual physical sensations at all. These sensations are different from yours in that they tend to be rather vaguely spread throughout the body and seem to most girls just general yearning feelings

– rather like looking at a beautiful sunset and wanting to keep it but not knowing how.[34]

W. B. Pomeroy, whose primers *Boys and Sex* and *Girls and Sex* circulated widely in the early 1970s, insisted that sex was less important to girls than 'public image'. 'Girls in fact seldom talk about sex as sex,' he asserted, 'and even when they do, they don't talk about it as boys do.'[35]

In 1970 the National Secular Society published a booklet entitled *Sex Education: The Erroneous Zone*, written by Maurice Hill and Michael Lloyd-Jones.[36] The authors aimed to cut through some of what they saw as the contemporary confusion over sex education. A preface was written by the novelist Brigid Brophy, who commended the authors for their wit and for their belief, following Freud's dictum, that 'to inhibit a child's sexual curiosity is to inhibit his capacity for intellectual thought'. Brophy also approved the authors' attitude to girls. Hill and Lloyd-Jones believed that sex education should stop suggesting that motherhood was the sole and sufficient satisfaction life offered to women, she noted. There was a pressing need 'to educate girls to think and earn for themselves'.[37]

Sex education should embrace more liberal objectives, Brophy continued, warming to her theme. Adolescents with homosexual inclinations should be reassured that they wouldn't necessarily 'grow out of it' and they should not be made to feel in the least guilty or disadvantaged. Girls as well as boys should be reassured that there was nothing wrong about masturbation, and indeed they should be encouraged to enjoy it. Addressing the girls, Brophy wrote:

Your masturbating is no-one's business but your own, so privacy is appropriate. Make the most of it. You might find it useful to practise coming quickly, in case you take as your lover a boy who hasn't been fortunate enough to read Maurice Hill and Michael Lloyd-Jones. If your lovers are to be girls, the need to hurry is one minor nuisance, among several others, which you will luckily avoid. If you turn out bisexual, you will want to practise both speediness and prolongation, which should make for admirably varied masturbatory experience.[38]

This was dynamite enough, but Brophy ran gaily on. She suggested that sexual contentment could bring peace of mind and free girls up for independent thinking and living. Current social arrangements reduced too many girls to seeking economic dependence in marriage. Autonomy was infinitely more desirable, and indeed neither true love nor even celibacy could flourish in the absence of personal independence and freedom.

Such ideas were of course anathema to the moral right, who predictably pounced on the pamphlet as offensive and liable to corrupt. Brophy's views were trounced and denounced as beyond the pale. The Conservative Party politician John Selwyn Gummer, whose book *The Permissive Society: Fact or Fantasy?* was published in 1971, quoted her in a tone of sarcastic incredulity, commenting: 'Now there's a fine preparation for any girl setting out in life! No wonder parents are not entirely happy about the prospect of some kinds of sex education in schools!'[39] 'We must of course feel very sorry for Brigid Brophy,' he continued, insultingly, 'What a deprived and sad person she seems from this.'[40] In the event, the National Secular Society withdrew *The Erroneous Zone*.[41] Yet Brophy's robust defence of young women's sexual orientations and choice was routinely sneered at by Mary Whitehouse, Valerie Riches and other critics of permissiveness over the next few years.

Along with sex education, contraception was a major bugbear of the right. If contraceptive advice was too easily available, they warned, the young would abandon chastity. The fear of illegitimacy was considered a valuable safeguard against 'vice'. Sir Brian Windeyer, as Chancellor of the University of London, threw his weight behind such views in a public address, declaring that

> In our increasingly permissive society, the pill has taken away an important constraint, and has contributed to a greater laxity in sexual morals and to greater promiscuity.[42]

In the late 1960s, and particularly in the early 1970s, the pill became much more generally accessible to unmarried girls. Researchers such as Michael Schofield continued to emphasise that it was the more responsible, and often the *least* promiscuous girls who sought contraceptive advice. In his opinion, it was important to make it much easier still to get hold of prescriptions for the pill in order to help the less responsible and more feckless type of young girl to avoid unwanted pregnancy.[43] In addition, he deplored the way that moral conservatives linked the pill with the idea of promiscuity because he thought that this would discourage shy young girls from asking for it. Like Brophy, Schofield was heartened by what he saw as the ways in which more reliable techniques of birth control were increasing girls' sexual confidence, suggesting that

> The modern generation of young women are not content to be sex objects whose role is to provide satisfaction for the men merely as a favour. They are much more aware of the possibilities of female sexual arousal ... Furthermore, girls now demand a higher standard of sexual performance from their partners.[44]

'Would you let your teenage daughter go to a birth control clinic?' *Daily Mirror* journalist Audrey Whiting had asked in 1963, reporting on what she described as 'the boldest and most dramatic step ever taken in the field of sex education', that is, the decision of the Marie Stopes clinic in London to provide contraceptives to girls under the age of sixteen without their parents knowing about it.[45] By 1971 there were thirteen Brook Advisory Centres providing advice on contraception for single girls: they were seeing around 10,000 new clients each year. Paul Ferris, writing in the *Observer*, reflected on 'Teenage Sex: The New Dilemma', which he described as 'an increasingly disturbing family problem'. How were parents to react if they learned that their teenage daughters were sexually active? What if they were under sixteen years of age?[46] Professionals and politicians were as confused as parents: it seemed that no one was sure what the guidelines were. Controversy and confusion mounted in 1971 when Dr Robert Browne, a GP in Birmingham, took it upon himself to inform the parents of a sixteen-year-old girl that the local Brook Advisory Centre had supplied their daughter with oral contraceptives. He was accused of misconduct, though subsequently cleared by the General Medical Council of the British Medical Association. Browne, a religious conservative, had argued that 'it was not God's will' that young people should indulge in pre-marital sex.[47] The whole question of whether it was legal and ethical for doctors to prescribe the pill to young girls without their parents' consent remained highly controversial.

Even more explosive was the issue of abortion, of course, both before and after the Abortion Law Reform Act of 1967. Opponents of permissiveness saw 'abortion on demand' as a major social evil, although it was hardly an accurate description of what was available in the 1970s. In many parts of the country facilities for abortion were remote and difficult to access, delays and waiting lists were long, and unmarried pregnant girls might still have to negotiate hostility and contempt from medical authorities. Anti-abortionists spread scare stories. John Selwyn Gummer contended that even those with 'the hardest hearts and the weakest heads' must feel squeamish 'when fully-formed children, able to cry, are thrown in the incinerator'.[48] A full-scale moral panic erupted in 1974 following the publication of *Babies for Burning,* a book by Michael Litchfield and Susan Kentish.[49] This purported to be a work of 'dispassionate' investigative journalism. It read like a gothic horror story. Young girls were depicted as haunting dark alleyways, 'shopping for abortion bargains'. There were frequent references to butchery, abattoirs, and doctors with genocidal tendencies. One gynaecologist was accused of selling aborted foetuses to a soap factory. This Harley Street practitioner was made to sound like a cross between Herod and Bluebeard. He was said to have confessed:

> Now, many of the babies I get are fully-formed and are living for quite a time before they are disposed of. One morning I had four of them crying their heads off. I hadn't the time to kill them there and then because we were so busy. I was loath to drop them in the incinerator because there was so much animal fat that could have been used commercially.[50]

Diane Munday, active in the cause of abortion law reform and a spokesperson for the British Pregnancy Advisory Service, contacted the *Sunday Times*. An article headed 'Abortion Horror Tales Revealed as Fantasies', which appeared in this newspaper on 30 March 1975, effectively discredited most of the 'evidence' of Litchfield and Kentish. In April 1975, *New Scientist* reported that the BPAS had taken out a libel writ on the two authors and their publishers on twenty-three counts, and suggested that there were more challenges to follow.[51] Neither the General Medical Council nor the Director of Public Prosecutions found any substance in the charges of Litchfield and Kentish.[52] *Babies for Burning*, full of blood, gore and fevered imaginings, was nevertheless widely read and influenced many opponents of abortion. James White, the Labour MP for Glasgow Pollok, who in 1975 led a campaign to limit the terms of the 1967 Abortion Act, was said to have been much influenced by the book.[53]

Another subject guaranteed to needle moral conservatives was that of teenage pregnancy. The press regularly stoked controversy on the subject in the 1970s with headlines about 'schoolgirl mothers' or 'gymslip mums'. In the 1960s, it had been widely feared that the raising of the school leaving age to sixteen would exacerbate the problem: however, the very perception of youthful pregnancy as a 'problem' was itself a product of changing social expectations. In a context where the age of marriage was falling, young brides and young mothers were looked upon with some indulgence: 'young love' could be celebrated along with roses in springtime. As the 1960s progressed, such sentimentality was rather less in evidence, particularly when there was no engagement ring in the offing and the fruits of young love might equate with single mothers on benefits. Unmarried mothers still attracted social disapproval.[54] In 1974, the twenty-two-year-old Helen Morgan, newly crowned as winner of the Miss World beauty competition, was forced to resign, four days after her victory, when it was discovered that (unmarried) she had an eighteen-month-old son.[55] The moral right was in a particular quandary over teenage pregnancy, which may have accounted for some of the virulence often expressed in discussions of the subject. There were regular attacks on young mothers who 'sponged' off the state at a cost to taxpayers. But this often went alongside opposition to sex instruction, contraceptive advice and easier access to abortion.[56]

In the 1980s there were endless disputes in Britain about the figures for teenage pregnancies: were these rising, stabilising or falling? What proportion were 'wanted' pregnancies? One study estimated that between 83,000 and 104,000 teenage girls became pregnant, annually, in England and Wales. Births to teenagers had increased during the 1960s but the numbers had fallen in the 1970s. In 1980, 61,000 teenage girls became mothers, compared with 81,000 ten years earlier. The numbers of abortions performed on teenage girls, in the meantime, had doubled, from around 15,000 in 1970 to 36,000 in 1980.[57] It was hard to generalise about young women's experiences, but there was rarely any shortage of hostile social commentary.

A research report for the Department of Health and Social Security, carried out by Madeleine Simms and Christopher Smith in 1986, found that teenage pregnancy was still a political football. They pointed out that the majority of teenage mothers came from rather deprived backgrounds, but they emphasised, nevertheless, that the majority of those they studied 'were delighted with their babies and their way of life and would not have [had] it otherwise'.[58] There was a complicated relationship between social deprivation and teenage motherhood, Simms and Smith suggested. For some girls, pregnancy seemed like the only route to self-respect and adult status. If society wanted to discourage teenage motherhood, better opportunities for girls and easier access to contraception and abortion were the obvious way forward.[59]

The question of whether doctors should prescribe the pill to sexually active girls under the age of sixteen remained difficult.

Most doctors felt that withholding contraceptive advice, or insisting on involving parents against the daughter's wishes, would do more harm than good. Victoria Gillick, a Roman Catholic mother of ten children, thought differently. When in 1980 a DHSS circular gave guidance on the subject which confirmed that the prescription of contraceptives to under-sixteen-year-olds without parental consent should be a matter for a doctor's discretion, Mrs Gillick sprang into action. She objected that doctors who prescribed contraceptives to under-sixteens would be encouraging sex with minors, and, further, that only parents could give consent to medical treatment.[60] After temporary success with an appeal court ruling, Gillick lost her case in the House of Lords, but went on battling against what she believed to be the social encouragement of promiscuity among young girls.[61] But the reaction against permissiveness could only go so far. The government and medical authorities charged with dealing with sexual health issues could scarcely ignore the importance of sex education, birth control and other public health issues. By the 1980s, panic over HIV and AIDS had added to this agenda. And so had feminism.

What is often referred to as 'second-wave' feminism really took off in Britain in the early 1970s. The first National Women's Liberation Movement conference was held at Ruskin College, Oxford in the spring of 1970. Four demands were originally formulated: equal pay, equal education and job opportunities, free contraception and abortion on demand, and free twenty-four-hour nurseries. Second-wave feminists saw themselves as building upon the achievements of the suffrage movement. Where suffragists, or 'first-wave' feminists, had concentrated on fighting for the vote, this new generation would question wider social structures, including the family.

Women's reproductive rights – the right to choose whether or not to bear children – were high on the agenda of second-wave feminists from the beginning. Over the next few years, the political edge of the WLM in Britain was sharpened by a fight against attempts from the moral right to undermine the provisions of the 1967 Abortion Act. Anti-abortionists often resorted to deeply misogynist language, which helped to provoke the 'them and us' mentality that suffused the pages of the feminist newspaper *Spare Rib* in the 1970s. In 1975, for instance, mobilising support against James White's restrictive amendment to the 1967 Act, *Spare Rib* quoted Alan Clark, then Conservative MP for Plymouth, as having suggested that White's projected amendment would reduce 'the numbers of au pair girls and sundry slags' from the Continent drifting through the country to have abortions.[62] Readers were given a list of MPs 'who voted against us' on this issue and urged women to start lobbying them.

Our Bodies, Ourselves, produced by the Boston Women's Health Collective, was first published in the USA in 1971. It quickly established itself as one of the most influential texts of second-wave feminism. A British version, edited by Angela Phillips and Jill Rakusen, was published by Penguin in 1978, and reprinted in 1980, 1983, 1984 and 1986. Praised in the *British Medical Journal* as 'well-researched, informative and educational for both men and women', this compendious volume soon established itself as 'a bible of the women's health movement'.[63] The book covered a wide range of subjects pertinent to women's health and well-being, including sexual health and reproduction. It gave direct, no-nonsense advice on contraception and abortion, with directions about how to find a clinic appropriate to the reader's needs. It was a mine of information for young women unsure of their sexual preferences and orientation, explaining a diversity of lesbian and heterosexual practices in a completely non-judgemental and helpful way. The tone was never condescending or patronising. The authors recognised that male doctors could be intimidating. Women should not allow themselves to be controlled, they insisted: they should look upon their GPs as partners and advisers. When first meeting a male doctor, they suggested, a woman should introduce herself and shake him firmly by the hand. This should bring him to his feet. Contact on the level, eyeball to eyeball, was preferable to a situation in which a woman patient approached her doctor 'as supplicant, when he wearily raises his eyes from writing his notes to give you the once-over'.[64]

Charlotte Greig, who studied at the University of Sussex in the 1970s, drew upon her experiences for her novel *A Girl's Guide to Modern European Philosophy*, published in 2007.[65] The book conveys something of the difficulties experienced by young women in the era of permissiveness and rapidly changing values. Susannah, the central character, is pregnant and agonises over whether to have an abortion. Her friends urge her to visit the university health service. One points out that the doctors on campus are likely to be sympathetic, and even if they are not, the friends can get their women's group to exert pressure. After all, it is a woman's right to choose whether to have a baby or not. 'This is about control over our lives,' insists the friend. 'Haven't you read *Our Bodies, Ourselves*?'

> 'No I bloody haven't', said Cassie, 'and I'm not going to. It's all about getting the clap and looking up your fanny with a wing-mirror and a bike torch, isn't it?'[66]

Ideas about young women not relying on lovers for contraception, taking responsibility for their own bodies, even to the extent of wresting control from a male-dominated medical profession, and making their own choices, were radical at the time. Autonomy wasn't always easy: a message which emerges strongly from Greig's novel.

There was also the question of continuing double standards. Feminism was less than gung-ho about the joys of permissiveness, although there were differences of viewpoint here.[67] In the United States, Gloria Steinem had declared (in the first issue of the magazine *MS*), that the sexual revolution 'was not our war'. The sexual revolution, she insisted, was a revolution for men, but not for women. Some feminists believed that men proclaimed the joys of sexual freedom to get women into bed with them, and that women, comparatively powerless, found it hard to say no. Others emphasised that for women, sex could never be the emotionally neutral, noncommittal exercise that it was for some men; nor was it ever completely cost-free. Sexual adventure was still riskier for girls than for their male peers: a boy might gain a positive reputation as a Don Juan, or 'a bit of a lad', while girls were apt to be labelled 'sluts' or 'slags'. But while some feminists counted the cost of permissiveness for women, few would have wanted to turn the clock back to the 1950s. More reliable contraception and easier abortion had certainly been liberating. And feminism supplied the opposition to double standards, and the concern for women's well-being, that would challenge the more 'sexist' aspects of permissiveness. In addition to this, feminist writing opened up discussions about sexual orientation and the sources of women's sexual pleasure.

At root, the WLM, like first-wave feminism, encouraged women to speak for themselves. This was easier in a sympathetic context, which is why small 'consciousness-raising' groups were a mainstay of the early stages of the movement in the late 1960s and early 1970s. Participants often recorded a thrill of recognition when they realised that other women shared their experiences and concerns. In this way, the personal was redefined as political. Mary Kennedy, who attended the Ruskin College conference in 1970, remembered that

> there was a real buzz of excitement. As a child I had been very angry about being a girl, in terms of the way that I was treated, because the boys and the men had all the power. Then here came this turning point, and we were all able to speak up.[68]

Feminism blossomed in the 1970s. Simone de Beauvoir's *Le Deuxième Sexe*, originally translated from the French in 1953, was much more widely read in Britain fifteen years later. Betty Friedan's *The Feminine Mystique*, a dissection of the frustrations of the American housewife, appeared in 1963 and made a strong impact on both sides of the Atlantic. Most influential of all was probably Germaine Greer's brilliant, belligerent polemic *The Female Eunuch*, first published in 1970.[69] This spoke to women of all ages, but its richly witty account of how girls are conditioned to fit 'the feminine stereotype' probably had particular resonance for the young. No one who read it could forget Greer's advice to girls to try tasting their menstrual blood as a measure of the extent to which they felt comfortable with their own bodies. Forty years later, the journalist Laurie Penny recalled reading her mother's copy of *The Female Eunuch* as a young girl in the 1980s: 'at the time, it felt like a striplight had been switched on in my mind'.[70]

The resurgence of feminism helped bring about the Equal Pay Act of 1970 and the Sex Discrimination Act of 1975. These battles for equal pay and equal opportunities for women had a long history, going back (at least) to the early years of the twentieth century. But ideas about, and indeed, the very concepts of 'sexual discrimination' and 'equal opportunities' were being expanded and reinterpreted at this time. In 1968, Edward Heath, as leader of the Conservative Party, had asked Anthony Cripps QC to head a committee to investigate the legal status of women. This committee had produced a report, rather quaintly entitled *Fair Shares for the Fair Sex*, in 1969.[71] In 1968 the MP Joyce Butler made the first of her four attempts to get an anti-discrimination bill through Parliament. In 1971, anti- discrimination bills were introduced in both the House of Commons (by William Hamilton) and the Lords (by Baroness Seear). Both bills were referred to select committees.[72] Both Lords' and Commons' committees collected ample evidence relating to sexual discrimination. In 1973 the Conservatives committed themselves to legislative intervention. The Sex Discrimination Act (SDA) of 1975 outlawed both direct and indirect discrimination.

The massive amount of investigation, research, discussion, lobbying and controversy which surrounded these developments revealed a variety of viewpoints. Margaret Thatcher, for instance, then Secretary of State for Education and Science, had confessed that she found 'great difficulty in grasping the practical element of discrimination in education'.[73] Others were convinced that schools and universities were riddled with sexist practices. Some of these were pretty overt kinds of discrimination, such as the 'quotas' limiting the numbers of girls who could be admitted to medical or veterinary schools. Others – such as the existence of single-sex schools and colleges – were more complex. In the strongly male-dominated elite universities of Oxford and Cambridge, the existence of single-sex colleges in combination with quotas and practical limitations on women's entry came to look increasingly discriminatory. The processes by which historically all-male colleges came eventually to accept women students (and conversely, previously all-female colleges came to admit men) were extraordinarily tortured and troubled. But this dismantling of centuries-old traditions happened very quickly.[74] There can be no doubt that the introduction of the SDA acted as a powerful stimulus and catalyst. Twenty years after the passing of the SDA, there were hardly any single-sex colleges left.

Mrs Thatcher had expressed the opinion that there was virtually no scope for anti-discrimination legislation in schools. She could hardly have been more wrong. One of the strongest achievements of second-wave feminism was its thorough-going scrutiny of the ways in which girls become 'conditioned' or 'socialised' into sex roles. Beginning in the family, this process was seen to gain impetus during the school years. First of all there were the differences in the curriculum offered to girls and boys since Victorian times: cookery, needlework, and housecraft for girls; woodcraft and technical drawing for the boys. Sporting activities, of course, were often highly gendered, with girls doing netball, hockey and lacrosse to the boys' rugby, athletics and football. More insidious than these differences in the formal curriculum were the differences in what came to be referred to as the informal, or 'hidden curriculum'. This meant all the things that might be learned inadvertently: the covert, often taken-for-granted values inherent in organisation, uniform and dress codes, classroom interaction, textbooks and everyday speech. The hidden curriculum came into operation every time a teacher asked the 'big strong boys' for help with chair shifting, or banned girls from wearing trousers in cold weather on the grounds that trousers didn't look ladylike. It could be observed in boys' domination of teacher time and playground space. It was inherent in a great deal of everyday classroom speech.

The developmental psychologist Valerie Walkerdine recorded dialogue in a nursery school in the late 1970s, snippets of which were published in an article which was widely read, provoking both horror and recognition among feminists.[75] A three-year-old girl (Annie) resisted two four-year-old boys' attempts to grab a piece of Lego off her. One of the boys, Terry, told the girl, Annie that she was a 'stupid cunt', while the other, Sean, messed up another child's model. The teacher, Miss Baxter, tried to intervene, and then the dialogue proceeded as follows:

> Sean: Get out of it Miss Baxter paxter.
> Terry: Get out of it knickers Miss Baxter.
> Sean: Get out of it Miss Baxter paxter.
> Terry: Get out of it Miss Baxter the knickers paxter knickers, bum.
> Sean: Knickers, shit, bum.
> Miss B: Sean, that's enough, you're being silly.
> Sean: Miss Baxter, knickers, show your knickers.
> Terry: Miss Baxter, show your bum off.
> [They giggle][76]

There was more in this vein, with Sean and Terry continuing to make all sorts of rude suggestions to the hapless Miss Baxter while she helplessly admonished them not to be silly. More effectively than acres of academic discourse, this exchange illustrated how gender politics seeped into the language of (even) the nursery classroom.

Feminist researchers addressed themselves to exploring all dimensions of educational sexism. Much, but by no means all of this work took place in universities. Many organisations and 'initiatives' designed to conquer stereotyping mushroomed outside academia. These included groups producing newsletters such as *Cassoe* (Campaigning against Sexism and Sexual Oppression in Education), WedG (Women and Education Group), producing a magazine called *Gen*, and an astonishing array of local teachers' and pupil organisations.[77] Many of these were regularly listed in *Spare Rib*, which in October 1978 gave addresses for local Women and Education groups in London, Brighton, Manchester and Sheffield and further recorded a group called Schoolgirls against Sexism.[78] The [then] Inner London Education Authority (ILEA) was particularly active, publishing for instance a compendious Anti-Sexist Resources Guide for teachers. Funded by the Equal Opportunities Commission and the School Curriculum Development Committee, *Genderwatch!* was a fat pack of self-assessment schedules through which teachers could monitor their own practice in schools with a view to eliminating 'sexism'.[79]

Feminists both inside and outside academia generated a huge and impressive literature on the subject in the 1970s and 1980s. Sue Sharpe's *'Just Like a Girl': How Girls Learn to Be Women* was published by Penguin in 1976. In a preface, the author recorded her thanks to 'all the members of the Arsenal Women's Liberation Group' for their support.[80] The book was wide-ranging, paying attention to both social class and race. Most of the girls studied by Sharpe were working class, and at school in the London borough of Ealing. Some of the girls from Asian families found school particularly challenging. Their parents were often anxious about their daughters becoming tainted by Western permissive values. This was a theme explored further in Amrit Wilson's ground-breaking study *Finding a Voice*, which focused on the experiences of Asian women in Britain.[81] Ideas about *sharam* ('modesty', or 'shame' in Urdu) and *izzat* ('family pride and reputation') could complicate girls' relationships with boys and hence their behaviour in a mixed classroom. On the other hand, sometimes a parental embargo on free and easy relationships with boys encouraged girls to concentrate on their schoolwork.

Sharpe found that most of the girls in her study expected to be married by the time they reached twenty-five years of age. Their occupational ambitions were limited. Her finding was in line with those of researchers in the 1960s, who had similarly emphasised that the majority of adolescent girls saw their futures as entirely bound up with home making.[82] Educationalists observed time and again before the 1980s that while girls leapt ahead in the early years of schooling, their performance dropped off dramatically when they reached adolescence. The revival of feminism stimulated important new studies of female adolescence. Up until the 1970s, with a handful of exceptions, studies of 'youth' had been of boys. Now Angela McRobbie, Jenny Garber, Valerie Walkerdine and other scholars turned their attention to the girls.[83] New questions were asked about the impact of popular culture on girls, and their involvement in teenage subcultures. Was girls' apparent loss of interest in school as they reached their teens simply a consequence of their interest in boys and romance?

Angela McRobbie's 1977 study of the teenage girls' magazine *Jackie* started out as an MA thesis in the Centre for Contemporary Cultural Studies at the University of Birmingham. Reproduced in a variety of forms over the next few years, it was very widely read.[84] *Jackie* was a publishing phenomenon. First appearing in 1964, its sales rose steadily from 350,000 copies per week to an impressive 605,947 per week in 1976. For over a decade it was Britain's top-selling teenage magazine. *Jackie* was a melange of cartoon love stories, pop gossip and fashion: what McRobbie described as a claustrophobic and oppressive world of teenage romance. Girls were encouraged to practise looking doe-eyed, pathetic and helpless in order to appeal to boys. Attraction was represented as all about love: there was virtually no sex. The magazine's advice column, retailed by agony aunts 'Cathy and Claire', had the tone of a sensible grown-up sister. Cathy and Claire were sympathetic and reassuring about many of the issues which troubled adolescent girls: pimples, periods and the like. Family life was acknowledged to be difficult sometimes, but always worth cherishing. Hearts and pink-sugary flowers proliferated. The steamier and grittier conflicts associated with the sexual double standard or the imperatives of adolescent lust rarely got a look in.

Feminists had a field day deploring *Jackie* and its supposedly pernicious effects on the minds of young girls in the 1970s. These attitudes softened slightly in the 1980s, as more scholars began to investigate the appeal of romance literature to women. Writers such as Janice Radway and Cora Kaplan rejected the idea of the woman reader as blotting paper, passively soaking up stories.[85] Readers were in dialogue with what they read. The act of reading itself could give pleasure and be an expression of independence for women. However, by the time these new academic approaches were in vogue, the popularity of *Jackie* was waning. In the early 1990s sales fell to a point where the publisher, D. C. Thomson, decided to discontinue the magazine.

Jackie lost its appeal because teenage girls were becoming more worldly, sophisticated and independent-minded. They wanted to learn more about sex. In 1975 Judy Blume, writing fiction for teenage girls, scored a massive hit with *Forever*, a sensitive portrayal of a young girl's first sexual experiences.[86]

In *Forever* there were no *dot dot dots* indicating tactful silences, and the bedroom scenes have been termed 'as detailed as any clueless adolescent girl could hope for'.[87] Girls smuggled the book under mattresses or hid it at the back of wardrobes. In spite of repeated attempts to get the book banned in America, over the next thirty years *Forever* went on to sell over 3.5 million copies worldwide.

In place of *Jackie*, in the 1980s girls turned to magazines such as *Mizz* or *Just Seventeen*.[88] The editorial tone of these was less patronising than that of *Jackie*, and readers were assumed to have more grown-up tastes. There was less prevarication about sex. New magazines such as *Cosmopolitan* helped to encourage a more open attitude to sexual behaviour. In an issue of the magazine in 1973, for instance, journalist Irma Kurtz suggested that girls needed to experiment more, and that a certain amount of promiscuity should be considered 'research' into what was conducive to personal happiness.[89] It is almost impossible to imagine such a suggestion being made in a popular magazine for women before the 1970s. Encouraged by the success of *Spare Rib*, some young feminists founded their own magazine, *Shocking Pink*, in 1979.[90] This announced its intention to move away from the restrictive, 'fluffy' formula of magazines such as *Jackie*, *Blue Jeans* and *Oh Boy!* in order to deal with real issues such as sexism and racism in schools. *Shocking Pink* aimed to give space also to issues around sexual identity, especially to young women's experiences of coming out, lesbianism and bullying. The magazine appeared sporadically between 1979 and 1992, the product of 'collectives' on the *Spare Rib* model.

A collection of young women's writing which had originally appeared in *Spare Rib* was edited by Susan Hemming and published as *Girls Are Powerful* in 1982.[91] The contributions were wide-ranging. A poem by Sarah Hook began memorably 'I'm a sexist adolescent/ Boys are all I want at present'. There were essays describing experiences of racial abuse, on the age-of-consent laws and on campaigns against John Corrie's anti-abortion bill. A piece by a young woman critical of her Orthodox Jewish up-bringing caused a great deal of controversy. The editing collective felt obliged to insert a statement of concern from members of the London Jewish Feminist Group in all volumes sold from that point. To counter any unwelcome stereotyping, they also inserted an additional piece, written by a Jewish lesbian, describing her own family background as a model of liberalism. This kerfuffle was an example of the lengths to which the Spare Rib Collective would go in order to ensure fair-mindedness, or what some would label 'political correctness', in the 1980s.

Second-wave feminism turned the spotlight on girls' experi-ences and opportunities at a time when these were undergoing rapid change. This means that it isn't always easy to distinguish cause from effect. To what extent was feminism *responsible* for these changes? Deep-rooted social and economic change in post-Second World War Britain, especially the widening of employ-ment opportunities for women, also played a part in changing aspirations. So, too, did the increased opportunities for young women to control their fertility. It became easier to focus the mind on education when you were in control of your own body. But it is difficult to exaggerate the importance of education. In the first place, the WLM itself was a product of the educational changes which were put in place after the Second World War. Its leaders were the first generation of women in the UK to have been able to experience secondary education as a right, following the Butler Education Act of 1944. Second, a movement towards more equal opportunities had been gaining pace in the 1960s, with some support from all the major political parties. At the end of the 1960s, the WLM exploded upon the scene, generating massive activity and pressure. Educational feminism became a powerful force in government and educational circles. There was a decisive break with history, in that state schooling moved away from the assumption that girls and boys should be educated for very different roles in life: what the Victorians had understood as 'separate spheres', or what early twentieth-century policy makers had seen as the male breadwinner/female housewife model. At the same time a plethora of initiatives to promote 'girl-friendly schooling' ensured sustained attention to the question of girls' achievement.[92]

Girls did better and better in school. In the 1960s, boys out-performed girls in examinations at sixteen. Then girls drew level. However, from the late 1980s girls began to overtake. Only about eighty boys to every hundred girls were achieving five high-grade passes at GCSE by 1987.[93] Girls' ambitions and aspirations expanded at the same time. Sue Sharpe, in a follow-up study to her work on Ealing schoolgirls, originally carried out at the beginning of the 1970s, noticed a marked change. Whereas in 1972, some 67 per cent of the girls in her sample had wanted to leave school on reaching sixteen (or earlier), by 1991 she found the same kind of proportion determined to stay on at school.[94] For this new generation, work seemed to offer space for personal development and independence: it was no longer a case of finding any old job for as short a time as possible before marriage. More girls set their sights on higher education too. For middle-class girls, aspiring to university became taken for granted. In the following decade, female undergraduates would come to outnumber their male counterparts in British universities, a trend which would have been unimaginable half a century earlier.[95]

At school level, social class and ethnic background still made for very different experiences among girls. At the end of the 1980s, the sociologist Ellis Cashmore suggested that for some working-class women the value of education had remained uncertain, guiding them 'towards domesticity as effectively as if it had dumped them on a number eight bus to Tesco's'.[96] But there can be no doubt that for some girls battling poverty and deprivation, school could represent a lifeline. Andrea Ashworth's moving account of growing up in Manchester in the 1970s and 1980s makes this clear.[97] Ashworth's family was rent by domestic violence, they had very little money, and a sequence of abusive relationships had propelled her mother into deep depression. School wasn't exactly a bed of roses either. Ashworth's biological father had been half-Italian, half-Maltese: olive-skinned, she was constantly derided as a 'wog' or a 'dirty Paki' in the playground. Sharp-witted and clever, she survived. Books were her escape. 'Anti-sexist initiatives' reached inner-city Manchester. Andrea was good at science, and remembered filling in GIST forms, GIST being the acronym for a project designed to get Girls into Science and Technology. At secondary school she bloomed, and was encouraged to go on to university. Andrea later described how, as a student at Oxford, she had felt 'that the world opened up like a massive flower'. '… it was abracadabra – it was another world'.[98] Her education conferred self-respect. It also made it easier for her to write about her experiences, both to come to terms with them herself, and also in a way that she hoped would be of benefit to others.

Did Andrea Ashworth's experiences owe anything to feminism? Undoubtedly, although it may not be immediately obvious. The GIST project didn't appear to make a great impact on her future: she read English at Oxford. But Angela's chances of getting into Oxford, as a girl, would have been much slimmer before the equality legislation of the mid-1970s. In addition to this, the climate in which stories of sexual abuse and domestic violence could be told, by the end of the twentieth century, owed a great deal to women's increasing self-confidence and to the concerns of feminism. These issues were much discussed in the 1980s.

In that decade, more and more women were going public with stories of how they had suffered abuse, as young girls, in the domestic environment, and often from men within the family.[99] From attempts to provide shelters for battered wives in the 1970s through campaigns to improve the treatment of girls and women who had suffered rape and abuse in the 1980s, feminists set out to confront sexual violence. They were successful in keeping these issues in the public eye, and thus on the political agenda.

This very success could bring its own problems. To draw attention to subjects which were previously hidden from the public gaze, and break taboos of silence, could generate a backlash. In 1987 a scandal over child abuse erupted in Cleveland. Doctors and social workers were shocked by their sense of just how widespread the problem might be, and struggled to cope. Controversy erupted, locally and nationally, as many parents asserted their innocence and bitterly protested against their children being taken into care. This precipitated a major crisis over the way the child protection services functioned. The Cleveland affair resulted in a judicial inquiry, chaired by Elizabeth Butler-Sloss, which took pains to produce a balanced view.[100] However in the mass of newspaper coverage which accompanied events, it was clear that the women professional workers on the case, paediatrician Dr Marietta Higgs and social worker Sue Richardson, had become the targets of a great deal of misogyny.[101] They were seen by some as over-zealous, interfering feminists. On 30 June, the *Independent* published an editorial recommending caution. While applauding the work that TV personality Esther Rantzen had done in founding the child protection charity Childline, the article reminded its readers that 'militant feminists are inclined to consider all men sexually aggressive and rapacious until proved innocent'.[102] There is a sense in which some of the blame for child abuse seems to have been displaced on to the professionals unearthing it. They were in danger of being vilified as folk devils in the process.[103]

Feminists had always been vulnerable to 'stereotyping' of course. Just as in the early years of the twentieth century suffragists had been caricatured as ugly harridans, their descendants in the 1970s and 1980s were often represented as dungaree- and woolly-hat-wearing, cropped-headed lesbians. The satirical magazine *Private Eye* ran a series labelled 'A Compendium of Loony Feminist Nonsense' in the eighties, chortling over references to 'chairpersons', 'snowpeople', and 'phallocracy'. It was illustrated with cartoons of big-bummed women hovering malevolently with knives over the genitals of trussed-up, pleading males. The magazine *Viz* featured the activist 'Millie Tant' ranting on about all men being beasts and the importance of bringing up children in a man-free environment. The barbs weren't always satirical. Feminists often suffered direct abuse. The American feminist Andrea Dworkin, for instance, was a particular target, partly in consequence of her inveterate battles against pornography.

The right-wing press delighted in stories about feminists falling out with each other. 'Punch-up at the Women's Lib Peace Rally' had announced the *Daily Mirror*, happily, as early as 1971, reporting on a conference in Canada.[104] There had always been differences of opinion among feminists, of course, and to some extent this was a reflection of a strong and healthy movement. But the WLM in Britain lost coherence in the 1980s as divisions deepened. There was a great deal of heart-searching about whom the movement spoke for. Was it too middle class? Were black women being marginalised or excluded? There was bitterness among activists who considered that British feminists were ignoring the very different experiences of women elsewhere in the world. Controversies over sexuality and pornography also became divisive. Some academic feminists retreated into what could look like ivory-tower obsessions with the nature of language and identity. Some feminists looked around gloomily, seeing signs of backlash and reaction. But there had been profound shifts in culture, language and social expectation. This enabled others to be more sanguine, trusting that a new generation of younger women would take ideas about sexual equality as their birthright.

7 | BODY ANXIETIES, DEPRESSIVES, LADETTES AND LIVING DOLLS: WHAT HAPPENED TO GIRL POWER?

'Girl power' was much discussed in the 1990s and early 2000s. It was sometimes rendered – with the suggestion of a pleasing growl – as 'grrl power'. The *Oxford English Dictionary* notes that the term originated in the USA, where it was at first associated with popular music. Alternative punk rock Riot Grrrl bands brought feminist, political themes into the underground music scene. Later, the term 'girl power' was appropriated as a more general, celebratory slogan by the British group the Spice Girls. And girl power came to denote more than just a trend in underground or popular music. In Western societies, girls could appear more active and more confident than ever before. The *OED* defined girl power as 'a self-reliant attitude amongst girls and young women manifested in ambition, assertiveness and individualism'.

Strong girls were in fashion. Young female punks in the late 1970s perfected a new kind of stylish stroppiness.[1] From the 1980s, popular culture had begun to reflect a widespread enthusiasm for self-assertive female types. Stars such as Madonna and Courtney Love both celebrated and parodied femininity: they were anything but self-effacing, and modelled the possibilities of female entrepreneurship and ambition. The Riot Grrls of the 1990s built on these foundations and encouraged political expression at a grassroots level, through a variety of new media, such as home-produced fanzines. Feisty girl heroines began to crop up on cinema and television screens: Xena, Warrior Princess,

7.1 Rotherham punk Julie Longden and friends pose in a photobooth, 1977 (by kind permission of Tony Beesley and Julie Longden).

Charlie's Angels, Sabrina the Teenage Witch, Buffy the Vampire Slayer. Wilting heroines were wet and passé. Social observers began to analyse what they identified as a new cultural turn. The *OED* added its entry on girl power in 2001.

In sharp contradiction to all this, a steady stream of books began to emerge from major publishing houses on both sides of the Atlantic arguing that girls were being massively damaged and disadvantaged by social change. An early example of this trend was Naomi Wolf's *The Beauty Myth*, first published in 1990.[2] Wolf's book was based on work she had carried out as a Rhodes scholar in Oxford. The book's main message was that in spite of legal and material gains in status, young women's lives were increasingly ruined by pressure to conform to idealised standards of beauty. Eating disorders, Wolf claimed, had risen 'exponentially', and more and more girls were seeking cosmetic surgery.[3] In terms of how girls were feeling about themselves, she suggested, they were probably worse off than their grandmothers. *The Beauty Myth* became a best-seller, and proved lastingly influential, particularly with younger audiences.

From the USA, a few years after *The Beauty Myth*, came psychologist Mary Pipher's *Reviving Ophelia: Saving the Selves of Adolescent Girls* (1994), and historian Joan Jacobs Brumberg's *The Body Project: An Intimate History of American Girls* (1997).[4] Pipher's book was based on her clinical work with young girls. She contended that young women in American society were the victims of a 'girl-poisoning culture'. This culture 'smacked girls on the head' with 'girl-hurting "isms" such as sexism, capitalism and lookism' at their most vulnerable stage in growing up. Their experience was like that of 'saplings in a hurricane'. No wonder that they were prey to eating disorders, depression and despair. The book sold widely. So, too, did Joan Brumberg's *The Body Project*. A respected social historian, Brumberg suggested that where once girls had focused their attentions on improving their minds, they had now become obsessed with perfecting their bodies. Good looks had become more important than good works. The past century had undoubtedly brought gains in autonomy, but at the same time girls had lost the 'protective umbrella' which – in the form of single-sex groupings and environments – had previously sheltered them. They had freedom, but this was laced with peril. Adolescent girls and their bodies, Brumberg insisted, had borne the brunt of social change in the twentieth century.

Yet more alarms were sounded in the next decade. Ariel Levy, a staff writer on the *New Yorker* magazine, launched an attack on what she called 'raunch culture' in her witty and polemical *Female Chauvinist Pigs*, published in 2005.[5] Levy took issue with 'women who make sex objects of other women and themselves'.[6] Her text is rich in its denunciations of women 'who get their tits out for the lads', girls happy to strut around in white stilettoes and body glitter, sporting Playboy bunny rings, and rhinestone-studded thongs and G-strings. Feminists had taken a wrong turning if it they saw this kind of behaviour as 'empowering'. Bawdiness, she, reminded her readers, was not the same thing as liberation.[7]

Levy, like many others, was disturbed by statistics showing the rising popularity of breast augmentation procedures in the USA. This theme of the social pressure on young girls to achieve perfect bodies was taken up again in 2007 in Courtney E. Martin's *Perfect Girls, Starving Daughters: The Frightening New Normalcy of Hating Your Body*.[8] In Britain, the psychotherapist Susie Orbach, who had risen to fame in the late 1970s with the publication of her unforgettably entitled book *Fat Is a Feminist Issue*, expanded on the theme of body hatred and the damage done by the diet industries in *Bodies*, published in 2009.[9] The same year saw the publication in the UK of M. G. Durham's *The Lolita Effect*, which deplored the inappropriate 'sexualisation' of young girls.[10] The British cultural critic Natasha Walter's *Living Dolls: The Return of Sexism*, was published by Virago in 2010.[11] This took a similar line to Ariel Levy's polemic on raunch culture. Walter argued that girls are the victims of a newly intense, sexist culture which force-feeds them on a diet of fluffy pink and internet porn, presenting them with a hollow or even poisonous version of 'liberation'.

Disentangling the various strands of these contemporary anxieties isn't easy, because there are many ways in which they overlap. The literature on girls' anxieties about their bodies, for instance, is often closely related to that on eating disorders, unhappiness and depression. Nor is it easy to separate out hard evidence from social panic. Both polemical books written by journalists and social critics, and the findings of academic and professional researchers are taken up and amplified – and sometimes distorted – in the press. Since the 1970s, the media have shown an exaggerated interest in girls' bodies. Some historians have traced this back to the permissiveness of the late 1960s; others have seen the trend as part of a backlash against the rise of feminism.[12] The topless 'Page Three' girl first became a feature of the popular British newspaper *The Sun* in the 1970s, and has irritated feminists to a greater or lesser extent ever since.[13] 'Personal interest' stories about girls struggling to lose weight, or battling against 'the slimmer's disease' of anorexia nervosa began to appear in the pages of the *Daily Mirror* and the *Daily Mail* around the same time, but increasingly in the 1990s. More recently television documentaries detailing the stories of the prodigiously fat or the thin and emaciated, or the body transformations of those undergoing marathons of cosmetic surgery, have become a hallmark of several television channels. On top of all this, we have to consider the world-transforming influence of the internet. To observe that we live a culture increasingly dominated by visual imagery, and in particular by images of bodies, has become the cliché of all clichés.

Growing girls have probably always been sensitive to their body weight and appearance. There is a haunting passage in Pearl Jephcott's study of working-class girls, *Girls Growing Up*, which was published during the Second World War in Britain. One of the respondents in Jephcott's survey, 'Mary Smith', was an intelligent and articulate young woman who had struggled against unpromising odds to train as a nurse. Jephcott herself was sufficiently moved by Mary's story to reproduce it, verbatim, as the first chapter in her book. Mary's plucky and heart-warming story ended with a confession:

> I never bother the opposite sex & very, very seldom they bother me, but my biggest tragedy is I am fat & wear W.X. clothes, I don't like dancing because I think I am too fat. I

don't go swimming because I think I am too fat, I feel very
embaressed [sic] when in the company of males, I cannot
dress as I like because the styles of dress I like do not suite
[sic] fat people ...[14]

A study of adolescents published in 1950 found girls more
obsessed with their appearance than boys, and noted the widespread concern with 'fatness, thinness, tallness, shortness, lack
of development, exceptionally early development, blackheads,
pimples, bad eyes, irregular teeth, ugly noses and receding
chins'.[15] James Hemming, a humanist and educational reformer,
was awarded a PhD from the University of London for his work
on the problems of adolescent girls in the 1950s. His study was
subsequently published as a book.[16] Hemming analysed more
than three thousand letters written by young girls to a weekly
paper in the early 1950s. The girls sought advice on a range
of personal matters, including friendship, and relationships at
home and school, but one of the biggest areas of anxiety was
appearance. Hemming found very few girls content with how
they looked, and noted widespread dejection, and a desperate
striving for perfection in this area.[17]

Writers such as Naomi Wolf were much influenced by surveys such as one carried out by *Glamour* magazine in 1984,
which found that some three-quarters of the women polled
thought that they were too fat.[18] Only around one quarter of
these women would have been regarded as overweight using
the medical criteria of the time. The 1980s was a decade in
which the 'workout' became fashionable, and body consciousness may have increased. Whether this was altogether a bad
thing is debatable, particularly given generally rising rates of
obesity at the end of the twentieth century.[19] But a key question

for feminists is whether younger women's perceptions of their body image were becoming increasingly distorted, and whether this carried increasingly damaging implications for their health. Did such changes lead to an 'epidemic of eating disorders' as often suggested?

Anorexia nervosa was a term established in the late nineteenth century, but as a condition self-starvation has a long history. It can be traced back, for instance, to the saints and fasting girls of medieval times.[20] In the nineteenth century, the display of a healthy appetite could be viewed as unfeminine. Some Victorian girls developed troubled eating patterns, swallowing little in public, while consuming food furtively in private. There has been some suggestion that self-starvation was common among girls in the 1920s.[21] The press paid little attention to anorexia before the 1970s, although there were occasional features relating to the pioneering work of Professor Arthur Crisp on the subject. In 1979, for instance, the *Daily Mirror* included a brief mention of Crisp's suggestion that girl anorectics 'were victims of middle-class values' in a piece headed 'Peril of the Rich Twiggies'.[22] Dr Tony Smith, medical correspondent for *The Times,* on the other hand reported Crisp's work as showing the strains which society subjected girls to at adolescence, and suggested that anorexic girls were unconsciously rejecting adult sexuality.[23]

Newspaper references to the condition increased during the 1980s, but the real explosion of media interest came during the following decade. A quick search for 'anorexia' in the *Daily Mirror*'s digital archive, for instance, yields nearly eight hundred hits, clustering particularly in the years between 1995 and 2005. Brief reports on medical findings gave way to lengthy, personal stories. These were often illustrated by images of cadaverous women, their rib cages and pelvic bones jutting horribly from their emaciated bodies. Harrowing accounts of personal tragedy – a mother's loss of both of her daughters to the disease, for instance – then began to alternate with gossip and exposés.[24] Photographs of celebrities who were looking a bit on the slim side were accompanied by speculation from their friends about whether or not they had succumbed to anorexia. Princess Diana's thin arms inevitably provoked suspicion. When Diana's sister-in-law, Lady Victoria Spencer, admitted to the disease, the press had a field day.

Speculation about celebrities became feverish and intrusive. Some celebrities went in for personal confession, admitting struggles with anorexia, ostensibly to help others. There have been attacks on the fashion industry for featuring 'size zero' models, and horror stories about the ballet world, blamed for subjecting young dancers to rigid body-control regimes. Horror stories about 'sick' 'pro-ana' or 'thinspiration' websites, accused of encouraging young girls to starve themselves, drew attention in both the popular press and in television documentaries from the mid-2000s. Stories about anorexia have probably now lost some of their power to shock. More recently, media coverage of the disease has found eye-catching new angles on the subject. 'Anorexic mum who weighs less than her 7-year old', shrilled the *Daily Mirror* in November 2011.[25] The article was accompanied by a photograph labelled 'Frock shock', showing beaming mother and slightly embarrassed-looking daughter wearing identical, pink flower-patterned dolly dresses with Peter Pan collars.

Anorexia is a terrible disease and it kills. Has its incidence increased as much as some writers have suggested? Naomi Wolf stated that 'eating disorders rose exponentially' in the period just before she was writing and described anorexia as 'a killer epidemic'.[26] But it is very difficult to get a clear, statistical picture.

This is partly because less was known about the condition before 1960. One thing media exposure has ensured is that now, many more people know about the disease, and it is much more likely to be reported. Many parents understandably get concerned as soon as they see any signs of a daughter going on a diet. Another problem is that the statistics which we do have relate to hospital admissions, and not all sufferers are hospitalised.[27] Establishing long-term trends is difficult because we don't have reliable figures on incidence from before the 1970s. The evidence we have is fairly impressionistic. Arthur Crisp's figures have sometimes been used as a baseline. Crisp suggested that around one girl in every hundred in independent schools in London was suffering from some degree of anorexia in the 1970s.[28] Writing later, in 2006, he suggested that the form and content of the disease had changed little between 1960 and 1995, and even that it might have become somewhat *less* common.[29] The incidence of bulimia nervosa, on the other hand – cycles of eating and purging – had risen greatly. An important study of time trends in eating disorder incidence published in 2005 found that the incidence of anorexia nervosa detected by general practitioners had remained stable between 1988 and 2000. The authors of this study too found that the incidence of bulimia had shown a dramatic increase in the 1990s, but that this now appeared to be falling.[30]

The notion, then, of a sudden 'epidemic' of anorexia among young women in Britain at the end of the twentieth century is misleading. The eating disorders charity Beat suggests that between 1 and 2 per cent of young women in the UK may be suffering from anorexia.[31] The Royal College of Psychiatrists suggests that the condition affects approximately 1 in 150 fifteen-year-old girls. The mental health charity Mind gives the ratio of 1 in 100 women between the ages of fifteen and thirty.[32] The disease is not, of course, found only among young women. Men, children and older females can also develop the condition. Anorexia is not the only form of eating disorder suffered by young women. What about bulimia? Bulimia is not life-threatening like anorexia nervosa, but still carries health risks and can undoubtedly cause suffering. There are also many other forms of disordered eating, often referred to as 'Ednos' (eating disorders not otherwise specified), which include excessive dieting, binging, occasional purging, and similar behaviours. Do we include the kind of overeating that has led to widespread obesity under the label of an eating disorder? If we widen the definition in this way, it is far from evident that this is specifically a female problem.

There has always been a great deal of debate about the causes of anorexia nervosa. Arthur Crisp had little time for anyone blaming fashion, insisting that this was to trivialise the condition. Interestingly, he objected strongly to the idea of lumping anorexia together with other 'eating disorders'. He maintained that problems such as bulimia and susceptibility to diet fads bore 'the same relationship to the psychopathology of anorexia nervosa as does a cough to cancer of the lung'.[33] Anorexia is now generally recognised as a serious and complex pathological condition, what journalist Laurie Penny has described as 'a psychotic strategy of self-control'.[34] Another journalist, the *Guardian*'s Hadley Freeman (who like Penny has admitted to having suffered from anorexia in her youth), put the matter in a nutshell, asserting that 'eating disorders do not stem from a desire to be slim: they are an expression of unhappiness through food'.[35]

Only a small proportion of girls suffer from serious eating disorders. Affluent societies, and not just girls, are obsessed with body size and image. Binge eating, and obesity, affect both sexes. It may seem paradoxical that there is so much concern about thinness when obesity is increasingly defined as one of the major health problems of the age, affecting far greater numbers. Notwithstanding Professor Crisp's objection to classifying anorexia alongside other forms of disordered eating, it is possible to see all eating disorders as to some extent rooted in distortions of appetite. These distortions seem to pervade wealthy societies bent on consumption. Young women in our society are undoubtedly subject to many pressures, and they are relentlessly targeted as consumers.[36] It is tempting to suggest that some of them feel *stuffed*, and lose their appetite in consequence. The intake of food is one area over which they can exercise power, and feel in control.

The question of whether too much is expected of girls today has often surfaced in the press throughout the twenty-first century so far. Are girls exhibiting unprecedented rates of unhappiness and depression? Some have urged that this is the case. Two academic studies, one based on a sample of school-aged youngsters in the West of Scotland, the other coming from North America, provoked a great deal of discussion.[37] The Scottish study, published by Patrick West and Helen Sweeting in 2003, resulted in a paper entitled 'Fifteen, Female and Stressed: Changing Patterns of Psychological Distress over Time'. The authors argued that between 1987 and 1999, levels of worry increased among girls but not boys. The girls' worries were not least about school performance, as well as looks and weight, and the researchers thought that this might have to do with changing gender roles. They recognised that girls tended to internalise, and boys to externalise stress, and admitted that the boys may have found respite from pressure in 'laddish' pursuits. The American study which highlighted women's unhappiness was by Betsey Stevenson and Justin Wolfers; entitled 'The Paradox of Declining Female Happiness', it was published in 2009. Stevenson and Wolfers suggested that in spite of all the ostensible improvements in women's lives (better wages, control over fertility, freedom from domestic drudgery and the like), their sense of subjective well-being appeared to have diminished since 1970.

Both studies proved controversial. As philosophers have been aware for centuries, happiness is difficult to define, to pin down and to measure. Subjective experiences of well-being are often mercurial, much influenced by different reference groups and changing aspirations. How does education impact on happiness, for instance? It might bring a measure of happiness through self-respect, while conducing to unhappiness through an increased awareness of the miseries of others on a global scale. Whatever their limitations, both the Scottish and the American studies were eagerly seized upon by commentators. Some journalists with feminist leanings were keen to exploit the opportunity of drawing attention to problems still faced by girls. Other feminists smelt a rat. In the USA, for instance, the much-respected writer Barbara Ehrenreich penned a sharp attack on Stevenson and Wolfers for having opened the doors to those who triumphantly concluded, on the basis of their work, that all feminism had done was to make women miserable.[38]

The psychologist and TV pundit Oliver James weighed in with the opinion that young women were 'the most screwed up group' in society, despite living in an era of greater freedom and affluence than ever before. It was no coincidence, he thought, that girls' unhappiness had increased at around the time they started to outstrip boys at school. Girls were bent on having it all and blamed themselves if they didn't succeed. He likened girls' situation to that of canaries down a mine, whose suffering should warn others of their impending fate under 'selfish capitalism'.[39] But were teenage girls 'a stand-alone demographic in crisis', as the *Observer*'s social affairs correspondent, Amelia Hill, averred in 2010?[40] The British think tank Demos set out to investigate this issue in a report entitled *Through the Looking Glass*, published in 2011.[41] Demos researchers came up with a mixed picture. They reported that twice as many girls as boys suffered from 'teen angst'. Rates of binge drinking, teenage pregnancy and physical inactivity among British girls were higher than in other parts of Europe. However, in many ways girls were doing extremely well. They were 'significantly more successful than boys in making the transition to adulthood'. Their performance in education was exemplary, and, for the first time, women aged between twenty-two and twenty-nine had closed the pay gap, 'with young women getting paid 2.1% more than their male peers'.

A new theme – or at least buzzword – began to surface in these debates about the well-being of young women. This was the term *sexualisation*. During the first decade of the twenty-first century, girls were increasingly identified as being the targets of 'a sexualised culture', or the victims of a 'creeping' or 'inappropriate' sexualisation. There were a number of slants on this. A popular notion that girls were under pressure 'to grow up too soon' was sometimes bolstered by notions of childhood innocence. This tapped nostalgia for a presumed 'golden age' when children played with balls and hoops rather than Barbie dolls and Tomb Raider, and Freud had yet to disturb the middle-class parent's state of mind. There was also growing concern about the commercial exploitation of childhood. In itself this was nothing new, but exploitation was seen to take a particularly unacceptable turn when a multinational company such as Tesco's, one of the largest retailers in the world, started marketing pole-dancing kits as toys. The furore over this hit the headlines in 2006.

Tesco's pole-dancing kit came complete with 'a sexy garter' and some paper money – or 'Peekaboo Dance Dollars' – to tuck in the knickers, along with instructions about how to 'unleash the sex kitten within'. Parents' groups went wild. The *Daily Mail* leapt on to the moral high ground, suggesting that only the most depraved people determined to corrupt their children would want to buy such a thing. Tesco insisted that the 'toy' was for adult use, but it was too late, no one was really listening. Deluged by complaints, Tesco agreed to remove their kit from the toys and games section of their website, but would continue to market it as a fitness accessory.[42]

Opponents of the 'sexual commodification of childhood' turned their attention elsewhere. The *Daily Mail*'s Bel Mooney weighed in with attacks on the influence of girl pop groups, such as the Pussycat Dolls and Girls Aloud, in articles with titles like 'Erotic Girl Group Steals Innocence of Childhood' and 'Sexy Schoolgirls Are Poisoning Our Culture'.[43] In recent years, there have been campaigns against Primark, for instance, for selling padded bikini tops and T-shirts and knickers with 'inappropriate' slogans, and New Look for marketing shoes with three-inch heels to pre-pubescent girls. Pencil cases and stationery embellished with the Playboy bunny logo have also attracted a great deal of opprobrium from groups such as Mumsnet, which launched a 'Let Girls Be Girls' campaign on the internet in 2010, out of concern 'that an increasingly sexualised culture was dripping toxically into the lives of children'.[44]

A long list of individuals and groups queued up for the chance to jump on this particular bandwagon. Concerns were raised not only in Britain. M. G. Durham's book *The Lolita Effect* cites journalist Jill Parkin of Australia's *Courier Mail* deploring what she identified as a new trend of 'little girls dressed as sex bait'.[45] Meanwhile, in Los Angeles, columnist Rosa Brooks worried about whether American capitalism was 'serving our children up to pedophiles on a corporate platter'.[46] Politicians in the UK sensed a golden opportunity. In 2010, the Conservative leader David Cameron, for instance, spoke out in defence of parents against 'premature sexualisation'. Children were being bombarded by inappropriate messages, he thought.[47] In the same feature, the (now extinct) retail store Woolworth was reported to have recently withdrawn its Lolita range of girls' bedroom furniture.

Was this a moral panic? A few brave voices spoke up, suggesting that indeed it was. Laurie Penny shrewdly pointed out that the notion of 'sexualisation' needed unpacking, because it tended to assume girls had no sexual feelings of their own. She confessed that she herself 'would have killed for a padded bra when I was in primary school, if only to give an extra boost to the wodges of toilet roll I had already begun to stuff into my crop-top'.[48] Adolescents showed insecurity about growing sexual development in various ways. Penny detected something of a class agenda behind the attacks on stores such as Primark for 'trashy' merchandise. The British journalist Barbara Ellen, always a staunch defender of the autonomy of teenage girls, and uneasy about what she termed the 'sub-McCarthyist hysteria' about child sexualisation, made similar observations.[49] What stands out from the historian's point of view is just how quickly stores such as Primark capitulated to pressure groups, withdrawing the offending merchandise.

Moral outrage had developed its own momentum, nonetheless. Three British-government-backed investigations reported on the issue of premature sexualisation between 2009 and 2011.[50]

David Buckingham's report *The Impact of the Commercial World on Children's Wellbeing* was published in 2009 and brought an intelligent, balanced approach to issues such as sexualisation and body image. Buckingham warned that debate around these subjects had been conducted 'in rather sensationalised and moralistic terms'. Next, Linda Papadopoulos was commissioned by the Home Office to undertake a review of the sexualisation of young people. This was published in 2010. Papadopoulos asserted that 'hypersexualisation' was a problem for both girls and boys. She claimed that it pervaded the media and led to a climate in which violence against women and girls was thought acceptable. Some critics thought that these claims needed more scrutiny.[51] The third report was commissioned by the children's minister Sarah Teather, backed by the now Prime Minister David Cameron, in the same year. Teather asked Reg Bailey, Chief Executive of the Christian organisation Mothers' Union, to report on the commercialisation and sexualisation of childhood. Bailey's report, *Letting Children Be Children*, was published in June 2011. It called upon business and broadcasting to help to protect children from 'the sexualised wallpaper' deemed to surround them. Bailey's suggestions for intervention included more attention to TV watersheds, urging news vendors to sell lads' mags in plain wrappers, laptops with more parental controls on access, and so forth.

In the meantime a number of other British politicians and writers went into the fray. Journalist Tanith Carey produced a manual designed to help parents protect their daughters from a hostile culture, entitled *Where Has My Little Girl Gone?*[52] Conservative MP Nadine Dorries began a campaign to require schools to teach the benefits of abstinence to girls (but not boys) between the ages of thirteen and sixteen.[53] And veteran broadcaster Joan Bakewell was widely reported as having done an astonishing

U-turn on the reputation she had earned for liberalism in the 1960s by confessing that she had come to wonder whether, after all, Mary Whitehouse might not have been right.[54] Bakewell herself protested that she hadn't changed her views completely. But she was unhappy about a society where sex meant money: 'no wonder young girls get mixed messages and grow up to make bad decisions'.[55] One wonders exactly what Joan Bakewell thought was new here.

Much of the literature denouncing the sexualisation of girls presents girls as victims, as relatively passive, with limited power to make decisions of their own. On the other hand, another vein of concern runs through these debates. This represents girls as leaping on a handcart to ruin through their own incontinence and 'laddish' behaviour. Girls drinking too much, taking drugs, taking their clothes off, exhibiting loud-mouthed and vulgar behaviour, and creating mayhem in the streets began to dominate newspaper headlines in the 1990s. These girls were often described as 'ladettes' or as unrepentant participants in 'raunch culture'. Researchers Carolyn Jackson and Penny Tinkler have observed that the image of the 'ladette' harks right back to reports of cocktail-swigging flappers in the 1920s and 1930s.[56] In 1927 the *Daily Mail* had even described girls misbehaving at southern seaside resorts as 'boyettes'.[57] The crux of the matter was that the behaviour of these women could not be perceived as 'ladylike'.

Feeding into representations of ladettes in the 1990s was also the pejorative stereotype of the 'Essex girl'. The Essex girl – represented as unintelligent, promiscuous and vulgar – was disdained by her detractors, similarly, on grounds of class as well as gender. 'Essex girls' were mocked for their accents, as well as for their taste in fake tans, bleached hair, ankle bracelets and white stiletto shoes. None of these was regarded as 'classy' by the middle-class taste police. Some feminists protested about all this snobbishness. In an article headed 'Long Live the Essex Girl', for instance, Germaine Greer wrote half-admiringly of the image of the young woman as unashamedly fun-seeking, 'anarchy on stilts', the kind of girls who would descend on Southend for a rave, causing even the bouncers to grow pale.[58] Greer objected to the misogyny fuelling a seemingly endless series of jokes about Essex girls as drunken slappers.

The image of the ladette was more encompassing. Ladettes could come from anywhere in Britain and they didn't have to be working class. Female undergraduates at elite universities and even TV personalities could be and were described as 'ladettes'. Ladettes could be 'girly' and sport stilettos and revealing neck-lines, or they could butch up in baggy trousers, hooded anoraks and clumpy boots. Again, distinguishing features were held to be the ability to down large quantities of alcohol, along with complete obliviousness to ladylike decorum. Jackson and Tinkler found the word 'ladette' first appearing in the British press in 1995: the behaviour of ladettes had generated around four hun-dred newspaper articles by 2003, a figure that rose to over two thousand by 2005.[59] The press relished accounts of girls behaving badly: these usually encouraged commentary about feminism having taken a wrong turning. A feature headed 'Ladettes ... or Sadettes?' appeared in the *Daily Mirror* in 1998, claiming to be based on a telephone survey of five hundred women aged between eighteen and thirty-one. Reporter David Pilditch saw one of the defining characteristics of the ladette as a rejection of domestic skills. Ladettes allegedly vacuumed their bedrooms as little as once or twice per year, and 'More than a quarter admitted they change their sheets only once a month. A third said they had never washed their duvets ... two thirds didn't even know how to.'[60] In addition to bucking housework, ladettes went out hunting for men in packs and downed beer from pint glasses. They earned large sums of money, and they endlessly delayed starting families.[61]

In 2004, the then British Home Secretary David Blunkett was reported as having become increasingly concerned about 'lager loutettes'. Traditionally, he suggested, young women had acted as a brake on young men getting into fights and displaying anti-social behaviour. Now, he feared, young women were competing with men in their bad behaviour, countenancing or even encouraging violence rather than acting as a calming influence.[62] British media celebrities such as the television presenter Denise van Outen, and DJs Sara Cox and Zoe Ball, were criticised for their ladette-type behaviour. Trawling through press reports, Carolyn Jackson found ladettes variously blamed for rising levels of cancer, alcoholism, heart disease, child neglect, hospital treatment, violence, and crime and road accidents. The ladette had effectively become a folk devil. A popular UK television series featured attempts to convert 'ladettes' into 'ladies'.[63]

Ladettes were represented as the less acceptable face of female independence, as evidence for feminism having gone too far. Just as anxieties about 'brazen flappers' had accompanied the profound social changes of the 1920s and 1930s, the concerns over ladettes surfaced following the rise of girl power. Change brought unease. There was a tendency for negative press reports and representations to screen out a more balanced assessment of social trends. Barbara Ellen commented upon this in the *Observer* in 2010:

It seems to me that, these days, girls everywhere are depicted as brain-dead drunken slappers. It's rare to see a media image of a group of girls who are not preparing to have sex in a Burger King doorway at 4am. So virulent is this media construct of British maidenhood that even the Oxford-Cambridge types only make the headlines when they go in for a spot of ironic glamour modelling.[64]

The reference to glamour modelling hit a raw nerve. Feminists were increasingly disturbed by reports of girls allegedly rating personal beauty ahead of brains.[65] There was incredulity and near-despair when surveys suggested that many British teenage girls saw glamour model Katie Price as a 'role model'. Price had originally called herself Jordan, and her career dated from the late 1990s, when she became famous for the surgically enhanced breasts which helped establish her reputation as a 'page three' model. A talent for publicity, combined with shrewd entrepreneurship and a colourful personal life, kept her name in the headlines. Many wondered at her celebrity, and particularly, why she was so admired by teenage girls. The journalist Decca Aitkenhead, for instance, agonised over this in the *Guardian*.[66] Price's appeal to young girls might be based on her candour, she mused, or maybe her love of ponies, her ambition to make the best of everything; her body, her business, her love life. The fact that lots of bad things happened in Price's life and that she pressed on, seemingly undaunted, could inspire admiration. And her refusal to be shamed by the media had a kind of courage about it. Discussion forums on the internet were full of vicious and abusive comments about Price, while the press regularly sneered at her behaviour. At the height of her popularity with young girls, Price became for others a kind of folk devil.

There are some parallels here with the media treatment of 'celebrity' fashion model Kate Moss. Moss's career took off a little earlier in the 1990s, and particularly when she was photographed by her friend Corinne Day.[67] These now-famous images showed the then teenage Moss almost bare of make-up, slender and unsophisticated in an ordinary, rather shabby domestic setting. She was almost immediately subjected to a stream of negative comment in the press. On account of her pale and waiflike looks, she was accused of constituting a poor role model for other girls.[68] There was (gratuitous) speculation about whether she was anorexic, she was repeatedly vilified for looking too thin, and she was regularly criticised for smoking. Early rumours about drug taking spread fast when the kind of look associated with the young model and some contemporary female singers was labelled 'heroin chic'. Kate Moss soon established herself as one of – if not the – most successful model of her generation. Her personal life, in the meantime, was rocky. In 1995 the *Daily Mirror* conducted a relentless campaign against 'Cocaine Kate' for her alleged drug dependency.[69] This showed little of the tolerance which had sometimes been extended to Marianne Faithfull by the same newspaper some decades earlier. Nevertheless, neither the bad press (nor the wild partying) did more than temporary, minor damage to Moss's career. Historically, the public naming and shaming of young women had often had devastating effects. It was an effective means of controlling them. Looking back over the careers and public exposure of Kate Moss and Katie Price, it seems that things were now changing.

Glamour modelling and fashion modelling are often perceived very differently. It might be argued that judgements of class and taste intrude here. Even so, glamour modelling is often assumed to be about taking clothes off, rather than showing them off. Feminists concerned about young girls seeing themselves as sex objects will worry about both categories. The fashion industry might be blamed for encouraging thinness ('size zero models') and impossible standards of physical perfection: what Naomi Wolf castigated as 'beauty pornography'. Glamour modelling usually draws more opprobrium, as veering dangerously close to pornography. Glamour modelling conjures up images of seedy photographers, Playboy bunnies, lap dancing and other forms of 'sexual objectification'.

The problem for feminism is that many British women appear happy to aspire to glamour modelling. They buy red-and-black lace bustiers, suspenders and impossible shoes. As well as admiring Katie Price, young women in their droves post images of themselves, half-dressed and looking inviting, on the web. Presumably some women, somewhere, once even bought a Tesco's pole dancing kit. In the first chapter of her book *Living Dolls: The Return of Sexism*, Natasha Walter takes us into a night-club in Southend in 2007, where a group of young women are competing for a modelling contract with *Nuts*, a lads' magazine.[70] The atmosphere gets steamy and raucous as the competitors are exhorted to undress. Afterwards, some of the girls admit that they found the experience a bit degrading. Even so, they are ruefully aware of the fact that they had *chosen* to be there: no one had forced them into it.

Natasha Walter is herself also ruefully aware of women's complicity in glamour modelling and other aspects of 'raunch culture': girls can't be seen as victims in any simple sense of the word. But she argues that part of the problem stems from young women's continuing *lack* of choice, the fact that they perceive few routes open to them as having the potential to bring success. Walter contends that the range of cultural possibilities available to girls is actually shrinking, as glamour modelling, lap dancing and prostitution are now 'mainstream' activities.[71] In this sexualised culture, girls are encouraged to see such activities as 'empowering': they are being sold a false vision of success, liberation and empowerment. The process begins early, with girls being offered pink and glittery toys, or Bratz dolls in fishnets and miniskirts, their 'heavily painted faces looking as if they have been created by Jordan's make-up artist'.[72] This represents what Walter calls 'the new sexism' which turns girls into 'living dolls'.

Many other writers have taken up this theme. In the *Guardian* two years earlier, Polly Toynbee embarked on a rant against what she called 'girlification' and the colour pink. From infancy, she claimed, girls were subject to 'a poisonous pink assault': 'everything Barbie and Bratz, Princess tiaras, fairy and ballerina dressing up, pink, pink everywhere – and it damages girls' brains'.[73] The campaigning group Pinkstinks, established in 2008, set out to combat 'the pinkification' of girlhood, determined to fight against the limited and stereotyped roles it maintained that society offered to girls.[74] Much of this was reminiscent of the 1970s, when feminists contested gender stereotyping in the toyshops and rewrote fairy stories with similar objects in mind. Pinkstinks campaigners often argued that the gender stereotyping evident in toyshops and bookstores had notably worsened over the last twenty years. New stores such as Girl Heaven hawked sparkly hairslides and pink feathery tutus to three- to thirteen-year-olds. From the story of Cinderella to the popular television series *Sex in the City*, both little and grown-up women were being bombarded with the message that salvation would come through shoes.

But did tinsel, pink glitter – or even Playboy bunny pencil cases – really signify the slippery slope into lap dancing and living doll land? Girls are not always so gullible. Researchers Rachel Russell and Melissa Tyler looked at how young girls reacted to Girl Heaven and its merchandise, and found them often critical

and guarded in their response to the images of girlishness and
femininity they found on offer.[75] They were far from being passive
consumers. Do we need to see the colour pink as demeaning
or is the condemnation of girlishness itself a subtle form of
misogyny? It can seem precariously close to misogyny at times.
The *Daily Mail* columnist Liz Jones, for instance, responded to
Polly Toynbee's piece in the *Guardian* by raging against 'sickly
pink tat, adorned with fluff and sequins' and continuing:

> Toynbee cited a new trend called the 'girlification' of women.
> It is reinforced by the half-dressed trollops who masquerade
> as icons, such as the members of Girls Aloud, who would
> surely feel more at home plying their trade on the streets of
> Ipswich.[76]

Adult women infantilised themselves by wobbling around in
high-heeled shoes, Liz Jones insisted, asking: how could women
be so pathetic?

Do we have evidence to accept Natasha Walter's suggestion
that a sexualised culture is increasingly 'shrinking and warping
the choices on offer to young women'? It depends where one
looks. Walter's writing is persuasive and at times polemical,
although she punctuates her text with attempts to supply a balanced judgement. She admits, for instance, that opportunities
for women are 'far wider than they were a generation ago'. In
her final chapter she concludes that feminists in the West have
'set in motion the greatest peaceful revolution the world has
ever known'. The achievements have been impressive: political
rights, equal education and opportunities for work, rights over
contraception and reproduction. Aside from abortion rights,
which have proved consistently controversial and are constantly
being challenged, most of these achievements are now pretty

much taken for granted. Girls today drink, and misbehave, and may be persuaded into choices they will later regret. But by no means all girls behave in this way and among even those who do, many will soon grow out of it. In this, they are not wholly different from young men.

The bigger picture gives more cause for optimism. From a historical perspective, the gains since the 1980s have been impressive. Girls have made dramatic progress, for instance, in education. In 1999, three leading feminist educational researchers, Madeleine Arnot, Miriam David and Gaby Weiner published their important book *Closing the Gender Gap: Postwar Education and Social Change.*[77] In this they scrutinised long-term trends in school examinations in Britain, showing how girls had improved both their entry and performance in these public examinations, at ages sixteen and eighteen, particularly since 1987. Partly as a result of the introduction of a national curriculum, more girls took up subjects such as science and maths, previously dominated by boys. This new pattern was well established by the 1990s. The gender gap was closing. Moreover, girls not only caught up with boys, they began, in several areas, to outperform them. Boys were not making progress at the same rate. By 2001, some 56.5 per cent of girls were achieving good grades (A*–C) in five or more subjects at GCSE, compared with only 45.7 per cent of their male counterparts. At primary level, girls got off to a much better start than boys in their reading, and this advantage was sustained right through the school years. The researchers treat their findings with caution, since differences of social class and ethnicity complicate the picture: not all girls succeed, nor do all boys fail. Even so, they conclude that these patterns of female performance constitute 'one of the most significant transformations in the history of social inequality in education in the UK'.

Girls' successes in schooling were mirrored in higher education. Before 1970 the proportion of female undergraduates in
British universities had been relatively stagnant. Thereafter the
situation improved.[78] A number of factors came into play here:
the growth of the attractive 'new' universities of the 1960s, for
instance, and the closure of teacher training colleges, which
had previously functioned as a kind of higher-education-on-
the-cheap option for girls. As girls bettered their examination
results, 'quotas' limiting female entrants in elite forms of higher
education were declared illegal, and the process whereby colleges
in Oxford and Cambridge went coeducational accelerated.[79] With
women no longer hedged in and herded into separate com-
pounds in higher education, their share of undergraduate places
first rose above the 50 per cent level in 1996. And it continued to
rise. By the end of the twentieth century, female undergraduates
outnumbered the men. Even in the medical schools, once bas-
tions of rugby teams and patriarchy, women students began to
find themselves in the majority. This situation would have been
unimaginable in the 1960s.[80]

Overall, the changes in education amounted to something of
a quiet revolution. As Arnot, David and Weiner emphasise, for
the first time in Britain state schooling decisively 'broke with the
gender order'.[81] Girls were no longer offered a totally separate
curriculum designed to make them feminine and to turn them
into wives and mothers. They studied the same subjects and
were ostensibly assessed by the same criteria as boys. This would
have been unimaginable in 1900. Girls' conspicuous and runaway
successes unnerved many, who worried about boys being left
behind. The label of 'underperformance' switched from girls to
boys, and something of a moral panic about how to explain *boys'*
'failure' followed.[82] Educationalists and parents agonised about

whether schools expected too much conformity and girly compliance in the classroom. Were boys being bored senseless by the nagging demands of coursework? There was sometimes a whiff of misogyny about all this. Would male teachers have a better idea of boys' need to indulge in rough play and to let off steam? Had feminism contrived to upset the natural order of things?

The full implications of these educational changes are a matter of 'contemporary history': we have yet to find out where they are all leading. Girls' educational successes haven't always neatly translated into occupational advantage.[83] Recent evidence has shown female graduates doing better in first employment than their male peers, but they may still fall back in terms of salaries and prospects for promotion in their late twenties and early thirties, or if and when they decide to become mothers. History warns us that when women have in the past risen to dominance in any particular occupation or profession, the *status* of that profession may fall.[84] What will happen to the status and remuneration of GPs, for instance, if current predictions are correct and by 2017 most family doctors are female? Men still tend to dominate the top jobs in any particular area, and it may be that new patterns of gender segregation will emerge. In recent years, the impact of financial crisis and government attempts to curtail spending has had damaging effects on girls' occupational prospects, not least because many girls set their sights on working in social services and the public sector.[85] But in spite of all these caveats, the changes since the 1970s and 1980s have been marked. Women are now a force to be reckoned with in the workplace. Occupational advisory services and government jobcentres no longer draw a clear distinction between men's jobs and women's jobs. Girls have many more role models on offer. When women find themselves excluded from jobs on account of age and/or appearance there is often considerable public outcry. In itself, this might be taken to indicate that things are changing, even if change is slow and not without setbacks of various kinds.

Looking back over changes since the 1990s, it is clear that a new generation of strong, resourceful young women did appear on the cultural scene and that many of them stayed there well after their youth was over. The list would include singers and musicians, artists, actors, television and film personalities, models, sports personalities and entrepreneurs. The singer Madonna's career took off in the 1980s, reaching global proportions in the 1990s. The diversity of her activities in the 1990s made her both an inspiration to young women and a household name, and even in her fifties her performances, film making and charity work made headlines.[86] Like Madonna, the rock musician Courtney Love parodied and played with femininity in performance, celebrating girlishness while refusing its constraints. Annie Lennox and Sinead O'Connor performed powerfully, pushed back boundaries, and combined talent with strong social and political views. Girl groups flourished.[87] Sarah Lucas, Rachel Whiteread and Tracey Emin established themselves as rising young female talents and forces to be reckoned with on the British art scene. On television, a new breed of action heroines enthralled viewers. The American screenwriter Joss Whedon famously set out to create a girl character who would refuse victimhood when he dreamed up the idea of Buffy the Vampire Slayer. The series achieved cult status when it was imported from North America and aired on British TV between 1997 and 2003. Legions of schoolgirls were inspired. All this is just to scrape the surface of what was going on, but it hardly suggests that what was on offer to young women was a narrowing vision of what they might become. Girl power may have been exaggerated – and it was certainly exploited by advertisers and in the media – but the evidence suggests it was no empty concept.

There was much talk of 'postfeminism' in the 1990s. Its meaning was ill-defined. Some argued that women had achieved a sufficient measure of equality and that feminism was no longer relevant. Others identified a backlash, or a betrayal. As a political movement, feminism lost clear, cohesive goals, but has been far from disappearing. Something similar happened in the early part of the twentieth century, after the vote was won. There seem to be moments in history when feminism emerges as a force which powerfully impacts on contemporary culture, other times when its character appears more latent and diffuse. Some observers have heralded the appearance of third – or even fourth – 'waves' of feminism, more global and inclusive in their remit. The impact of the digital revolution has been profound. Where young women in the 1980s and 1990s produced fanzines, their counterparts today turn to websites and to blogging. Keeping in touch with what other young women are thinking has never been easier, and there are exciting possibilities both for self-expression and for making social and political connections.

Founded and originally edited by Catherine Redfern (since 2007 by Jess McCabe), in 2001 www.thefword.org.uk set out to create a new spirit of community among younger feminists. The American blogger Jessica Valenti's Feministing.com, which also set out to appeal to younger feminists, dates from 2004. UK Feminista, directed by Kat Banyard, was established as a grassroots campaigning organisation with an informative website (ukfeminista.org.uk) in 2010. A host of feminist websites in both the UK and North America address everything from how to combat patriarchy (Iblamethepatriarchy.com) through body image (www.about-face.org) and violence against women (www.

endviolenceagainstwomen.org.uk), to women in the media and pop culture (bitchmagazine.org). It isn't easy to give a comprehensive account of such a rich and moving picture: some websites prove ephemeral, others take deep root and thrive, but the array is dazzling.

One example of how quickly feminist campaigning has been changing under the influence of new media was the Slutwalk campaign of 2011. What began as a dispute in Canada quickly turned into a series of protest marches across the world. Early in 2011, women in Toronto were outraged when a local police officer suggested to a group of law students that girls might lessen their chances of being subjected to violent rape by not 'dressing like sluts'. Tired of hearing the victims of sex crimes blamed for their own sufferings, and determined to reclaim the right to dress however they chose, over 3,000 women gathered in the local park before marching in protest to Toronto police headquarters. Many of the women chose to march in 'provocative' clothing, joyously flaunting their fishnets and cleavage bras. They hoisted banners asserting 'My Dress Is Not a Yes' and 'Slutpride'. Assured of massive media coverage, the idea spread like wildfire. There were Slutwalks in New York, London and Melbourne. They stimulated plenty of controversy. In Britain, the right-wing columnist Melanie Phillips denounced 'these silly girls' for what she described as 'an international explosion of self-indulgent and absurd posturing'. In Phillips's view, Slutwalks exposed feminism for being 'well past its sell-by date'.[88] Jessica Valenti, on the other hand, celebrated both the energy with which women rejected the 'dangerous myth' that they invited rape through their 'suggestive' clothing and the exhilarating speed with which a new generation of feminists could now translate their anger into action.[89]

8 | LOOKING BACK

Historians often smile wryly at the idea of progress. Societies change, but it is not always easy to judge whether this is for better or for worse. Some Victorians thought that they had reached a high point of human civilisation; others, particularly towards the end of the nineteenth century, were haunted by a despair that things were getting worse.

The Victorian thinker Herbert Spencer judged that a society in which women were 'freed' from the labour force and 'protected' by men, so that females could stay within the home and rear children, was an excellent thing. Feminists who sought careers had got things wrong, he asserted, and it was a mischievous idea to think of educating girls to fit them for business or the professions.[1] Feminism, in Spencer's view, had probably only come about because there was a shortage of men, and it was unfortunate that some women had to reconcile themselves to the fact that they would never find husbands. The art critic and social reformer John Ruskin would have agreed warmly. In Ruskin's vision, girls were tender beings, like plants needing protection from damaging frosts. They required shelter provided by fathers or husbands, and their main job in life was to sanctify and purify the home. Women who failed to appreciate and to carry out this mission were responsible for all manner of social ills. Young ladies all over the country were presented with prettily bound copies of Ruskin's homilies, and particularly his essay 'On Queen's Gardens', in *Sesame and Lilies*, for right-minded contemplation of their future as wives and mothers.[2]

Feminists turned these ideas upside down. Some judged Ruskin sanctimonious drivel.[3] The women's movement stood for education, property rights, and what was often seen as an unwomanly involvement in work and politics. This struggle involved protracted battles. Gender politics were never completely straightforward: many men supported women's claims to equal rights, and some women rejected the need for enfranchisement. But in the early twentieth century, as agitation for the vote was stepped up in the face of obdurate opposition, the conflict took on the complexion of a sex war. Around suffragette militancy and the force-feeding of women political prisoners, just before the outbreak of war in 1914, this battle between the sexes reached its most vicious stage.

One of the skills historians can supply is perspective. Girls growing up in late Victorian Britain found their freedom and prospects extremely circumscribed. Experiences and opportunities varied, in the first instance, according to social class. Middle-class girls were often cushioned from the outside world. A young Molly Hughes, growing up in London in the 1880s, was certainly not encouraged to travel on a bus on her own.[4] But this kind of 'protection' depended upon having a father, brothers or other male relatives who could provide. When Molly's father died unexpectedly, she was thrown much more on her own resources. She had to contemplate earning some kind of living, possibly in teaching, and this required a more solid education than that hitherto provided for her by her mother, at home.[5] Working-class girls usually had to shift for themselves from an early age, as well as shifting for others. Their childhood was often short: responsibilities for domestic work and the care of younger siblings intruded even before they had the chance of going to school.[6]

Whatever their class background, girls in late Victorian and Edwardian times shared some experiences in common. They were brought up to think of self-sacrifice as a quintessentially feminine virtue, and to defer to fathers, brothers and male authority generally.[7] They were brought up very differently from boys. Any idea that their education should have the same purpose as their brothers' was unthinkable. Girls' opportunities to support themselves were limited. And they had perforce to learn the lesson that as young women their rights, educationally, socially and politically, barely existed.

Daughters who revolted against this situation were commonly regarded as a problem. But the system itself was under strain. There were, after all, the 'odd women', the 'surplus women' for whom a husband might never materialise. Both paternal provision – and patriarchy – had their limits: what was to become of those who could not be provided for? To equip daughters with some kind of education started to look like an insurance policy. It was frequently sold as such. But education could and did give girls ideas and self-respect. It might indeed make them strongminded. Would the strain on the female intellect wreak havoc with girls' reproductive potential? Many physiologists maintained that this was indeed a risk: girl graduates, they warned, might never become mothers. And even if their education hadn't flattened their chests and shrivelled up their ovaries, strong-minded women were widely perceived as having 'unsexed' themselves.

Women who unsexed themselves by fighting for their rights were regularly portrayed as ugly harridans with slatternly hairstyles: unbalanced, hysterical and devoid of judgement. A comic postcard industry throve on such imagery. Suffragists countered these representations with images of saintly martyrs, dressed in virginal white, often topped with academic robes and mortar boards to indicate trained intelligence and high-mindedness to boot. For some feminists, men in general became the enemy. Men were the brutish sex, who drank and whored and reduced all women to a state of sexual slavery, often infecting them with unspeakable diseases in the process. Votes for women and purity for men were the twin demands of the Women's Social and Political Union. In this fevered atmosphere, a moral panic about white slavery spread like an epidemic. White slavers were imagined as stalking the streets and lurking around ports, railway stations and even theatre foyers, chloroform at the ready, looking for girls to kidnap and carry off. Urban myths flourished on the basis of endless lurid stories and journalistic exposés. Moralists, religious campaigners, feminists, social conservatives who deemed girls in need of even more 'protection', and a public ready for titillating scandal all wanted to read more about it.

The First World War slackened constraints, and contemporaries worried about girls on the loose. Flappers and roaring girls replaced the revolting daughters and hysterical suffragettes in the minds of those who bewailed the loss of the old order, which now looked as if it might be gone for ever. Many observers were unsettled by the idea of uppity young women turning their backs on domestic service, painting their faces, and flocking into the cinemas and dance halls. Even worse was the spectre of these brazen hussies earning good wages at the expense of deserving ex-servicemen and the fathers of families with many mouths to feed.

In popular demonology, the pleasure-seeking flapper was gradually replaced by the good-time girl. The good-time girl was seen as out for what she could get; she exploited men, was probably promiscuous, and certainly a danger to health, home and family. Social workers and medical professionals helped the media to construct a stereotype, so that there would be no mistaking her. This spectre of the good-time girl continued to haunt respectable society in the post-1945 world. Crimes committed by young women were comparatively rare, but when they did occur, they claimed disproportionate media attention and allowed for a great deal of public moralising. Young women who were judged to wear too much lipstick and 'flaunt' fur coats and nylon stockings provoked head shaking and muttered tut-tutting. A common moral judgement was that such hussies 'had it coming to them'.

In the 1950s and 1960s there was growing concern about new forces in society with potential to lead girls astray and turn them into rebels. These included American crooners, jukeboxes, coffee bars and jazz cellars, Teddy boys, and rock 'n' roll. The Profumo affair troubled the establishment male: upstarts such as Christine Keeler and Mandy Rice-Davies were disconcertingly eager to contact the newspapers and to speak up for themselves. They were apparently shameless and could bring a man down. In respectable middle England, even away from the excesses of the metropolis, a burgeoning teenage culture threatened to exclude parents altogether from any supervision of courtship: daughters were increasingly perceived as out of control and as running after the wrong kind of men. Bad boys with raw sex appeal gave middle-class fathers headaches: their intentions didn't look particularly honourable. There was no National Service any more to knock them into shape, nor was it apparent that these youths had prospects. Films such as *Beat Girl* played on horror stories of an aimless generation of youngsters, the girls, like the boys, out for kicks, contemptuous of family values, and dicing with fast cars alongside their reputations.

Pre-marital pregnancy and illegitimacy were still sources of great social shame. Young people were marrying at much younger ages than before the Second World War, and some of these unions were shotgun marriages, with pregnant brides. Social tensions arising from these new patterns of behaviour were reflected in a marked increase in the 1950s in the number of parents – largely fathers – who tried to have their daughters made wards of court. The courts complained that they could barely cope with this rise in demand for their services. Magistrates were further frustrated by the alacrity with which appellants tried to undo such arrangements for wardship once it became clear that a daughter was actually pregnant. Even a bad choice of son-in-law was seen as better than an illegitimate grandchild. Dissatisfaction with the way wardship cases were clogging up the courts was one of the main reasons why in the late 1960s there was reconsideration of the age of majority. After the Family Law Reform Act of 1969, young women were no longer classed as 'infants', and could marry even without parental consent, from the age of eighteen.

By the time that the age of majority was reduced from twenty-one to eighteen, the pattern was again changing. Beatlemania had swept the country, and young people were caught up in the story of Swinging Britain. The contraceptive pill was allowing young women to experiment with sex without having to risk pregnancy. Legalised abortion meant that fewer of those who did conceive out of wedlock felt that they had no choice other than to marry. The seemingly relentless fall in the age of marriage which had characterised the 1960s halted, and even went into reverse. Young women grew more independent still, increasing numbers of them going off to university or living in flats and bedsits, away from the watchful eye of parents. This new, 'permissive' social ethos elicited a variety of responses: some girls experienced it as liberating. Others, particularly in retrospect, confessed that in some ways they had felt more pressured into sexual encounters with men. But by the 1970s, a flourishing women's liberation movement made it easier to speak out and to share stories. It also provided support for young women's views, of whatever persuasion.

The 1970s were a watershed. Second-wave feminism threw its strength behind equality legislation, particularly equal pay and the Sex Discrimination Act of 1975. It can be argued that the women's liberation movement took root in Britain not least as a result of changes in schooling after the Second World War. The 1944 Education Act introduced secondary education for all, and the first generation of girls who took this education for granted were often perplexed to encounter limited opportunities on leaving school, and a sexually segregated labour market. Second-wave feminists turned their attention to the structures of work and the family, which both came in for sustained critical analysis. A third area of concern was education itself. 'Educational feminism' was one of the most obvious achievements of the WLM. It took the form of a mass of projects and initiatives to combat stereotyping and to encourage girl-friendly schooling. In the 1970s and 1980s, schooling and higher education in Britain were transformed, in that the traditional assumptions which held that boys and girls should be educated differently were swept away. The feminist project was aided by the introduction of a national curriculum, which helped to erode gender differentiation through subject choice. In higher education, gender quotas, which had held down a lid on the numbers of girls who could study medicine or veterinary science, were deemed unlawful. After much heart-searching and tortuous politicking in the elite universities of Oxford and Cambridge, all the formerly exclusively male colleges

8.1 Two pairs of twin sisters celebrate their A-level results at Putney High School, south London, in August 2011. Girls leaping with joy at their exam successes had become a photographic convention by this time (© Steve Parsons/PA Archive/Press Association Images).

turned their backs on centuries of tradition and opened their doors to female students. This was a move of great importance, not all of it symbolic: the fact that there had been so few women's colleges, all of them much poorer than the wealthy male foundations, had made it impossible to admit more than a minority of girls to Oxbridge in the 1960s. From the 1990s, the numbers began to equalise. With women students no longer confined to the hencoops, their proportions in universities all over Britain began first to catch up with, and then even to overtake, those of the men.

By the end of the twentieth century, girls' performance had drawn level with that of boys at each stage of education. Indeed, in some areas they were doing markedly better than their male peers. The newspaper-reading public became accustomed to celebratory photographs of girls leaping in the air like spring lambs each year, when their GCSE or A-level examination results were announced. Feminist researchers whose careers had focused on girls' underachievement were in danger of finding themselves sidelined, as public attention shifted to boys, who were increasingly seen as 'losing out' in formal education. There was something of a panic about boys in schools: were they bored, deprived of inspiring role models, perhaps, or maybe constitutionally unsuited to the constant demands of coursework? Lurking under the surface of such debates was a question about whether feminism had brought about some kind of imbalance in the natural order of things. Feminists in the 1970s had seen potential in single-sex classrooms as a way of increasing girls' confidence. Now there were suggestions that boys-only groupings might focus on hard physical challenge or bring adventure back into the curriculum.

The closing of the gender gap in education, together with marked changes in young women's aspirations, led some observers to talk again about social and sexual revolution. A 1994 study by Helen Wilkinson for the think tank Demos popularised the idea of a 'genderquake'. Entitled *No Turning Back: Generations and the Genderquake*, the study identified 'a historic shift in the relations between men and women', held to be particularly evident in younger age groups.[8] For others, the 1990s witnessed the rise of 'girl power' as a cultural phenomenon, reflected in music, media, fashion and patterns of consumption. Some argued feminism had done its work and was no longer relevant: young women, it seemed, were shying away from 'the f-word'. Others claimed that older forms of oppression – such as the violence towards women exhibited in some kinds of pornography

– were intensifying, or they identified new sources of concern. Naomi Wolf saw what she defined as 'beauty pornography' as a form of 'radiation sickness', or as a virulent social disease. Others claimed that young women showed rising rates of depression, body anxiety and self-loathing. Girls were criticised for 'laddish' behaviour, and for drinking too much. Or they were represented as the victims of a 'sexualised' culture.

Waves of anxiety, horror stories and panic, then, have accompanied social change affecting women since Victorian times. A particular unease over the position of young women seems to have been a concomitant of modernisation. It is not always easy for the historian to read what was going on in any particular period for a number of reasons. In the first place, strong cultural expressions about femininity or girlhood (such as those formulated by Ruskin or the Victorian poet Coventry Patmore)[9] may be understood as prescriptions for – rather than descriptions of – contemporary social behaviour. In other words, Ruskin preached at schoolgirls precisely because they were increasingly dissatisfied, and bent on fulfilment outside the sanctuary of the home. Second, the image of girlhood innocence has always carried rich symbolic associations and emotional meanings: young women have had a hard time escaping these. In Victorian times, girls were either pure or they had fallen. Their chastity had a property value, especially if they were middle or upper class, and this property was vested in fathers and future husbands. Once she was 'fallen', a girl's assets, or indeed her value as a person, were considered to have been lost. Innocent girls might carry some kind of redemptive power. But once fallen, many predicted that there was no stopping them on the road to ruin, and they would most probably drag men into worldly perdition with them. Girls' behaviour has regularly been judged as innocent or corrupt, white or black, with no shades of grey in between. A consequence of this has been the tendency to portray girls as either victims or villains, rather than ordinary, curious, fallible human beings.

The social thinker and criminologist Stanley Cohen introduced the idea of 'moral panics' into academic sociology when he published his influential *Folk Devils and Moral Panics* in 1972.[10] His book explored social reactions to youth subcultures in the 1960s, and in particular, the activities of Mods and Rockers. Cohen showed how the media could overreact to behaviour which was seen to challenge existing social conventions. The media response can amplify and distort: representations cannot always be read as reflecting social reality. In a later edition of his book, Cohen emphasises that calling something a 'moral panic' does not imply that the something didn't actually exist, or that the reaction to any particular social problem is based purely on fantasy or delusion.[11] It does, however, allow us to see social problems as socially constructed and selectively highlighted, and to ask questions about culture and power. How and why do some issues steal the headlines as urgent social problems while others, arguably more serious, fail to attract the attention they deserve? Cohen's book did not deal centrally with girls, although he later signalled his awareness that there was more to be said about the social reaction to female Mods and indeed about moral panics around what was perceived to be socially challenging, 'unfeminine' female behaviour.[12]

Since the early twentieth century, the lives of young women in the 'Western' world have been transformed. They have gained educational and political rights. Girls are no longer driven into domestic service in their droves in early adolescence. They are schooled along much the same lines as boys and are extremely successful in examinations. Female undergraduates outnumber men in higher education and they now have access to the most prestigious institutions. Girls have more opportunities for personal and sexual self-expression and more control over their bodies than ever before. Contraception and abortion are widely available and the terrible social shame that used to attach to illegitimacy has gone. Opportunities for work and employment have widened dramatically. None of this has come about without acute problems of adjustment. There has been a great deal of anxiety, generating regular crops of horror stories and panic. Indeed, a continuing vein of anxiety about girls has been a subtext of the twentieth century and more. Young women who deviated from convention in late Victorian times were often stigmatised and pathologised. Similarly, 'the modern girl' has regularly been seen as both threatened by and threatening to, a social order undergoing profound social change.

Feminism has played an important part in this process of social change. As a political movement, feminism has never been monolithic: it has always encompassed diverse viewpoints. Some would argue that feminism has privileged the voices of white, middle-class women, and that the movement has paid insufficient attention to difference and diversity. The struggle for the vote in the 1900s brought some degree of unity between women from different backgrounds and around strategic goals – though not always around the strategies for pursuing them.[13] There was similarly a degree of consensus around rights to education and equal pay, and to some extent around reproductive rights, in the 1970s. At other times over the last century and more, it is arguably easier to point to tensions and dissensions within feminism rather than to consensus. There were conflicts in the nineteenth century, for instance, between feminists who insisted on women's education matching up to existing male standards and patterns, and those prepared to contemplate a different, more 'feminine' course.[14] In the 1970s and 1980s, feminists were divided over whether women should receive wages for housework: what was then described as the 'domestic labour debate'.[15] Another source of contention – echoing similar divisions in the 1900s – involved how to relate to men. Radical and separatist feminists wanted as little as possible to do with them. Socialist feminists, on the other hand, wanted women and men to work together for a brighter social future. Ten years later there was a great deal of often acrimonious disagreement about pornography: should *all* pornography be dismissed as degrading to women or was it a whole lot more complicated than that? Disagreements over pornography continue to divide feminists.

But an awareness of the diversity of affiliations and viewpoints within feminism today has to be balanced by an appreciation of some of the ways in which feminists are working together internationally, to improve girls' lives. Plan International's 'Because I Am a Girl' campaign aims to fight gender inequalities worldwide, seeking to promote girls' rights and education and to lift millions of girls out of poverty.[16] The organisation brings together many other foundations with similar aims and equally dedicated to improving the welfare of adolescent girls.

There has been a recurrent tension between a feminist tendency to portray women and girls as victims and a counterbalancing insistence on women's agency and capacity for self-determination. Looking back through history we can see that too much emphasis on victimisation can produce odd political results. It is difficult to forge a political identity out of victimhood. Victims call for protection, and too much protection can easily begin to look like control. This was very evident in the 1900s when some feminists campaigned alongside evangelical religious groups for 'social purity' and against what was depicted as the mass menace of a white slave trade. Much of this was chimerical and a result of moral panic. It conduced to some strange political alliances between social purity feminists and men who were wholly opposed to women's suffrage, but keen to protect a sex the image of whose frailty reassured them.

There have been times over the last century and a half when feminism has gathered strength and power, and other times when it has appeared less a political movement with clear-cut goals and more a state of mind – something akin to recognising women as fully human beings with agency and autonomy. Rebecca West famously confessed that she wasn't sure what a feminist was, but that everyone labelled her as such when she expressed sentiments which differentiated her from a doormat.[17] One of the main achievements of Caitlin Moran's exuberant best-seller *How to Be a Woman*, is that it makes feminism sound like common sense.[18] Equally important, though, has been the need for women to share stories, since the sharing of experience makes for understanding and the strength which is necessary for political action. This is what consciousness raising set out to achieve in the 1970s. The digital revolution has opened up opportunities for the sharing of stories and experiences on an unprecedented scale.

To highlight the ways in which girls' and young women's lives have changed for the better is not to suggest that there aren't still problems deriving from double standards and inequality. Of course there are. Sexual double standards still distort and damage young women's lives. Material inequalities – and the ways in which these appear to be widening – give profound cause for concern. These inequalities constrain and distort the life chances of girls, particularly those from less privileged social backgrounds. The historian bent on taking the long view may discern clear signs of progress, but this is not in any way to surrender to complacency. For history also demonstrates the ever-present possibilities of backlash, reaction and new oppressive forces. Young women need feminism as much as ever, if they are to see their lives in context and to live them fully.

NOTES

Introduction

1 See for instance, McRobbie, A., *The Aftermath of Feminism: Gender, Culture and Social Change*, London: Sage, 2009, especially the Introduction; Harris, Anita, *Future Girl: Young Women in the Twenty-first Century*, London: Routledge, 2004; Ringrose, J., 'Successful Girls? Complicating Post-Feminist, Neoliberal Discourses of Educational Achievement and Gender Equality', *Gender and Education*, 19:4, 2007, pp. 471–89; Gonick, M., 'Between "Girl Power" and "Reviving Ophelia": Constituting the Neoliberal Girl Subject', *National Women's Studies Association Journal*, 18:2, 2006, pp. 1–23. There is a wide range of viewpoints in Harris, A., (ed.), *All About the Girl: Culture, Power and Identity*, Abingdon: Routledge, 2004; see also Aapola, S., Gonick, M., and Harris, A. (eds), *Young Femininity: Girlhood, Power and Social Change*, Houndmills: Palgrave, 2005.

2 Purvis, J., 'The Prison Experiences of the Suffragettes in Edwardian Britain', *Women's History Review*, 4:1, 1995, pp. 103–33.

3 In 1963, the Conservative politician John Profumo was at the centre of a widely publicised scandal involving sex and fears about national security.

4 For example, Gillis, S., and Munford, R., 'Genealogies and Generations: The Politics and Praxis of Third Wave Feminism', *Women's History Review*, 13:2, pp. 165–82; Baumgardner, J., and Richards, A., *Manifesta: Young Women, Feminism and the Future*, New York: Farrar, Straus and Giroux, 2000.

1 White slavery

1 Robins, E., *Where Are You Going To?* London: Heinemann, 1913; John, Angela V., *Elizabeth Robins: Staging a Life, 1862–1952*, London: Routledge, 1995, p. 185.

2 Thomas, S., 'Crying "the Horror" of Prostitution: Elizabeth Robin's *"Where Are You Going To...?"* and the Moral Crusade of the Women's Social and Political Union', in *Women, A Cultural Review*, 16:2, 2005, pp. 203–21.

3 Martindale, L., *Under The Surface*, Brighton: Southern Publishing Company, 1909. There were at least six editions of the book. Pankhurst, C., *The Great Scourge and How To End It*, London: E. Pankhurst, 1913.

4 John, *Elizabeth Robins*, p. 185.

5 Pankhurst, *The Great Scourge*, p. 152.

6 Kent, S. Kingsley, *Sex and Suffrage in Britain, 1860–1914*, London: Routledge, 1995, pp. 5–7 for a summary of the different ways in which *The Great Scourge* has been received. See also Savage, G., '"The Wilful Communication of a Loathsome Disease": Marital Conflict and Venereal Disease in Victorian England', *Victorian Studies*, 1990, 34:1, pp. 35–54.

7 Pankhurst, *The Great Scourge*, Appendix, p. 134, 'The Truth about the Piccadilly Flat Case'.

8 Information on the Piccadilly Flat case comes mainly from Home Office Papers in the National Archives (HO 45/24649). This file includes press cuttings and contemporary pamphlets. See also James Keir Hardie's *The Queenie Gerald Case: A Public Scandal*, Manchester and London: National Labour Press, 1913. There is further material on Queenie Gerald's activities in the Metropolitan Police Files in the National Archives (MEPO 3/1352). Hansard records details of the questions Keir Hardie asked about the case in the House of Commons, on 6 August 1913, together with the Home Secretary's answers.

9 'The Midwife', Report of Central Midwives' Board, in *British Journal of Nursing Supplement*, 15 November 1913, p. 415.

10 Hardie, *Hansard*, 6 August 1913, p. 16.

11 National Archives, HO 45/24649.

12 http://hansard.millbank systems.com/commons/1913/aug/05/queenie-gerald-prosecution.

13 National Archives, MEPO 3/228. See also MEPO 2/1763, 2/1610.

14 Willis, W. N., *White Slaves in a Piccadilly Flat*, London: Anglo-Eastern Publishing Company, 1915.

15 Ibid., esp. pp. 10, 22, 38 and 49.

16 HO 45/24649.

17 See Chief Inspector's report of visit to Queenie Gerald's flat at 85 Newman Street in December 1927. This contains a mass of fascinating detail. Mrs G. was reported as having greeted her visitor 'dressed in a loose kind of white silk sleeveless dress or covering, apparently of the best quality, which was scalloped round the bottom and which showed at the sides at least 5 inches of her naked thigh above the knees. She also wore white silk stockings worked with sequins on the front, with large garters with ornaments above her knees, white high heeled shoes, also worked with sequins.'

'I have never, during my career, ever seen a person dressed in this condition when calling to make an enquiry respecting any matter,' commented the inspector somewhat breathlessly. A note is appended to the description suggesting that 'no officer should call alone to see this woman'; further, 'no junior officer should call to see her on any enquiry whatever'. All this is in MEPO 3/1352.

18 See press cuttings from *John Bull* and correspondence 1917–1920 in HO 45/24649.

19 The W. T. Stead Resource site www.attackingthedevil.co.uk/ is a good introduction, and has the complete text of Stead's 'Maiden Tribute' articles as originally published in the *Pall Mall Gazette*. See also Walkowitz, J., *City of Dreadful Delight: Narratives of Sexual Danger in Late Victorian London*, Chicago, IL and London: Virago, 1992. There is an older, less academic account by Charles Terrot, *The Maiden Tribute: A Study of the White Slave Traffic of the Nineteenth Century*, London: Muller, 1959. This was published in the USA in 1960 as *Traffic in Innocents: The Shocking Story of White Slavery in England*. See also Plowden, A., *The Case of Eliza Armstrong, 'A Child of 13 Bought for £5'*, London: BBC Publications, 1974.

20 Report of the Select Committee of the House of Lords on the Law Relating to the Protection of Young Girls from Artifices to Induce Them to lead a Corrupt Life, PP. 1881, vol. XIII and 1882, vol. IX.

21 'The Maiden Tribute of Modern Babylon: The Report of Our Secret Commission', serialised in the *Pall Mall Gazette,* from 6 July 1885, reproduced at www.attackingthedevil.co.uk/.

22 For an interesting discussion of this, see Deborah Gorham's 'The "Maiden Tribute of Modern Babylon" Re-Examined: Child Prostitution and the Idea of Childhood in Late Victorian England', *Victorian Studies,* 21:3, Spring 1978, pp. 353–79.

23 See, for instance, Bristow, Edward J., *Vice and Vigilance: Purity Movements in Britain since 1700,* Dublin: Gill and Macmillan, 1977; Bland, L., *Banishing the Beast: English Feminism and Sexual Morality 1885–1914,* London: Penguin, 1995.

24 See particularly Doezema, J., 'Sex Slaves and Discourse Masters: The Historical Construction of "Trafficking in Women"', D. Phil. thesis, University of Sussex, Institute of Development Studies, 2005. A version of this thesis was published as *Sex Slaves and Discourse Masters: The Construction of Trafficking,* London: Zed Books, 2010. See also Irwin, Mary Ann, '"White Slavery" as Metaphor: Anatomy of a Moral Panic', *Ex Post Facto: The History Journal,* 1996, vol. V, San Francisco State University, www.walnet.org/csis/papers/irwin-wslavery.html.

25 See collections in the Women's Library, London Metropolitan University, which holds the records of the National Vigilance Association, 1885–1969, including a large collection of pamphlets on the white slave trade, e.g. 'White Slave Trade Official Documents 1905–7', 'White Slave Traffic 1912 and After'. Pamphlets in papers of the Ladies' National Association for the Abolition of the State Regulation of Vice and the Promotion of Social Purity, 1869–1915, also held in the Woman's Library. See also: Report of International Conference on 'The White Slave Traffic' held in Paris 1902, presented to Parliament August 1905 (Cd 2667, HMSO). There is relevant material in the National Archives, especially MEPO 2/558 and MEPO 2/1312. Jens Jäger has brought some of this material together in 'International Police Co-Operation and the Associations for the Fight Against White Slavery', *Paedagogica Historica,* 38:2, pp. 565–79.

26 Report of International Conference on 'The White Slave Traffic' held in Paris 1902.

27 National Archives, MEPO 3/228, MEPO 2/1610. MEPO 2/1763.

28 See reports in the *Manchester Guardian,* 'White Slave Traffic, The King's Message', 2 July 1913, p. 10, and 'The White Slave Traffic Conference', 5 July 1913, p. 10.

29 See, for instance, Lindsey, Shelley Stamp, 'Is Any Girl Safe? Female Spectators at the White Slave Films', *Screen,* 37:1, Spring 1996, pp. 1–15. See also Bristow, *Vice and Vigilance,* pp. 189–90.

30 Lindsey, 'Is Any Girl Safe?' p. 10. On concern over white slavery in the US see, *inter alia,* Donovan, B., *White Slave Crusades: Race, Gender and Anti-Vice Activism 1887–1917,* Urbana and Chicago: University of Illinois Press, 2006.

31 Malvery, Olive Christian (Mrs Archibald MacKirdy), and Willis, W. N., *The White Slave Market,* London: Stanley Paul, 1912.

32 Ibid., p. 13.

33 Bell, Ernest A., *Fighting the Traffic in Young Girls; or, War on the White Slave Trade,* G. S. Ball, 1910.

34 *White Slave Traffic, 1912, and After,* pamphlet published by the Ladies' National Association for the Abolition of State Regulation of Vice, London: Halsey Brothers, 1913.

35 Bristow, *Vice and Vigilance,* p. 193.

36 Hansard, House of Commons 11 December 1912, vol. 45, cc. 699–734.

37 See Fletcher, Ian C., 'Opposition by Journalism? The Socialist and Suffragist Press and the Passage of the Criminal Law Amendment Act of 1912', *Parliamentary History,* 25:1, 2006, pp. 88–114.

38 'White Slave Traffic, Lord Lytton's Branding Proposal', *Manchester Guardian,* 29 November 1912, p. 13; 'The White Slave Traffic, The New Act in Operation', *The Times,* 14 December 1912, p. 6.

39 'Flogging Under the White Slave Act: A Woman's Protest', *Manchester Guardian,* 6 March 1914, p. 10.

40 West, Rebecca, essay on the White Slave Traffic Bill originally published in the *Clarion,* 22 November 1912, reprinted in Marcus, J., (ed.), *The Young Rebecca: Writings of Rebecca West, 1911–17,* London: Macmillan and Virago, 1982, p. 122.

41 Billington-Greig, T., 'The Truth about White Slavery', *English Review,* June 1913, pp. 428–46.

42 Ibid., p. 441.

43 Ibid., p. 439.

44 Ibid., p. 445.

45 Correspondence Respecting International Conferences on Obscene Publications and the White Slave Traffic, Paris 1910, London: HMSO, 1912, Cd 6547, with notes added 1913 by F. S. Bullock, the Women's Library.

46 Ibid., Notes, p. 6.

47 Letter from D. J. Bigham, New Scotland Yard, to A. Maxwell, dated 14 February 1919, in the National Archives, MEPO 2/1763.

48 Hale, K., *A Slender Reputation: An Autobiography,* London: Warne, 1998, p. 52.

49 Gorham, D., *Vera Brittain: A Feminist Life,* Cambridge, MA: Blackwell, 1996, p. 51.

50 Vera Brittain, diary entry for March 1913, cited in Gorham, *Vera Brittain,* p. 51.

51 Vera Brittain, *Testament of Youth,* London: Gollancz, 1933, pp. 46–7.

52 Marshall, D. (edited by David Edge Marshall), *The Making of a Twentieth Century Woman: A Memoir,* London: Blazon Books, 2003, p. 24.

53 Ibid.

54 Papers of Travellers' Aid Society in the Women's Library. The British Library has some reports of the Metropolitan Association for Befriending Young Servants (MABYS), founded by Jane Nassau Senior. There are more reports in with Joan Bonham Carter's papers in Hampshire Record Office (94M72/F519). For rescue work at railway stations, see among others, Anon., ('London, Offices of "M.A.P"'), *In the Grip of the White Slave Trader,* London: c. 1910.

55 (Anon.), *The Dangers of False Prudery, by the Author of 'The White Slave Trade': A Book for Parents,* London: C. Arthur Pearson, 1912.

56 See Bristow, *Vice and Vigilance,* and Bland, *Banishing the Beast;* also Hunt, A., *Governing Morals: A Social History of Moral Regulation,* Cambridge University Press, 1999.

57 For William Alexander Coote see entry in *Dictionary of National Biography.* See also Coote, W. A.,

A Romance of Philosophy, London: National Vigilance Association, 1916; *A Vision and Its Fulfilment,* London: National Vigilance Association, 1910; *The White Slave Traffic,* London: C. Arthur Pearson, 1916.

58 For the Contagious Diseases Acts see Walkowitz, J. R., *Prostitution and Victorian Society: Women, Class and the State,* Cambridge University Press, 1980.

59 Morgan, S., *A Passion for Purity: Ellice Hopkins and the Politics of Gender in the Late Victorian Church,* University of Bristol Press, 1999, and the same author's '"Wild Oats or Acorns?" Social Purity, Sexual Politics and the Response of the Late-Victorian Church', *Journal of Religious History,* 31:2, June 2007.

60 See reports of MABYS (1877–1880; 1881–1883; 1884–1886) in the British Library, which also has Reports of the Moral Reform Union, 1882–1897; Higson, J. E., *Women and Social Purity,* London: SPCK, 1918.

61 Money, Agnes L., *A History of the Girls' Friendly Society,* London: Gardner, 1897 (revised edition 1911); Heath-Stubbs, M., *Friendship's Highway: Being a History of the Girls' Friendly Society, 1875–1925,* London: GFS Central Office, 1926; Harrison, B., 'For Church, Queen and Family: The Girls' Friendly Society 1874–1920, *Past and Present,* 61:1, 1973, pp. 107–38. See also the Women's Library online exhibition 'Bear Ye One Another's Burdens' by Vivienne Richmond at www.londonmet.ac.uk.

62 Richmond, V., '"It Is Not a Society for Human Beings but for Virgins": The Girls' Friendly Society Membership Eligibility Dispute 1875–1936', *Journal of Historical Sociology,* 20:3, 2007, pp. 304–27.

63 Harrison, 'For Church, Queen and Family', p. 109.

64 Heath-Stubbs, *Friendship's Highway,* p. 50.

65 Ibid., pp. 51–3.

66 Miss Nunneley, 'Snowdrop Bands', in *Women Workers, Papers read at a Conference convened by the Birmingham Ladies' Union of Workers among Women and Girls in November 1890,* Birmingham: 1890. See also issues of *The Snowdrop,* 'Official organ of Snowdrop and White Ribbon bands', issues for 1912 in the British Library.

67 Ibid.

68 Ruskin, J., *Sesame and Lilies,* London: Smith, Elder and Co., 1865.

69 See for instance Krugovoy Silver, A., *Victorian Literature and the Anorexic Body,* Cambridge University Press, 2002, pp. 63–4.

70 On Ruskin generally see Batchelor, J., *John Ruskin: No Wealth but Life,* London: Chatto and Windus, 2000; on beauty queens see Cole, M., *Be Like Daisies: John Ruskin and the Cult of Beauty at Whitelands College,* St Albans: Brentham Press, 1992. Roehampton University has the archives of Whitelands College, including papers relating to the connection with John Ruskin, 1864–1978, and material relating to the annual May Day ceremonies, 1881–2001. The dresses, ornaments and bouquets of the May Queens have been preserved in the collection.

71 There was also a flourishing trade in primers for the guidance of schools when using Ruskin's texts, such as *Sesame and Lilies.* See, for instance, Modlen, W., *Notes for the Use of Schools on Ruskin's Sesame and Lilies,* Huntingdon: K. Modlen, 1912.

72 Mrs Parker, *A Year's Work*

amongst Factory Girls, London: GFS and Hatchards' Piccadilly, 1884, p. 11.

73 Report of the Social Purity Alliance for 1887–1888, Westminster: 1888, p. 14.

74 Heath-Stubbs, *Friendship's Highway,* pp. 111–12.

75 Girls' Statement Books from 1880s, in Archives, Salvation Army Heritage Centre.

76 Richmond, "'It Is Not a Society for Human Beings but for Virgins'".

77 File relating to Dronfield Sex Education case in the National Archives, ED 50/185. The case is discussed in Mort, F., *Dangerous Sexualities: Medico-Moral Politics in England since 1830,* London: Routledge and Kegan Paul, 1987, p. 121ff.

78 Salvation Army Girls' Statement Books, Archives, Salvation Army Heritage Centre.

79 Royden, A. Maude (ed.), *Downward Paths: An Inquiry into the Causes Which Contribute to the Making of the Prostitute,* London: G. Bell and Sons, 1916.

80 Ibid., Introduction, p. xii.

81 Ibid., p. 49.

82 Ibid., p. 50.

83 Ibid., p. 54.

84 Ibid., pp. viii, 110–15.

85 Ibid., pp. 110, 114.

86 Hansard, House of Commons Debates, 10 June 1912, vol. 39, paras 574–5.

87 Terrot, C., *Traffic in Innocents: The Shocking Facts about the Flesh Markets of Europe; A Story of Lust and Moral Depravity Unequalled in Civilized Times,* New York: Bantam/E. P. Dutton, 1961.

2 Unwomanly types

1 Ibsen's *A Doll's House* was performed at the Novelty Theatre in London in 1889 with Janet Achurch as Nora. It aroused a storm of public controversy. Walter Besant, who had already revealed a deep-rooted antipathy to feminism in his satirical novel *The Revolt of Man* (1882), wrote a short story entitled 'The Dolls' House – and After', which appeared in the *English Illustrated Magazine* in January 1890. This cautionary tale catalogued the disasters which Besant imagined that Nora's desertion would have perpetrated on her family; her husband driven to drink, her son to forgery, her daughter to suicide. A spate of alternative endings and sequels to the play followed, with G. B. Shaw, Israel Zangwill and Eleanor Marx defending Ibsen's viewpoint. See Shaw, G. B., 'Still After the Doll's House', *Time,* February 1890, and Marx, E., and Zangwill, I., 'A Doll's House Repaired', *Time,* March 1891.

2 Crackenthorpe, B. A., 'The Revolt of the Daughters', *Nineteenth Century,* 35, January 1894, pp. 23–31.

3 Jeune, M., 'The Revolt of the Daughters', *Fortnightly Review,* 55, February 1894, pp. 267–76.

4 Pearsall Smith, Alys W., 'A Reply from the Daughters', *Nineteenth Century,* 35, March 1894, pp. 443–50.

5 Hemery, G., 'The Revolt of the Daughters: An Answer – by One of Them', *Westminster Review,* 141, June 1894, pp. 679–81.

6 Amos, Sarah M., 'The Evolution of the Daughters', *Contemporary Review,* 65, April 1894, pp. 515–20.

7 Nightingale, F., 'Cassandra', printed as an appendix to Strachey, R., *The Cause: A Short History of the Women's Movement in Great Britain,* Bath: Cedric Chivers, 1974, p. 402.

8 Strachey, *The Cause,* pp. 14, 44.

9 See Dyhouse, C., *Girls Growing*

Up In Late Victorian and Edwardian Britain, London: Routledge and Kegan Paul, 1981.

10 There is a useful exploration of the governess in Hughes, K., *The Victorian Governess,* London: Hambledon Press, 1993.

11 The best treatment is probably still Stephen, B., *Emily Davies and Girton College,* London: Constable, 1927. See also Sara Delamont's entry for Emily Davies in the *Oxford Dictionary of National Biography*, and references.

12 Dyhouse, *Girls Growing Up,* Chapter 2. See also Dyhouse, C., 'Miss Buss and Miss Beale: Gender and Authority in the History of Education', in Hunt, F. (ed.), *Lessons for Life: The Schooling of Girls and Women, 1850–1950,* Oxford: Blackwell, 1987, pp. 22–39.

13 Dyhouse, *Girls Growing Up*; on the GPDS (later GDS) see Kamm, J., *Indicative Past: 100 Years of the Girls' Public Day School Trust,* London: Allen and Unwin, 1971.

14 See McWilliams Tullberg, R., *Women at Cambridge,* London: Gollancz, 1975 (revised edition published by Cambridge University Press, 1998); Dyhouse, C., *No Distinction of Sex? Women in British Universities 1870–1939,* London: UCL Press, 1995.

15 Dyhouse, *No Distinction of Sex?* pp. 91–125.

16 'Honour to Agnata Frances Ramsay', *Punch,* 2 July 1887.

17 On women students and college rooms see Hamlett, J., '"Nicely Feminine, yet Learned": Student Rooms at Royal Holloway and the Oxbridge Colleges in Late Nineteenth-century Britain', *Women's History Review,* 15:1, 2006, pp. 137–61.

18 Dyhouse, *No Distinction of Sex?*

19 On Sophie Bryant see Sheila Fletcher's entry in the *Oxford Dictionary of National Biography*, also Drummond, I. M. (ed.), *Sophie Bryant, DSc, Litt D, 1850–1922,* London: private publication.

20 'George Egerton' (Mrs Mary Chavelita Dunne), *Keynotes,* London: Elkin Mathews and John Lane, 1893.

21 'Borgia Smudgiton', with 'Japanese Fan-de-Siècle illustrations by Mortarthurio Whiskersly' in *Punch,* 106, 10 March 1894; Part II, 106, 17 March 1894. See the discussion of the ways in which the New Woman was parodied as a symbol of disorder in Richardson, A., *The New Woman in Fiction and in Fact: Fin-de-Siècle Feminisms,* London: Palgrave Macmillan, 2001, especially the Introduction.

22 Grant Allen, *The Woman Who Did,* London: John Lane, 1895.

23 Fawcett, M. Garrett, 'The Woman Who Did', *Contemporary Review,* vol. LXVII, 1895, pp. 625–31.

24 See, for instance, Victoria Crosse, *The Woman Who Didn't,* London: Roberts Bros, Boston: John Lane, 1895; 'Lucas Cleeve' (Adelina Kingscote), *The Woman Who Wouldn't,* London: Simpkin Marshall and Co., 1895.

25 See, for instance, Stutfield, Hugh E. M., 'Tommyrotics', *Blackwoods Magazine,* June 1895, and 'The Psychology of Feminism', *Blackwoods Magazine,* January 1897.

26 The Rational Dress Society, founded in London in 1881, argued for bloomers and bifurcated garments that came into their own when cycling rose in popularity in the 1890s. See Cunningham, Patricia A., *Reforming Women's Fashion 1850–1920: Politics, Health and Art,* Kent State University Press, 2003; Marks, P.,

Bicycles, Bangs and Bloomers: The New Woman in the Popular Press, Lexington: Kentucky University Press, 1990.

27 Glendinning, V., *A Suppressed Cry: Life and Death of a Quaker Daughter*, London: Routledge and Kegan Paul, 1969, p. 71; Marshall, M. Paley, *What I Remember*, Cambridge University Press, 1947, p. 20.

28 Glendinning, *A Suppressed Cry*, p. 73.

29 From Lennox, G. R., *Echoes from the Hills*, Devon: Arthur H. Stockwell, 1978, p. 24.

30 Delamont, S., 'The Contradictions in Ladies' Education', in Delamont, S., and Duffin, L. (eds), *The Nineteenth Century Woman: Her Cultural and Physical World*, London: Croom Helm, 1978, p. 146; see also Dyhouse, *Girls Growing Up*, p. 68.

31 *The Journal of Marie Bashkirtseff*, translated, with an introduction, by Mathilde Blind, London: Cassell and Co., 1890.

32 *Journal of Marie Bashkirtseff*, Virago Press edition, 1985, offset from 1891 edition, introduced by Rozsika Parker and Griselda Pollock, p. 133.

33 Stead, W. T., 'The Journal of Marie Bashkirtseff: The Story of a Girl's Life', *Review of Reviews*, June 1890, pp. 539–49.

34 Ibid., p. 549.

35 Shaw, G. B., 'The Womanly Woman', in *The Quintessence of Ibsenism*, London: 1891.

36 *Journal of Marie Bashkirtseff*, p. 290.

37 The issue of femininity as performance was explored fully a century later by Judith Butler in her (now) classic analysis *Gender Trouble*, New York and London: Routledge, 1990.

38 Spencer, H., *Principles of Biology*, London: Williams and Norgate, 1867, vol. II, pp. 485–6.

39 Clarke, Edward H., *Sex in Education; or, A Fair Chance for Girls*, Boston, MA: James R. Osgood, 1875. Project Gutenberg eBook, p. 9.

40 Maudsley, H., 'Sex in Mind and in Education', *Fortnightly Review*, new series, 15, 1874, pp. 466–83.

41 Ibid., p. 468.

42 Ibid., p. 477.

43 See Presidential Address by Dr Withers Moore, annual meeting of the British Medical Association in Brighton, 1886, reported in *British Medical Journal*, 14 August 1886, pp. 338–9. For more discussion see Dyhouse, *Girls Growing Up*, pp. 151–9. See also Burstyn, J. N., 'Education and Sex: The Medical Case Against Higher Education for Women in England, 1870–1900, *Proceedings of the American Philosophical Society*, 117:2, April 1973, pp. 79–89.

44 Lawson Tait, R., *Pathology and Treatment of Diseases of the Ovaries*, Birmingham: Cornish Brothers, New Street, 1883; Clouston, T. S., 'Psychological Dangers to Women in Modern Social Developments', in *The Position of Women, Actual and Ideal. A Series of Papers Delivered in Edinburgh, 1911, with a preface by Sir Oliver Lodge*, London: Nisbet, 1911, pp. 108–11; Thorburn, J., *Female Education from a Physiological Point of View*, Manchester: Owen's College, 1884.

45 Tylecote, M., *The Education of Women at Manchester University, 1883–1933*, Publications of the University of Manchester no. 277, 1941, p. 31.

46 Histories of women's fight for medical education include: Bell, E. Moberley, *Storming the Citadel: The Rise of the Woman Doctor*, London: Constable, 1953; Lutzker, E., *Women*

Gain a Place in Medicine, New York: McGraw Hill, 1969; Blake, C., *The Charge of the Parasols: Women's Entry to the Medical Profession,* London: Women's Press, 1990; Bonner, T. Melville, *To the Ends of the Earth: Women's Search for Education in Medicine,* London and Cambridge, MA: Harvard University Press, 1992. See also Dyhouse, C., 'Driving Ambitions: Women in Pursuit of a Medical Education 1890–1939', in the same author's *Students: A Gendered History,* London and New York: Routledge, 2006.

47 On Elizabeth Garrett Anderson see Anderson, L., *Elizabeth Garrett Anderson, 1836–1917,* London: Faber and Faber, 1939.

48 Garrett Anderson, E., 'Sex in Mind and Education: A Reply', *Fortnightly Review,* 15, 1874, pp. 582–94.

49 Annie G. Howes (chair), *Health Statistics of Women College Graduates: Report of Special Committee of the Association of Collegiate Alumni, together with Statistical Tables Collated by the Massachusetts Bureau of Statistics of Labour,* Boston, MA: Wright and Potter, 1885.

50 Mrs H. Sidgwick, *Health Statistics of Women Students of Cambridge and Oxford and of Their Sisters,* Cambridge University Press, 1890.

51 Pfeiffer, E., *Women and Work: An Essay,* London: Trübner, 1888.

52 Ibid, pp. 89–101.

53 Atkinson, P., 'Fitness, Feminism and Schooling', in Delamont, S., and Duffin, L. (eds), *The Nineteenth Century Woman.*

54 Tylecote, *The Education of Women at Manchester University,* p. 31.

55 See Chisholm, C., *The Medical Inspection of Girls in Secondary Schools,* London and New York: Longmans Green and Co., 1914.

56 On the WSPU and suffrage battles generally see, among others, Purvis, J., and Holton, S. Stanley, *Votes for Women,* London: Routledge, 2000, and Purvis, J., and Joannou, M., *The Women's Suffrage Movement: New Feminist Perspectives,* Manchester University Press, 1998.

57 Liddington, J., and Norris, J., *One Hand Tied behind Us: The Rise of the Women's Suffrage Movement,* Virago: London 1978, reprinted by Rivers Oram Press, 2000.

58 For details of suffragette processions and spectacle see Tickner, L., *The Spectacle of Women: Imagery of the Suffragette Campaign, 1907–1914,* London: Chatto and Windus, 1988.

59 West, R., 'A Reed of Steel', in Marcus, Jane (ed.), *The Young Rebecca,* p. 243.

60 Lytton, Lady Constance and 'Wharton, J., Spinster', *Prison and Prisoners: Some Personal Experiences,* London: Heinemann, 1914.

61 Liddington, J., *Rebel Girls: Their Fight for the Vote,* London: Virago, 2006.

62 Ibid.

63 Rosen, A., *Rise Up Women! The Militant Campaign of the Women's Social and Political Union 1903–1914,* London: Routledge, 1974, p. 125.

64 The admirer was Henry Nevinson. See John, Angela V., *War, Journalism and the Shaping of the Twentieth Century: The Life and Times of Henry W. Nevinson,* London: I. B. Tauris, 2006, p. 100.

65 Tickner, *The Spectacle of Women.* The Women's Library has several postcard images of the Women's Coronation Procession, 17 June 1911, 129, postcard box 04.

66 Crawford, E., *The Women's Suffrage Movement, a Reference Guide, 1866–1928*, London: UCL Press, 1999, pp. 322–3.

67 Dyhouse, *No Distinction of Sex*, pp. 217–18.

68 For Emmeline Pankhurst and her relationships with her daughters see Purvis, J., *Emmeline Pankhurst: A Biography*, London: Routledge, 2002.

69 Brittain, *Testament of Youth*, pp. 38–9.

70 Marjorie Anderson , interview with Winifred Starbuck, first broadcast on *Woman's Hour*, c. 1958, www.bbc.co.uk/archive/suffragettes/8323.shtml.

71 Dyhouse, *Girls Growing Up*, Chapter 3.

72 Davin, A., 'Imperialism and Motherhood', *History Workshop Journal*, 5:1, 1978, pp. 9–66.

73 Dyhouse, C., 'Good Wives and Little Mothers: Social Anxieties and the Schoolgirl's Curriculum, 1890–1920', *Oxford Review of Education*, 3:1, 1977, pp. 21–35.

74 See for instance, Bremner, C. S., *The Education of Girls and Women in Great Britain*, London: Swann Sonnenschein, 1897, pp. 47–8; Dyhouse, *Girls Growing Up*, pp. 170–1.

75 Chorley, K., *Manchester Made Them*, London: Faber and Faber, 1950, p. 248.

76 Hall, G. Stanley, *Adolescence: Its Psychology and Relation to Physiology, Anthropology, Sociology, Sex, Crime, Religion and Education*, New York: Appleton, 1904.

77 See also Hall, G. Stanley, *Educational Problems*, New York: Appleton, 1911; and his *Youth: Its Regimen and Hygiene*, New York: Appleton, 1906.

78 See discussion of Hall's views in Dyhouse, *Girls Growing Up*, Chapter

4, 'Adolescent Girlhood: Autonomy versus Dependence'.

79 Cole, M., *Marriage, Past and Present*, London: J. M. Dent and Sons, 1938, p. 95.

80 Hall, 'The Budding Girl', in *Educational Problems*, vol. II, p. 1.

81 Ibid., p. 33.

82 Ibid., p. 34.

83 Hall, *Youth: Its Regimen and Hygiene*, pp. 303–19.

84 Ibid., pp. 320–1.

85 Hall, *Educational Problems*, p. 29.

86 Ibid., pp. 29–33.

87 Quoted in Stacey, J., Béreaud, S., and Daniels, J. (eds), *And Jill Came Tumbling After: Sexism in American Education*, New York: Dell, 1974, p. 277.

88 Ross, D., *G. Stanley Hall: The Psychologist as Prophet*, University of Chicago Press, 1972, pp. 9, 97–8.

89 Campbell, J. M., 'The Effect of Adolescence on the Brain of the Girl', paper presented to the Association of University Women Teachers in London, 23 May 1908 , pp. 5–6.

90 Barnard, A. B., *The Girl's Book about Herself*, London: Cassell, 1912, pp. 21–2.

91 Blanchard, P., *The Care of the Adolescent Girl*, London: Kegan Paul, 1921, esp. p. 67.

92 See, for instance, Saywell, E., *The Growing Girl*, London: Methuen, 1922.

93 Dangerfield, G., *The Strange Death of Liberal England*, London: Constable, 1936, described the suffragettes in such terms.

3 Brazen flappers

1 The relationship between modernity, young women and femininity was much discussed not only in Britain but also on a global

level. 'The Modern Girl Around the World' research group, based at Duke University in North Carolina but incorporating scholars from all over the world, has been focusing on these issues, particularly in relation to representations and the appearance of 'the modern girl'. See Weinbaum, E., Thomas, Lynn M., Barlow, Tani E., Ramamurthy, P., Poiger, Uta G., and Yue Dong, M. (eds), *The Modern Girl Around the World,* Durham, NC: Duke University Press, 2008. An earlier statement of research findings was published by the same group in *Gender and History,* 17:2, 2005, pp. 245–94. See also Søland, B., *Becoming Modern: Young Women and the Reconstruction of Womanhood in the 1920s,* Princeton University Press, 2000.

2 The argument that women's war effort earned them the vote was popularised by Arthur Marwick in his widely read *The Deluge: British Society and the First World War,* London: Bodley Head, 1965. Different viewpoints are put forward in Braybon, G., *Women Workers in the First World War: The British Experience,* London: Croom Helm 1981, and more recently Noakes, L., *Women in the British Army: War and the Gentle Sex, 1907–1948,* London and New York: Routledge, 2006.

3 Smith, Harold L., *The British Women's Suffrage Campaign, 1866–1928,* London and New York: Longmans, 1998, esp. pp. 70–1.

4 Melman, B., *Women and the Popular Imagination in the 1920s,* London: Palgrave Macmillan, 1988.

5 Mrs Alec Tweedie, *Women and Soldiers,* London: John Lane, Bodley Head, 1918, Chapter VIII, 'War Hysteria'.

6 Woollacott, A., '"Khaki Fever"

and Its Control: Gender, Class, Age and Sexual Morality on the British Home Front in the First World War', *Journal of Contemporary History,* 29, 1994, pp. 325–47.

7 Tweedie, *Women and Soldiers,* p. 93.

8 Voeltz, Richard A., 'The Antidote to "Khaki Fever"? The Expansion of the British Girl Guides during the First World War', *Journal of Contemporary History,* 27, 1992, pp. 627–38; see p. 632.

9 Dyhouse, *Girls Growing Up in Late Victorian and Edwardian England,* pp. 110–14.

10 See Reports on Guiding by Agnes Baden-Powell published in the women's magazine, *Home Notes,* 1910–1911; also Agnes Baden-Powell's *The Handbook for Girl Guides; Or, How Girls Can Help Build the Empire,* London: Thos Nelson and Sons, 1912.

11 Kerr, Rose, *The Story of the Girl Guides 1908–1938,* London: Girl Guides Association, 1976; Baden-Powell, O., *Window on My Heart: The Autobiography of Olave, Lady Baden-Powell, as told to Mary Drewery,* London: Hodder and Stoughton, 1973.

12 Lady Baden-Powell, *Training Girls as Guides: Hints to Commissioners and All Who Are Interested in the Welfare and Training of Girls,* London: Pearson, 1917, pp. 13–14.

13 Ibid., pp. 13–21.

14 See, among others, Bingham, A., *Gender, Modernity and the Popular Press in Inter-War Britain,* Oxford University Press, 2004.

15 *Shingled, Bingled and Bobbed* was the title of a play written for the Girls' Friendly Society by J. A. S. Edwards in 1929. www.londonmet. ac.uk/thewomenslibrary/gfs/ branches/branches-3.html.

16 Gillies, M., *Amy Johnson: Queen of the Air*, London: Weidenfeld and Nicolson, 2003; London: Orion Books, 2004, p. 23.

17 Hale, *A Slender Reputation*, p. 7.

18 Dyhouse, C., *Glamour: Women, History, Feminism*, London: Zed Books, 2010, esp. Chapters 2 and 3.

19 Cited in Voeltz, 'The Antidote to "Khaki Fever" ...', p. 632.

20 'The 1920 Girl: Competition for "The Elusive Male", Britain's Surplus of Women', *The Times*, 5 February 1920, p. 9.

21 Levine, P., 'Battle Colors: Race, Sex, and Colonial Soldiery in World War I', *Journal of Women's History*, 9:4, 1998, pp. 104–30; Bland, L., 'White Women and Men of Colour: Miscegenation Fears in Britain after the Great War', *Gender and History*, 17:1, 2005, pp. 29–61.

22 Report in *British Medical Journal*, 3 April 1915, pp. 613–14.

23 Levine, 'Battle Colors', p. 116.

24 Tabili, L., 'Women "of a Very Low Type": Crossing Racial Boundaries in Imperial Britain', in Frader, Laura F., and Rose, S. (eds), *Gender and Class in Modern Europe*, Ithaca, NY: Cornell University Press, 1996, pp. 165–90.

25 Kohn, M., *Dope Girls: The Birth of the British Drug Underground*, London: Lawrence and Wishart, 1992.

26 The first of Sax Rohmer's series of novels about Fu Manchu, epitome of 'the Yellow Peril' was *The Mystery of Dr Fu Manchu*, published in Britain in 1913.

27 For stories of Billie Carleton and Freda Kempton see Kohn, *Dope Girls*, pp. 96–141.

28 'Clemence Dane' (Winifred Ashton), *Regiment of Women*, London: Heinemann, 1917.

29 'Clemence Dane', *The Women's Side*, London: H. Jenkins, 1926, See the chapter 'A Problem in Education' and p. 64.

30 See Love, H., 'Radclyffe Hall', in Kastan, David Scott, (ed.), *The Oxford Encyclopaedia of British Literature*, vol. I, p. 499.

31 Faderman, L., *Surpassing the Love of Men: Romantic Friendship and Love Between Women from the Renaissance to the Present*, London: Women's Press, 1985. See esp. Chapters 3 and 4.

32 Waites, M., 'Inventing a "Lesbian Age of Consent"? The History of the Minimum Age for Sex Between Women in the UK', *Social and Legal Studies*, 11:3, 2002, pp. 323–42; Cohler, D., *Citizen, Invert, Queer: Lesbianism and War in Early Twentieth Century England*, Minneapolis: University of Minnesota Press, 2010, p. 143.

33 Littlewood, M., 'Makers of Men: The Anti-Feminist Backlash of the National Association of Schoolmasters in the 1920s and 1930s', *Trouble and Strife*, 5, 1985, pp. 23–9.

34 Quoted by Nicholson, V., *Singled Out: How Two Million Women Survived without Men after the First World War*, London: Viking, 2007, p. 20.

35 Kenealy, A., *Feminism and Sex Extinction*, London: T. Fisher Unwin, 1920.

36 Ibid., pp. 85, 128 and passim.

37 Ibid., p. 230.

38 Board of Education, *Report of the Consultative Committee on Differentiation of the Curriculum for Boys and Girls Respectively in Secondary Schools*, London: HMSO, 1923. See Preface for terms of reference.

39 Ibid., p. 126.

40 Ibid., p. 132.

41 Dyhouse, C., 'Women Students

and the London Medical Schools, 1914–39 : The Anatomy of a Masculine Culture', *Gender and History,* 10:1, 1998, pp. 110–32. A version of this article appeared as Chapter 7 in the same author's *Students: A Gendered History.*

42 See for instance Hutchinson, A. S. M., *This Freedom,* London: Hodder and Stoughton, 1922.

43 Dyhouse, *Students,* Chapter 2, reference to sardine factory p. 49.

44 Dyhouse, C., "'Signing the Pledge?" Women's Investment in University Education and Teacher Training before 1939', *History of Education,* 26:2, 1997, pp. 207–23.

45 Butler, C. V., *Domestic Service; An Inquiry, by the Women's Industrial Council,* London: G. Bell and Sons, 1916. See pp. 16–17, 22, 34, 46–9.

46 Foley, W., *A Child in the Forest,* London: Hutchinson, 1978, p. 184.

47 Ibid., p. 229.

48 Jephcott, A. P., *Girls Growing Up,* London: Faber and Faber, 1942. Mary Smith's story, pp. 11–34.

49 Glucksman, M., *Women Assemble: Women and New Industries in Inter-War Britain,* London: Routledge, 1990; Todd, S., *Young Women, Work and Family in England, 1918–1950,* Oxford University Press, 2005.

50 *Hutchinson's Women's Who's Who,* London: Hutchinson, 1934.

51 Strachey, R., *Careers and Openings for Women,* London: Faber and Faber, 1935; papers of Women's Employment Federation in the Women's Library; see press cuttings albums. Volume 3 has the cutting from the *Daily Mail* (5 March 1936) quoted in the text.

52 Holtby, W., *Poor Caroline,* London: Cape, 1931.

53 For the 'pledge' taken by intending schoolteachers in order to secure funding for a university education, see Dyhouse, '"Signing the Pledge"'.

54 All information on Amy Johnson from Gillies, *Amy Johnson.*

55 Phillips, T., *We Are the People: Postcards from the Collection of Tom Phillips,* London: National Portrait Gallery, 2004, p. 230.

56 Brader, C., '"A World on Wings": Young Female Workers and Cinema in World War I', *Women's History Review,* 14:1, 2005, pp. 99–117; Singer, B., 'Female Power in the Serial-Queen Melodrama: The Etiology of an Anomaly' , in Abel, R. (ed.), *Silent Film,* London: Athlone, 1996.

57 Hammerton, J., *For Ladies Only? Eve's Film Review, Pathé Cinemagazine, 1921–1933,* Hastings: Projection Box, 2001.

58 Dyhouse, *Glamour,* esp. Chapters 2 and 3.

59 Matthews, J., 'They Had Such a Lot of Fun: The Women's League of Health and Beauty', *History Workshop Journal,* vol. 30, 1990, pp. 22–54.

60 Horwood, C., '"Girls Who Arouse Dangerous Passions": Women and Bathing, 1900–1939', *Women's History Review,* 9:4, pp. 653–73.

61 Dyhouse, C., 'Boat Racing, Women and Sport', in the same author's *No Distinction of Sex?,* pp. 202–6.

62 Allen, M., *The Pioneer Policewoman,* London: Heinemann, 1925, pp. 36, 257–61, cited in Brader, 'A World on Wings', p. 111.

63 *The Cinema: Its Present Position and Future Possibilities; Being the Report of, and Chief Evidence Taken by the Cinema Commission of Inquiry instituted by the National Council of*

Public Morals, London: Williams and Norgate, 1917.

64 Hammerton, *For Ladies Only,* p. 47.

65 Priestley, J. B., *English Journey,* London: Heinemann, 1934, p. 401; Orwell, G., *The Road to Wigan Pier,* Harmondsworth: Penguin, 1972 (1937), p. 79.

66 Burt, C., 'The Causes of Sex Delinquency in Girls', in British Social Hygiene Council, *Health and Empire,* London: Constable, 1926, pp. 251–71. Quotation from p. 265.

67 The story is told in full in Weis, R., *Criminal Justice: The True Story of Edith Thompson,* London: Penguin, 1990.

68 See Bland, L., 'The Trials and Tribulations of Edith Thompson: The Capital Crime of Sexual Incitement in 1920's England', *Journal of British Studies,* 47, July 2008, pp. 624–48.

69 Ibid., p. 631.

70 *Daily News,* 13 December 1922, quoted in Bloom, C., *Bestsellers, Popular Fiction since 1900,* Basingstoke: Palgrave Macmillan, 2002, pp. 38–9.

71 For Edith Roberts see *Leicester Mercury,* 7 and 8 June, 19 July 1921; file in National Archives, PCOM 8/298. See also Grey, D. J., 'Discourses of Infanticide in England, 1880–1922'. D.Phil. dissertation, Department of History, University of Roehampton, 2008.

72 National Archives, PCOM 8/298.

73 East Sussex Coroners' Records, 1931, East Sussex Records Office.

74 The Wellcome Library in London houses some 4,000 case cards compiled by Sir Bernard Spilsbury between 1905 and 1933. These contain reports on numerous cases of illegal abortion and cases of suspicious infant death.

75 Gissing, G., *The Odd Women,* London: T. Nelson and Sons, 1907; the Penguin reprint, 1994, has a useful introduction by Elaine Showalter. See also Orwell, G., *The Clergyman's Daughter,* London: Gollancz, 1935.

76 Bennett, A., *Our Women,* London: Cassell, 1923, pp. 30–6; 58–71.

77 The story of Hayley Morris and Pippingford Park comes from press reports in *The Times* and *Daily Mirror,* April to October 1925, and the National Archives, MEPO 3/400. This file also contains numerous press cuttings from the *Sussex Daily News.*

78 MEPO 3/400, National Archives.

79 Stopes, M., *Married Love,* London: A. C. Fifield, 1918; *Wise Parenthood,* London, A. C. Fifield, 1918. Rose, J., *Marie Stopes and the Sexual Revolution,* London: Faber and Faber, 1992. See also Geppert, A. C. T., 'Divine Sex, Happy Marriage, Regenerated Nation: Marie Stopes's Marital Manual, *Married Love* and the Making of a Best-Seller, 1918–1955', *Journal of the History of Sexuality,* 8:3, 1998, pp. 389–433; Chow, K., 'Popular Sexual Knowledges and Women's Agency in 1920s England', *Feminist Review,* no. 63, 1999, pp. 64–87.

80 Huxley, E., *Love among the Daughters,* London: Chatto and Windus, 1968, pp. 64–5.

81 Ibid.

82 Houghton, S., *Hindle Wakes,* London: Sidgwick and Jackson, 1912.

83 See for instance, Taylor, D. J., *Bright Young People: The Rise and Fall of a Generation, 1918–1940,* London: Chatto and Windus, 2007.

84 Shute, N., *We Mixed Our Drinks: The Story of a Generation,* London: Jarrolds, n.d. (c. 1945)

85 Ibid., p. 14

86 Ibid., p. 87.

87 *Miss Modern*, January 1931, p. 76.

88 *Miss Modern,* January 1938.

89 Ibid., p. 8.

4 Good-time girls

1 See file in National Archives, 'Juvenile Courts, Children, Immorality Amongst Young Girls, 1934–1937', HO 45/21072, which includes the newspaper cuttings referred to.

2 Letter from Travers Humphreys to Home Secretary dated 5 October 1934, in HO 45/20172.

3 See correspondence in HO 45/20172.

4 Reply to Travers Humphreys from Home Office dated 21 November 1934, in HO 45/20172. The term 'Approved School' came into use in the 1930s. Approved schools were residential institutions to which young people could be committed for criminal offences or because they were considered to be beyond parental control. They effectively replaced the earlier reformatory or industrial schools.

5 Letter from Home Office to Archbishop of Canterbury, 15 March 1935, HO 45/21072.

6 See notes of meeting on 'Lax Conduct Amongst Girls: Increasing Amount of', in HO 45/20172.

7 Hall, G. M., *Prostitution: A Survey and a Challenge*, London: Williams and Norgate, 1933, see Introduction by Charles E. Raven.

8 Ibid., p. 30.

9 Ibid., p. 32.

10 Ibid., p. 26. Burt, 'The Causes of Sex Delinquency in Girls'. Quotation from p. 265.

11 Hall, *Prostitution*, p. 32.

12 Rose, S. O., 'Sex, Citizenship and the Nation in World War II Britain', *American Historical Review*, 103:4, 1998, pp. 1147–76.

13 Ibid., p. 1157.

14 Brighton Probation Committee, Correspondence about young girls associating with soldiers, in National Archives, MH 102/1146.

15 Raymond, R. Alwyn, *The Cleft Chin Murder*, London: Claud Morris, 1945. National Archives, MEPO 3/2280; DPP 2/1325. See also Bechofer Roberts, C. E., *The Trial of Jones and Hulten*, London: Jarrolds, 1945. Press reports generally, esp. 'U.S. Soldier and Girl For Trial', *The Times*, 28 November 1944, p. 2; 'The "Cleft Chin" Murder', *The Times*, 17 January 1945, p. 2; and regular reports in *The Times* through January 1945. The account in the text is based primarily on these sources.

16 Orwell, G., 'Decline of the English Murder', first published in *Tribune,* 15 February 1946.

17 Hulten's appeal file in the National Archives, DPP 2/1325.

18 Orwell, 'Decline of the English Murder'.

19 Alwyn Raymond, *The Cleft Chin Murder*, p. 6.

20 La Bern, A. J., *Night Darkens the Streets,* first published 1947, this edition London: Transworld Publishers, 1958.

21 Ibid., pp. 37, 47, 97.

22 'Fight in a Reformatory', *Picture Post,* 3 May 1947.

23 National Archives, MH 102/1137–1141; see also Robertson, James C., '*Good Time Girl*, the BBFC and the Home Office: A Mystery Resolved', *Journal of British Cinema and Television*, 3:1, 2006, pp. 159–63.

24 Correspondence in MH 102/1137, National Archives.

25 Correspondence in MH 102/1139, National Archives.

26 Letter from Chuter Ede to Rank, 15 July 1947, MH 102/1139.

27 Comments in MH 102/1141.

28 See collection of press cuttings and reviews in MH 102/1140.

29 Ibid., *Newcastle Journal*, 14 June 1948.

30 *Evening Standard,* 30 April, 1948; *Daily Graphic,* 30 April 1948, both in MH 102/1140.

31 *Sunday Times,* 2 May 1948.

32 Anyone who doubts this should try Googling 'Reform School Girls'.

33 See, among others, Richardson, H. J., *Adolescent Girls in Approved Schools,* London, Routledge, 1969; Slater, E., Cowie, J., and Cowie, V., *Delinquency in Girls,* London: Heinemann, 1968; Cox, P., *Gender, Justice and Welfare: Bad Girls in Britain, 1900–1950,* London: Palgrave Macmillan, 2003.

34 See file 'Borstal Training for Young Female Offenders', HO 144/21905, in National Archives, esp. newspaper cutting of article on 'The Borstal Girl' from the *Magistrate,* April 1929, by Lilian Barker.

35 National Archives, Kenilworth Training School Revolt, HO 45/14545; also MH 102422–434, 1939–1948. See also archives relating to Knowle Hill Community Home in Warwickshire County Record Office: CR 2366, including Log Book 1910–1942, Girls' Minute Book Joint Committee, Minutes of Ladies' Committee, Punishment Book 1916–1943.

36 See notes of Dr Norris visit to Knowle Hill and marginal annotations in HO 45/14545.

37 May 1923, note in HO 45/14545.

38 Knowle Hill Community Home, Punishment Book 1916–1943, in Warwickshire County Record Office. See four-page 'Report of Inquiry into Allegations of Irregular Punishment at Knowle Hill School', dated 29 September 1959, folded into the punishment book.

39 www.geograph.org.uk/ photo/1974349, retrieved 6 July 2011.

40 'The Unstable Adolescent Girl', *British Medical Journal,* 19 December 1946, pp. 909–12.

41 Ibid., p. 910.

42 Burt, 'The Causes of Sex Delinquency in Girls'. Quotation from p. 265.

43 'The Unstable Adolescent Girl', p. 909.

44 Willcock, H. D., *Report on Juvenile Delinquency,* London: Falcon Press, 1949, p. 54.

45 The Knowle Hill affair features on www.corpun.com/index.htm, which has various links.

46 On Ruth Ellis and her appearances in court see Marks, L., and Van Den Bergh, T., *Ruth Ellis: A Case of Diminished Responsibility?* Harmondsworth: Penguin, 1990, esp. p. 134.

47 Fabian, R., *London After Dark: An Intimate Record of Night Life in London, and a Selection of Crime Stories from the Case Book of Ex-Superintendent R. Fabian,* London: Naldrett Press, 1954, p. 52.

48 Ibid., p. 54.

49 The journalist Duncan Webb published a report on prostitution in the West End pointing a finger at the Messina brothers in a well-known article in the *People,* 3 September 1950; see also his article 'Messina Gang Women Flout the Police' in the same newspaper, 1 October 1950. Material on the Messina brothers and their various activities (and feud

with Duncan Webb) is available in the National Archives, esp. HO 45/25638, MEPO 2/9004, MEPO 2/9845, MEPO 2/9633, MEPO 3/2582.

50 HO 45/25638, esp. MEPO 3/2582.

51 www.screenonline.org.uk/film/id/1071678/index.html.

52 See note 49.

53 'Confidential Report of Investigation into Conditions of the Coloured Population in a Stepney Area', produced by a local committee chaired by the Revd St John Groser, Rector of St George's, Stepney, 1944. Phyllis Young was the main investigator. In Tower Hamlets Local History Library, P/RAM/2/1/2.

54 Ibid., pp. 20–1.

55 Edith Ramsay collection, Tower Hamlets Local History Library, Notes on prostitution in the Commercial Road/Cable Street Area, P/RAM/2/1/7.

56 See Fabian's spoken introduction to Passport to Shame, and note 51, also Fabian, 'The Street Girls of Soho' in London After Dark.

57 Richardson, Adolescent Girls in Approved Schools, p. 1.

58 Ibid.

59 Slater, Cowie and Cowie, Delinquency in Girls, p. 59.

60 'Millions Like Her', Picture Post, 13 January 1951, pp. 10–15.

61 Mass Observation, 'A Report on Teen-Age Girls', 1949, report no. 8150, Mass Observation Archive, University of Sussex.

62 Wilkins, L., The Adolescent in Britain, London: Central Office of Information, 1955.

63 See Joyce Joseph's report 'A Research Note on Attitudes to Work and Marriage of 600 Adolescent Girls', British Journal of Sociology, 12:2,

1961, pp. 176–83, on a study carried out by Thelma Veness.

64 Joseph, 'A Research Note', p. 182.

65 Statistical Evidence submitted to the Committee on Age of Majority (Latey Committee), 1967, in National Archives, RG 48/3089, Grebenik, E., and Rowntree, G., 'Factors Associated with the Age of Marriage in Great Britain', Proceedings of the Royal Society, 1963, vol. 159, pp. 178–202. See also Dyhouse, Students, pp. 92–4.

66 Ollerenshaw, K., Education for Girls, London: Faber and Faber, 1961, p. 38.

67 See, for instance, Evans, M., A Good School: Life at a Girls' Grammar School in the 1950s, London: Women's Press 1991; Ingham, M., Now We Are Thirty: Women of the Breakthrough Generation, London: Eyre Methuen, 1981.

68 Nabokov, V., Lolita, New York: G. P. Putnam, 1958.

69 Some representations were by women writers. See, for instance, Taylor, M., The Nymphet, London: New English Library, 1970.

70 The fashion writer Alison Settle complained about what she called 'The Frightening Passion for Childhood's Look'; see her Viewpoint in the Observer, 2 February 1958: newspaper cuttings collection in Alison Settle Archive, University of Brighton. See also Dyhouse, Glamour, Chapter 4.

71 De Beauvoir, S., Brigitte Bardot and the Lolita Syndrome (trans. Bernard Fretchman), London: New English Library, 1962.

72 Newsom, J., The Education of Girls, London: Faber and Faber, 1948.

73 Ibid., pp. 82, 109, 112–13.

74 Report of Central Advisory Council for Education, Fifteen to

Eighteen, London: HMSO, 1959, pp. 32, 34.

75 Report of Central Advisory Council for Education, *Half Our Future*, London: HMSO 1963, pp. 135–6.

76 This was sometimes related to social class, and the supposition that middle-class girls would be able to pay someone else to do the housework. But the 'domestication' of the curriculum was also opposed on feminist grounds. See Dyhouse, *Girls Growing Up in Late Victorian and Edwardian England*, p. 164ff.

77 Greer, G., *The Female Eunuch*, London: Paladin, 1971, p. 92.

78 Brown, C., *Lost Girls*, London and Southampton: Camelot Press, 1955, p. 65.

79 Tennant, E., *Girlitude; A Portrait of the 1950s and 1960s*, London: Cape, 1999, p. 123.

80 Tweedie, J., *Eating Children*, London: Viking, 1993, p. 122.

81 Ibid., p. 127.

82 Barber, L., *An Education*, London: Penguin, 2009.

83 Ibid., p. 47.

84 Tweedie, *Eating Children*, p. 153.

85 Miller, J., *Relations*, London: Cape, 2003, p. 80.

86 Ibid., p. 82.

87 Duffy, M., *That's How It Was*, London: Virago, 1983, p. ix.

88 Sage, L., *Bad Blood*, London: Fourth Estate, 2000.

89 Ibid., p. 172.

90 Ibid., p. 195.

91 Ibid., p. 234.

92 Forster, M., *Dames' Delight*, London: Jonathan Cape, 1964.

93 Newman, A., *A Share of the World*, London: Bodley Head, 1964.

94 Delaney, S., *A Taste of Honey*, London: Eyre Methuen, 1959.

95 Banks, Lynne Reid, *The L-Shaped Room*, London: Chatto and Windus, 1960.

5 Coming of age

1 www.screenonline.org.uk/film/id/1022053/index.html.

2 www.imdb.com/title/tt0047841/.

3 www.screenonline.org.uk/film/id/482602/index.html.

4 www.mybrightonandhove.org.uk/page_id_8033_path_op224p1363p.aspx; see also www.bygones.org.uk/page_id_223_path_op2p13p.aspx; 'The Blue Gardenia Murder, 1961' in D'Enno, D., *Foul Deeds and Suspicious Deaths Around Brighton*, Barnsley: Wharncliffe Books, 2004.

5 See Jackson, Louise A., '"The Coffee Club Menace", Policing Youth, Leisure and Sexuality in Post War Manchester', *Cultural and Social History*, 5:3, 2008, pp. 289–308; Osgerby, B., '"The Sexpresso Kids": Coffee Bars and Teenage Culture in Britain, 1945–70', paper given at the 37th Annual Conference of the Social History Society, at the University of Brighton, 3–5 April 2012.

6 Press cuttings and reports in Edith Ramsay Collection, Tower Hamlets Local History Library, File P/RAM/2/1/2.

7 Hansard, Debate over Magistrates' Powers and Control of Clubs in House of Lords, 1 June 1960, vol. 224, para. 231. http://hansard.millbanksystems.com/lords/1960/jun/01/magistrates-powers-and-control-of-clubs (Lord Stonham's speech).

8 Tarr, Carrie T., '"Sapphire", "Darling" and the Boundaries of Permitted Pleasure', *Screen*, 26:1, 1985, pp. 50–65; Hill, J., 'The British "Social Problem" Film: "Violent Playground"

and "Sapphire"', *Screen*, 26:1, 1985, pp. 34–48; www.screenonline.org.uk/film/id/440288/index.html.

9 For Ramsay see Sokoloff, B., *Edith and Stepney: The Life of Edith Ramsay*, London: Stepney Books, 1987.

10 Ibid., p. 138; see also P/RAM/2/1 in Tower Hamlets Local History Library.

11 P/RAM/2/1/5 and P/RAM/2/2/14, Tower Hamlets Local History Library.

12 'Confidential Report of Investigation into Conditions of the Coloured Population in a Stepney Area', produced by a local committee chaired by Revd St John Groser, Rector of St George's, Stepney, 1944. Investigator Phyllis Young, in Tower Hamlets Local History Library, P/RAM/2/1/2P/RAM/2/1/2.

13 Williamson, Revd J., letter to LCC, 20.1.1960, in P/RAM/2/1.

14 P/RAM/2/4/2. (Notes on Prostitution in Stepney). 'Homo-Sexuals, known locally as "Pouffes": People claim to distinguish between "common pouffes", who are East Enders, and "Select pouffes", said to come from Chelsea. Long hair, blue boots, clearly abnormal. Why are they there and what do they do? I have no idea, except that they add to the prevailing sense of evil.'

15 Note dated 1.5.1960, in P/RAM/2/1.

16 P/RAM/2/1; P/RAM/2/1/10.

17 Hansard, Debate over Magistrates' Powers and Control of Clubs in House of Lords, 1 June 1960, vol. 224, para 231. See note 7.

18 Ibid., Baroness Ravensdale of Kedleston speech, para. 241.

19 Ibid., para. 242.

20 Ibid., para. 244.

21 Ibid., para. 242–3.

22 Ibid.

23 Ibid., Speech by Lord Bishop of Carlisle, para. 265.

24 See cuttings in P/RAM/2/1/2.w.

25 See Self, Helen J., *Prostitution, Women, and the Misuse of the Law: The Fallen Daughters of Eve*, London: Frank Cass, 2003; Slater, S. A., 'Containment: Managing Street Prostitution in London, 1918–1959', *Journal of British Studies*, 49:2, 2010, pp. 332–57.

26 P/RAM/2/1/7, Tower Hamlets Local History Library.

27 Ibid., Edith Ramsay suggested that earnings could range from £30 to £175 per week.

28 Mort, F., *Capital Affairs: London and the Making of the Permissive Society*, New Haven, CT: Yale University Press, 2009. See Chapter 7 on the Profumo Affair. Denning, A. T., *The Scandal of Christine Keeler and John Profumo*, Lord Denning's Report, 1963, London: Tim Coates, 2003.

29 Press coverage was too extensive for detailed footnotes but see, for instance, 'Last Act in the "Saga" of Christine Keeler: In the World of the Rich and Famous', *Daily Mirror*, 7 December 1963, pp. 6–7.

30 Rice-Davies, M., *The Mandy Report*, London: Confidential Publications, n.d.

31 Mort, *Capital Affairs*, p. 314.

32 Rice-Davies, *The Mandy Report*, n.p.

33 Mort, *Capital Affairs*, p. 314.

34 *Sunday Mirror*, 4 August 1963, pp. 14–15.

35 Proops, M., 'Naughty Girls Don't Show a Profit', *Daily Mirror*, 8 May 1963, pp. 8–9.

36 Jackson, Louise A, '"The Coffee Club Menace"', pp. 289–308.

37 Ibid., p. 298.

38 Ibid.

39 See, for instance,www.my-brightonandhove.org.uk/.

40 Hansard, Debate over Magistrates' Powers and Control of Clubs in House of Lords, 1 June 1960, vol. 224, quoted in Lord Stonham's speech.

41 Horn, A. M., *Juke Box Britain: Americanisation and Youth Culture, 1945–1960*, Manchester University Press, 2009.

42 Sage, *Bad Blood*, p. 174.

43 Ibid., p. 193.

44 www.screenonline.org.uk/film/id/439003/index.html.

45 Jackson, B., *Working Class Community*, London: Routledge and Kegan Paul, 1968; see chapter 'School Ends', esp. p. 142.

46 www.britishpathe.com/video/beatnik-beauty-aka-beautiful-beatnik/query/Beatnik+Beauty, 'Beatnik Beauty', 1963.

47 Rowbotham, S., *Promise of a Dream*, London: Allen Lane, 2000, p. 86.

48 Laurie, P., *The Teenage Revolution*, London: Anthony Blond, 1965, p. 151.

49 Ibid., p. 7.

50 Ibid.

51 'Welcome Home Beatles', *Daily Mirror*, 22 February 1964, p. 1.

52 '"Beatlemania" at Buckingham Palace', *Daily Mirror*, 27 October 1965.

53 Quoted in 'We've Got to Beat the Beatles – MP tells Women Tories', *Daily Mirror*, 5 December 1963.

54 Johnson, P., 'The Menace of Beatlism', *New Statesman*, 28 February 1964, pp. 326–7. Quoted in Fowler, D., *Youth Culture in Modern Britain , c. 1920–1970*, Basingstoke: Palgrave Macmillan, 2008, p. 171.

55 'Beatles Have No Sex Appeal, Says Doctor', *Daily Mirror*, 28 May 1964, p. 13.

56 Adler, B., *Love Letters to the Beatles*, London: Anthony Blond, 1964, and see article in *Daily Mirror*, 5 September 1964, p. 9.

57 Landau, Cécile, *Growing Up in the Sixties*, London: Macdonald Optima, 1991, p. 63; see also p. 32.

58 'Fifteen Tiddly Schoolgirls on the Mat', *Daily Mirror*, 28 October 1963.

59 'Beatlemania! It's Happening Everywhere – Even in Sedate Cheltenham', *Daily Mirror*, 2 November 1963, p. 3.

60 Ehrenreich, B., Hess, E., and Jacobs, G., *Remaking Love: The Feminization of Sex*, New York: Anchor Press/Doubleday, 1986, esp. pp. 17–35.

61 Ibid., p. 6.

62 Brown, H. Gurley, *Sex and the Single Girl*, London: Frederick Mueller, 1963. The influence of *Sex and the Single Girl* was discussed in many of the obituaries which followed her death in 2012. See, for example, 'Why the Sexual Revolution Needed a Sexual Revolutionary', *Atlantic*, 13 August 2012. www.theatlantic.com/entertainment/archive/2012/08/why-the-sexual-revolution-needed-a-sexual-revolutionary/261492/.

63 For an interesting discussion of Helen Gurley Brown, see Berebitsky, J., 'The Joy of Work: Helen Gurley Brown, Gender and Sexuality in the White-Collar Office', *Journal of the History of Sexuality*, 15:1, 2006, pp. 89–127.

64 Ouellette, L., 'Inventing the Cosmo Girl: Class Identity and Girl-Style American Dreams', *Media, Culture and Society*, 21:3, 1999, pp. 359–83.

65 Abrams, M., *The Teenage Consumer*, London: London Press Exchange, 1961.

66 'Call Them Spendagers!', *Daily*

Mirror, 1 October 1963, p. 9; 'Peter Pans in Never Never Land', *Daily Mirror,* 3 October 1963, p. 9; 'Boom-Girls! They run sports cars and pay for boyfriends on dates', *Daily Mirror,* 10 February 1960, p. 21.

67 Anant, V., 'Big City Loneliness', *Picture Post,* 3 March 1956, pp. 12–13.

68 Pringle, A., 'Chelsea Girl', in Maitland, S., *Very Heaven: Looking Back at the 1960s,* London: Virago, 1988, p. 38.

69 Carstairs, G. M., 'Teenage Sexual Behaviour', *The Listener,* 25 November 1965, pp. 835–7.

70 Schofield, M., with Bynner, J., Lewis, P., and Massie, P., *The Sexual Behaviour of Young People,* London: Longmans, 1965.

71 Ibid., pp. 124, 107.

72 Barlow, J., *Term of Trial,* London: Hamish Hamilton, 1961; www. imdb.com/title/tt0056568/.

73 The St Trinian's series began with Searle, R., *Hurrah for St Trinian's and Other Lapses,* London: Macdonald, 1948. For recent compilations of the drawings see *The Curse of St Trinian's: The Best of the Drawings,* London: Pavilion, 1993; *St Trinian's, the Cartoons,* London: Penguin, 2007.

74 The first St Trinian's film was *The Belles of St Trinian's* (1954). This was followed by *Blue Murder at St Trinian's* (1957), *The Pure Hell of St Trinian's* (1960), *The Great St Trinian's Train Robbery* (1966), *Wildcats of St Trinian's* (1980), *St Trinian's* (2007), *St Trinian's 2, The Legend of Fritton's Gold* (2009) and, most recently, *St Trinian's Versus the World,* 2012.

75 www.imdb.com/title/tt00 58169/.

76 'Erskine, R.' (Roger Erskine Longrigg), *The Passion Flower Hotel: A Novel,* London: Jonathan Cape, 1962;

see also article in *Books Monthly,* www.imdb.com/title/tt0058169/ (retrieved 9 April 2012); obituary of Roger Longrigg in *The Times,* 16 March 2000.

77 Obituary of Roger Longrigg in *The Times,* 16 March 2000.

78 Schofield, *Sexual Behaviour of Young People,* p. 107.

79 Galloway, J., *All Made Up,* London: Granta, 2011.

80 Ryle, A., *Student Casualties,* London: Allen Lane, 1969, pp. 120, 124.

81 McCance, C., and Hall, D. J., 'Sexual Behaviour and Contraceptive Practice of Unmarried Female Undergraduates at Aberdeen University', *British Medical Journal,* 17 June 1972, pp. 694–700.

82 Lively, P., *A House Unlocked,* London: Penguin, 2001, p. 178.

83 See Dyhouse, *Students,* p. 106.

84 Useful on the history of pressure to legalise abortion are Kandiah, M., and Staerck, G. (eds) *The Abortion Act 1967,* which brings together material from a seminar held by the Institute of Contemporary History in the School of Advanced Study at the University of London in July 2001, www.kcl.ac.uk/innovation/groups/ ich/witness/archives/PDFfiles/ AbortionAct1967.pdf; see also the collection of leading campaigner Diane Munday's papers, held in the Bishopsgate Institute in London..

85 Kandiah and Staerck, *The Abortion Act 1967;* see introduction by Stephen Brooke.

86 Cook, H., *The Long Sexual Revolution: English Women, Sex and Contraception, 1800–1975,* Oxford University Press, 2004.

87 Dyhouse, *Students,* Chapter 5; Dyhouse, *No Distinction of Sex?,* Chapters 2 and 5 for the history

of separate treatment of female students.

88 See *Report of the Committee on the Age of Majority* (Latey Report), Cmnd 3342, London: HMSO, 1967, section 'Historical Background'. The report was written in the main by Katharine Whitehorn.

89 There are far too many references to detail but see, for instance, 'Three "Brides" Visit Gaol', *Daily Mirror*, 8 September 1959, pp. 12–13; 'The Corsican Lovers Elope to Gretna', *Daily Mirror*, 15 April 1957, p. 24; 'Gretna Grief', *Daily Mirror*, 30 November 1961, pp. 8–9.

90 Ibid., p. 29, para. 79.

91 Dyhouse, *No Distinction of Sex?*, Chapters 2 and 5; see also Dyhouse, *Students*.

92 Dyhouse, *No Distinction of Sex?*, p. 214.

93 Latey Report, p. 21, para. 38.

94 See evidence submitted to the Latey Committee on the Age of Majority in National Archives, LCO17/1–25; also RG 48/3089.

95 Latey Report, p. 27, para. 66.

96 A subject much debated at the time. See Hansard, Debate on Family Law Reform Bill, 1968–9, vol. 778, ibid pp. 38–106.

97 Cilla Black, quoted in *Honey*, April 1970, p. 9.

98 Maitland, *Very Heaven*, p. 15.

99 Grant, L., *Sexing the Millennium,* London: HarperCollins, 1993, pp. 15–16.

100 Ibid.

6 Taking liberties

1 *Daily Mirror*, 23 June 1964, p. 17.

2 *Daily Mirror*, 4 July 1970, p. 12.

3 Interview in the *Independent*, 1 September 1996, p. 18; See also Faithfull, M. (with Dalton, D.), *Mem-

ories, Dreams, Reflections*, London: Fourth Estate, 2007.

4 'I really do want to be good', interview in *Daily Mirror*, 15 February 1969, pp. 6–7.

5 'The Lusty Dreams of a Girl on Two Wheels', *Daily Mirror*, 13 September 1968, pp. 22–3.

6 This remark is cited in the current Wikipedia entry for Marianne Faithfull (retrieved 10 April 2012) Faithfull ruefully admitted to having made the remark in an interview with *New Musical Express* in 1973; see Faithfull with Dalton, *Memories, Dreams, Reflections*, p. 114.

7 Ibid., p. 126.

8 Proops, M., 'Why Wed?', *Daily Mirror*, 9 October 1968, pp. 8–9; Short, D., 'The Courage of Marianne', *Daily Mirror,* 29 July 1972, p. 15.

9 Marianne Faithfull, interview with Ginny Dougary in *The Times,* 21 January 2000. Britney Spears's lyric, 'I'm Mrs Lifestyles of the Rich and Famous/I'm Mrs Oh My God That Britney's Shameless', would echo something of this attitude forty years later.

10 See, for instance, Weatherhead, L. D., 'A Nation in Danger', *The Times*, 20 September 1961, p. 13; 'Countering the New Morality', *The Times,* 29 September 1966, p. 11.

11 www.screenonline.org.uk/ people/id/479374/index.html.

12 'High Intelligence of Prison Girls', *The Times*, 8 October 1963, p. 5.

13 'Countering the New Morality', *The Times,* 29 September 1966, p. 11.

14 'Parents' Responsibility', letter from Professor Ivor Mills, in *The Times*, 9 October 1972, p. 13.

15 Regan, S., 'Are We Getting Our Money's Worth out of the Students?', *News of the World,* 11 November 1968.

16 Regan, S., 'Sex in the Universities', *News of the World*, 17 November 1968.

17 'A Girl with a Man in Her Cupboard', *Daily Mirror*, 26 June 1971, p. 5.

18 See 'Procedures on Expelled Student "Full of Holes"', *Guardian*, 29 June 1971, p. 5; 'Sex and the Single Student: Richard Bourne on Lord Denning's Decision', *Guardian*, 10 July 1971, p. 11; 'Lord Denning: Students and Morals', in *Guardian*, 16 July 1971, p. 10.

19 Alan Simpson, 'Lord Denning: Students and Morals', *Guardian*, 16 July 1971, p. 10.

20 Whipple, A., 'Speaking for Whom? The 1971 Festival of Light and the Search for the "Silent Majority"', *Contemporary British History*, 24:3, 2010, pp. 319–39.

21 Ibid., pp. 335–6.

22 Riches, V., *Sex and Social Engineering: How the Sex Education Lobby Is Undermining Society*, The Responsible Society, 1986.

23 Palmer, T., *The Trials of Oz*, London: Blond and Briggs, 1971.

24 'More Girls in London Have VD', *The Times*, 21 July 1970, p. 2.

25 Whitehouse, M., *Whatever Happened to Sex?* Hove: Wayland Publishing, 1977, p. 9.

26 Schofield, *Promiscuity*, p. 162.

27 Schofield, *The Sexual Behaviour of Young People*.

28 Hampshire, J., and Lewis, J., '"The Ravages of Permissiveness": Sex Education and the Permissive Society', *Twentieth Century British History*, 15:3, 2004, pp. 290–312.

29 Riches, *Sex and Social Engineering*; The Responsible Society was one of the predecessors of the Family Education Trust, see website of Family Education Trust. www.famyouth.org.uk/about.php, retrieved 11 April 2012.

30 Limond, D., '"I never imagined that the time would come"; Martin Cole, the *Growing Up* Controversy and the Limits of School Sex Education in 1970s England', *History of Education*, 37:3, 2008, pp. 409–29. The film *Growing Up* is reproduced as part of a two-DVD set produced by the British Film Institute (BFI), entitled *The Joy of Sex Education*.

31 Muscutt was later reinstated. See Limond, '"I never imagined that the time would come"', pp. 418–19.

32 Paul Ferris, 'Teenage Sex/The New Dilemma', *Observer*, 18 July 1971, p. 21; 'Sex Debate Cancelled Because of Publicity', *The Times*, 6 July 1971, p. 3.

33 Hoffman, Mary M., 'Assumptions in Sex Education Books', *Educational Review*, 27:3, 1975, pp. 211–220.

34 Perry, P., *Your Guide to the Opposite Sex*, London: Pitman, 1970, as cited in Hoffman, *Your Guide*, p. 216.

35 Pomeroy, W. B., *Boys and Sex*, cited in Hoffman, *Your Guide*, p. 216.

36 Hill, M., and Lloyd-Jones, M., *Sex Education: The Erroneous Zone*, London: National Secular Society, 1970.

37 Ibid., Introduction by Brigid Brophy, p. iv.

38 Ibid.

39 Gummer, J. Selwyn, *The Permissive Society: Fact or Fantasy?* London: Cassell, 1971, p. 58.

40 Ibid., p. 61.

41 There is a copy in the Archive of the National Secular Society in the Bishopsgate Institute in London.

42 Sir Brian Windeyer, address to RSA, quoted by Schofield in *Promiscuity*, p. 22.

43 Schofield, *Promiscuity*, pp. 24–5.

44 Ibid., pp. 68–9.

45 Whiting, A., 'Would You Let Your Teenage Daughter Go to a Birth Control Clinic?', *Daily Mirror*, 8 November 1963, p. 9.

46 Paul Ferris, 'Teenage Sex/The New Dilemma', *Observer*, 18 July 1971, p. 21.

47 'God's Will – By Doctor in the Pill Case', *Daily Mirror*, 6 March 1971, p. 5; 'GPs in Sex Secrets Revolt', *Daily Mirror*, 15 May 1974, p. 1.

48 Selwyn Gummer, *The Permissive Society*, p. 39.

49 Litchfield, M., and Kentish, S., *Babies for Burning: The Abortion Business in Britain*, London: Serpentine Press, 1974.

50 Ibid., p. 148.

51 Lewin, R., 'Abortion – Getting the Facts Right', *New Scientist*, 3 April 1975, p. 2.

52 Hansard, debates in House of Lords, 6 August 1975, vol. 363, cc. 1654–1655; debates in House of Commons, 26 July 1977, vol. 936, cc. 573–575; 22 June 1979, vol. 968, cc. 1651–1652.

53 Francome, C., *Abortion Freedom: A Worldwide Movement*, London: Routledge, 1984, p. 165ff; Newburn, T., *Permission and Regulation: Law and Morals in Postwar Britain*, London: Routledge, 1992, pp. 151–2; Diane Munday papers in Bishopsgate Institute.

54 E.g. 'Unmarried Mothers: Some Opposing Views', in *The Times*, 5 December 1966, p. 13; 'Parents of Schoolgirl Mothers Blamed', *The Times*, 11 March 1966, p. 6; 'Campaign to Combat Teenage Pregnancies', *The Times*, 28 April 1981, p. 4; 'Anguish of the Teenage Mothers', *The Times*, 18 October 1985, p. 15. 'Concern at High Rate of Illegitimacy', *The Times*, 19 August 1985, p. 3.

55 See *Independent*, 6 November 2011, looking back on the story of Helen Morgan's experience, www.independent.co.uk/news/uk/home–news/miss-world-who-gave-up-her-crown-returns-to-the-pageant-for-the-first-time-6258022.html, retrieved 11 April 2012.

56 E.g. Rhodes Boyson, 'Free Contraceptives', in *The Times*, 17 April 1974, p. 15.

57 Simms, M., and Smith, C., *Teenage Mothers and Their Partners: A Survey in England and Wales*, London: HMSO, Department of Health and Social Security Research Report no. 15, 1986.

58 Ibid., p. 8.

59 Ibid., p. 103.

60 http://news.bbc.co.uk/onthisday/hi/dates/stories/july/26/newsid_2499000/2499583.stm, retrieved 11 April 2012; De Cruz, S. P., 'Parents, Doctors and Children: The Gillick Case and Beyond', *Journal of Social Welfare Law*, 9:2, 1987, pp. 93–108; NSPCC Factsheet, 'Gillick Competency and Fraser Guidelines', December 2009, www.nspcc.org.uk/inform/research/questions/gillick_wda61289.html.

61 Weale, S., '"I Will Not Let It Go"', article on Victoria Gillick, *Guardian*, 21 November 2000. www.guardian.co.uk/theguardian/2000/nov/21/features11.g22, retrieved 11 April 2012.

62 'Abortion Act Threat', *Spare Rib*, no. 34, 1975, p. 17. See also no. 35.

63 British edition of *Our Bodies, Ourselves*, edited by Phillips, A., and Rakusen, J., London: Penguin and Allen Lane, 1978.

64 Ibid., p. 558.

65 Greig, C., *A Girl's Guide to Modern European Philosophy*, London: Serpent's Tail, 2007.

66 Ibid., pp. 179–80.

67 Compare, for instance, Jeffreys, S., *Anticlimax: A Feminist Perspective on the Sexual Revolution,* New York: New York University Press, 1991, with Grant, *Sexing the Millennium.*

68 Quoted by Kira Cochrane in 'Forty Years of the Women's Liberation Movement', *Guardian,* 26 February 2010. www.guardian.co.uk/lifeandstyle/2010/feb/26/forty-years-womens-liberation.

69 De Beauvoir, S., *The Second Sex,* London: Cape, 1953; Friedan, B., *The Feminine Mystique,* London: Gollancz, 1963; Greer, G., *The Female Eunuch,* London: Paladin, 1971.

70 Penny, L., 'The Female Eunuch Forty Years On', *Guardian,* 27 October 2010. www.guardian.co.uk/books/booksblog/2010/oct/27/female-eunuch-40-years-on, retrieved 13 April 2012.

71 See Conservative Party Archives in Bodleian Library, CCO 20/36/4 and CCO 20/36/7. Geoffrey Howe later redrafted the Cripps Committee Report to make it more inclusive; see CRD 3/38/2. A published version of the report, written by Beryl Cooper and Geoffrey Howe, *Opportunity for Women,* was published by the Conservative Political Centre in September 1969.

72 House of Lords, *Special Report from the Select Committee on the Anti-Discrimination Bill,* London: HMSO 27 March 1973; House of Lords, *Second Special Report from the Select Committee on the Anti-Discrimination Bill,* Session 1972–73, London: HMSO, 18 April 1973; House of Commons, *Special Report from the Select Committee on the Anti-Discrimination (No. 2) Bill,* London: HMSO, 26 June 1973.

73 See Minutes of Evidence taken before Select Committee of House of Commons on Anti-Discrimination Bill, paras. 258–305, pp. 38–49.

74 See Dyhouse, *Students,* esp. Chapters 6, 8 and 9 for a detailed narrative and analysis of coeducation in Oxford and Cambridge colleges.

75 Walkerdine, V., 'Sex, Power and Pedagogy', *Screen Education,* no. 38, Spring 1981, pp. 14–24.

76 Ibid., p. 15.

77 Collection in author's possession.

78 *Spare Rib,* October 1978, no. 75.

79 ILEA Learning Resources Branch, *Anti-Sexist Resources Guide,* compiled by Sue Adler and Annie Cornbleet, London: Television and Publishing Centre, Yale Press, 1984; *Genderwatch! Self-Assessment Schedules for Use in Schools,* devised by Kate Myers, London: SCDC Publications, 1987.

80 Sharpe, S., *'Just Like a Girl': How Girls Learn to Be Women,* London: Penguin, 1976.

81 Wilson, A., *Finding a Voice: Asian Women in Britain,* London: Virago, 1978.

82 Sharpe, *'Just Like a Girl';* compare with Joseph, J., 'A Research Note on Attitudes to Work and Marriage of Six Hundred Adolescent Girls', *British Journal of Sociology,* 12:2, 1961, pp. 176–83, and Rauta, I., and Hunt, A., *Fifth Form Girls: Their Hopes for the Future,* survey carried out on behalf of the Department of Education and Science, London: HMSO, 1975.

83 Early examples of a new attention to girls were McRobbie, A., and Garber, J., 'Girls and Subcultures', in Hall, S., and Jefferson, T. (eds), *Resistance through Rituals,* London: Hutchinson, 1976; McRobbie, A.,

'*Jackie*: An Ideology of Adolescent Femininity', Birmingham, Centre for Contemporary Cultural Studies, 1977. A version of this is now available as '*Jackie* Magazine: Romantic Individualism and the Teenage Girl' at www. gold.ac.uk/media/jackie-magazine. pdf (retrieved 13 April 2012). Walkerdine, J., and Lucey, H., *Democracy in the Kitchen; Regulating Mothers and Socialising Daughters*, London: Virago, 1989. See also Dyhouse, C., 'Adolescent Girlhood: Autonomy versus Dependence', in *Girls Growing Up in Late Victorian and Edwardian England*.

84 McRobbie, '*Jackie*: An Ideology'; see note 83.

85 Radway, J., *Reading the Romance: Women, Patriarchy and Popular Literature*, Chapel Hill: University of North Carolina Press, 1984; Kaplan, C., '*The Thorn Birds*: Fiction, Fantasy, Femininity', in Burgin, V., Donald, J., and Kaplan, C. (eds), *Formations of Fantasy*, London: Routledge, 1986.

86 Blume, J., *Forever*, London: Pan Horizons, 1986 (1975).

87 Courtney Sullivan, 'Judy Blume Showed Innocence Isn't Forever', www.npr.org/templates/story/story. php?storyId=127482114, retrieved 13 April 2012.

88 McRobbie, A., *Feminism and Youth Culture: From Jackie to Just Seventeen*, Basingstoke: Macmillan Education, 1991.

89 Kurtz, I., 'The Simple Secret of Successful Sex', *Cosmopolitan*, August 1973, p. 111.

90 For *Shocking Pink* , 1979–1983, see www.thefword.org.uk/features/ 2011/08/shocking_pink and for 1987–1992, www.grassrootsfeminism. net/cms/node/165 (retrieved 13 April 2012).

91 Hemmings, S., (ed.), *Girls Are Powerful: Young Women's Writings from Spare Rib*, London: Sheba Feminist Publishers, 1982.

92 There are too many sources to list here but see, for instance, Whyte, J., Deem, R., Kant, M., and Cruickshank, M. (eds), *Girl Friendly Schooling*, London: Methuen, 1985.

93 Arnot, M., and Phipps, A., 'Gender and Education in the UK', paper commissioned for the EFA Global Monitoring Report, 2003/4, *The Leap to Equality, 2004*; Arnot, M., David, M., and Weiner, G., *Closing the Gender Gap: Postwar Education and Social Change,* Cambridge: Polity Press, 1999.

94 Sharpe, '*Just Like a Girl*'.

95 Dyhouse, C., 'Gaining Places: The Rising Proportion of Women Students in Universities after 1970', in Dyhouse, *Students*.

96 Cashmore, Ellis, *United Kingdom?: Class, Race and Gender since the War*, London: Unwin Hyman, 1989, p. 194.

97 Ashworth, A., *Once in a House on Fire*, London: Picador, 1998.

98 Harriet Swain, interview with Andrea Ashworth, *Times Higher Education Supplement*, 20 March 1998.

99 See for instance, Bass, E., and Thornton, L. (eds), *I Never Told Anyone: Writings by Women Survivors of Child Sexual Abuse*, New York: Harper and Row, 1983; Fraser, S., *My Father's House*: London: Virago, 1989; Spring, J., *Cry Hard and Swim: The Story of an Incest Survivor*, London: Virago, 1990. Just after this book went to press, revelations about media personality Jimmy Savile's exploitation of young girls from the 1960s to the 1980s show just how difficult it could be for young women to speak out about

sexual abuse, and to have their stories listened to and taken seriously.

100 Butler-Sloss, E., *Report of the Inquiry into Child Abuse in Cleveland 1987,* London: HMSO, July 1988; Bell, S., *When Salem Came to the Boro,* London: Pan, 1988; Campbell, B., *Unofficial Secrets: Child Sexual Abuse – the Cleveland Case,* London: Virago, 1988.

101 Nava, M., 'Cleveland and the Press: Outrage and Anxiety in the Reporting of Child Sexual Abuse', *Feminist Review,* 28, Spring 1988, pp. 103–21; Donaldson, L. J. and O'Brien, S., 'Press Coverage of the Cleveland Child Sexual Abuse Enquiry: A Source of Public Enlightenment?' *Journal of Public Health Medicine,* 17:11, pp. 70–6.

102 Miles Kington, 'The Danger of Labelling Parents Guilty Until Proved Innocent', *Independent,* 30 June 1988, reproduced in Nava, 'Cleveland and the Press'.

103 Nava, 'Cleveland and the Press'.

104 *Daily Mirror,* 13 April 1971, p. 5.

7 What happened to girl power?

1 The best-known history of punk is Savage, J., *England's Dreaming: Sex Pistols and Punk Rock,* London: Faber, 2001. A number of local studies include material on girls and punk. See, for instance, Beesley, T., *Our Generation: The Punk and Mod Children of Sheffield, Rotherham and Doncaster 1976–1985,* Peterborough: Fastprint Publishing, 2009. This serves as the first volume of a trilogy, the other two titles being *Out of Control,* Rotherham: Days Like Tomorrow Books, 2010, and *This Is Our Generation Calling,* Rotherham: Days Like Tomorrow Publishing, 2010. Vols. 2 and 3 contain

the most information on female punks.

2 Wolf, N., *The Beauty Myth: How Images of Beauty Are Used against Women,* London: Vintage, 1990.

3 Ibid. The claim that 'eating disorders rose exponentially' appears on pp. 10 and 11 of this edition.

4 Pipher, M., *Reviving Ophelia; Saving the Selves of Adolescent Girls,* New York: Putnam, 1994; Brumberg, J. J., *The Body Project: An Intimate History of Adolescent Girls,* New York: Random House, 1997.

5 Levy, A., *Female Chauvinist Pigs: Women and the Rise of Raunch Culture,* New York: Free Press, 2005.

6 Ibid., p. 4.

7 Ibid., pp. 6, 16 and passim.

8 Martin, Courtney E., *Perfect Girls, Starving Daughters: The Frightening New Normalcy of Hating Your Body,* New York: Free Press (Simon and Schuster), 2007.

9 Orbach, S., *Fat Is a Feminist Issue: The Anti-Diet Guide to Permanent Weight Loss,* New York, London: Paddington Press, 1978; Orbach, S., *Bodies,* London: Profile, 2009.

10 Durham, M. Gigi, *The Lolita Effect,* London: Duckworth, 2009.

11 Walter, N., *Living Dolls; The Return of Sexism,* London: Virago, 2010.

12 Collins, M., 'The Pornography of Permissiveness: Men's Sexuality and Women's Emancipation in Mid-Twentieth Century Britain', *History Workshop Journal,* 47, 1999, pp. 99–120.

13 Loncraine, R. 'Bosom of the Nation: Page Three in the 1970s and 1980s', in Gorji, M. (ed.), *Rude Britannia,* London: Routledge, 2007.

14 Jephcott, *Girls Growing Up,* p. 33.

15 Frazier, A., and Lisonbee, K. L., 'Adolescent Concerns with Physique', *School Review*, 58, 1950, pp. 397–405, as quoted by Hemming, James, in 'Some Problems of Adolescent Girls', DPhil thesis, University of London, 1957, p. 231. Copy in Bishopsgate Institute.

16 Hemming, James, 'Some Problems of Adolescent Girls'; see also Hemming, J., *Problems of Adolescent Girls*, London: Heinemann, 1967.

17 Hemming, James, 'Some Problems of Adolescent Girls', pp. 231–4.

18 Wolf, *The Beauty Myth*, p. 151. For *Glamour* magazine's update on the 1984 survey see www.glamour. com/health-fitness/2009/03/women-tell-their-body-confidence-secrets.

19 See, for instance, Zweiniger-Bargielowska, I., 'The Body and Consumer Culture' in the same author's edited collection, *Women in Twentieth Century Britain*, London: Longmans, 2000.

20 Brumberg, J. J., *Fasting Girls: The History of Anorexia Nervosa*, New York: Vintage, 2000 (originally published Cambridge, MA: Harvard University Press, 1988).

21 Crisp, A., Gowers, S., Joughin, N., McClelland, L., Rooney, B., Nielson, S., Bowyer, C., Halek, C., and Hartman, D., 'The Enduring Nature of *Anorexia Nervosa*', *European Eating Disorders Review*, 14, 2006, pp. 147–52, p. 147. Professor Crisp and his colleague S. G. Gowers interviewed an eighty-year-old woman with anorexia. Born in 1908, she maintained that women's magazines in the 1920s contained many more articles on dieting than their successors in the 1980s.

22 'Peril of the Rich Twiggies', *Daily Mirror*, 18 July 1979, p. 13.

23 Smith, T., 'When a Teenage Girl Refuses to Eat', *The Times*, 18 April 1975, p. 13; 'Psychiatry: Anorexia Nervosa', *The Times*, 4 June 1976, p. 18.

24 For instance: 'Must My Daughter Die Like Her Twin?', *Daily Mirror*, 6 August 1997, p. 20; 'Is Ally Wasting Away?', *Daily Mirror*, 7 September 1998, p. 9.

25 'Anorexic Mum Who Weighs Less than Her 7-Year-Old', *Daily Mirror*, 8 November 2011.

26 Wolf, *The Beauty Myth*.

27 My thanks to Nicole Albutt, of the eating disorders charity *Beat*, for discussion of some of these issues: the conclusions, of course, are my own.

28 Science Report, 'Psychiatry: Anorexia Nervosa', *The Times*, 4 June 1976, p. 18.

29 Crisp et al., 'The Enduring Nature of *Anorexia Nervosa*', pp. 147–52.

30 Currin, L., Schmidt, U., Treasure, J., and Jick, H., 'Time Trends in Eating Disorder Incidence', *British Journal of Psychiatry*, 186, 2005, pp. 132–5.

31 www.disordered-eating.co.uk/ eating-disorders-statistics/anorexia-nervosa-statistics-uk.html (retrieved 14 April 2012).

32 Ibid.

33 Crisp et al., 'The Enduring Nature of *Anorexia Nervosa*', p. 151.

34 Penny, L., 'An Aching Hunger', *Guardian*, 11 March 2009, pp. 16–17.

35 Hadley Freeman, 'We all know that the way the media judge women's bodies is sick – but how directly this leads to eating disorders is less clear', *Guardian*, 3 August 2011, p. 5.

36 There is a huge literature on women and eating disorders. See, among others, Chernin, K.,

The Hungry Self: Women, Eating and Identity, New York: Times Books, 1985; Bordo, S., *Unbearable Weight: Feminism, Western Culture and the Body,* Berkeley: University of California Press, 1993.

37 West, P., and Sweeting, H., 'Fifteen, Female and Stressed: Changing Patterns of Psychological Distress over Time', *Journal of Child Psychology and Psychiatry,* 44:3, 2003, pp. 399–411; Stevenson, B., and Wolfers, J., 'The Paradox of Declining Female Happiness', Institute for the Study of Labour (IZA),Discussion Paper no. 4,200, May 2009. Both of these studies received a great deal of press attention.

38 Ehrenreich, B., 'Are Women Getting Sadder?', *Huffington Post,* 13 October 2009, www.huffingtonpost.com/barbara-ehrenreich/are-women-getting-sadder_b_319436.html.

39 James, O., 'Too Much, Too Young', Channel 4 at 25 book, British Association of Film and Television Award, http://25by4.channel4.com/chapter_14/article_4/print (retrieved 30 April 2010).

40 Hill, A., 'After Feminism: What Are Girls Supposed to Do?', *Observer,* 21 February 2010. www.guardian.co.uk/society/2010/feb/21/after-feminism-girls-supposed (retrieved 17 April 2012).

41 Darlington, R., Margo, J. Sternberg, S., and Burks, B, *Through the Looking Glass,* London: Demos, 2011, www.demos.co.uk/publications/throughthelookingglass.

42 See, for instance, Fernandez, C., 'Tesco Condemned for Selling Pole Dancing Toy' Mailonline, 24 October, 2006, www.dailymail.co.uk/news/article-412195/Tesco-condemned-selling-pole-dancing-toy.html; http://

www.mirror.co.uk/news/uk-news/tescos-toy-pole-dance-kit-646625; Laura Barton, *Guardian,* www.guardian.co.uk/lifeandstyle/2006/oct/25/1. All originally posted 2006, retrieved 17 April 2012.

43 Mooney, B., 'Erotic Girl Group Steals Innocence of Childhood', Mailonline, 3 February 2003, and 'Sexy Schoolgirls Are Poisoning Our Culture', 9 February 2007; www.dailymail.co.uk/femail/article-433601/Erotic-girl-group-steals-innocence-childhood.html; www.dailymail.co.uk/femail/article-434995/Sexy-schoolgirls-poisoning-culture.html, retrieved 17 April 2012.

44 E.g. www.telegraph.co.uk/finance/newsbysector/retailandconsumer/7589004/Primark-withdraws-padded-bikini-tops-for-seven-year-old-girls.html; for Mumsnet campaign see http://www.mumsnet.com/campaigns/let-girls-be-girls.

45 Jill Parkin cited in Durham, *The Lolita Effect,* p. 69.

46 Ibid.

47 BBC News, 18 February 2010, 'Stop Sexualising Children, Says David Cameron' http://news.bbc.co.uk/1/hi/uk_politics/8521403.stm, retrieved 17 February 2012.

48 Penny, L., 'Let Girls Wear Primark's Padded Bikinis', *Guardian,* 15 April 2010, http://www.guardian.co.uk/commentisfree/2010/apr/15/primark-padded-bikinis-mumsnet-sexuality.

49 Ellen, B., 'Powerless to Protect Our Kids? Oh, Do Grow Up', *Observer,* 5 June 2011, www.guardian.co.uk/commentisfree/2011/jun/05/children-sexuality-naipaul-kate-moss.

50 Buckingham, D., *The Impact of the Commercial World on Children's Wellbeing: Report of an Independent*

Assessment, Departments for Children Schools and Families, and Culture, Media and Sport, December 2009, www.education.gov.uk/publications/ standard/publicationDetail/Page1/ DCSF-00669-2009; Papadopoulos, L., *Sexualisation of Young People Review*, Home Office Publication, 2010, available in National Archives at http://webarchive.nationalarchives. gov.uk/+/http://www.homeoffice. gov.uk/documents/Sexualisation- of-young-people.html; Bailey, R., *Letting Children Be Children: Report of an Independent Review of the Commercialisation and Sexualisation of Childhood*, Department for Education, June 2011, https://www.education.gov. uk/publications/standard/publication Detail/Page1/CM%208078.

51 See for instance, Smith, C., review of Papadopoulos in *Participations: Journal of Audience and Reception Studies*, 7:1, May 2010; or, more brutally, Toby Young, 'The Home Office Report on Child Sexualisation Is a 100-page Cosmopolitan Article', *Telegraph*, 26 February 2010.

52 Carey, T., *Where Has My Little Girl Gone?*, Oxford: Lion, 2011.

53 The Bill prompted protest campaigns from the National Secular Society and on Facebook, as well as widespread opposition from feminists, www.guardian.co.uk/educa- tion/2012/jan/20/nadine-dorries- sexual-abstinence-bill-withdrawn (retrieved 17 April 2012).

54 BBC News, 1 June 2010, 'Dame Joan Bakewell Says Mary Whitehouse Was Right', www.bbc. co.uk/news/10202116; and Bakewell, J., 'Sorry Mrs Whitehouse – I Still Disagree', *Telegraph*, 2 June 2010, www.telegraph.co.uk/culture/ tvandradio/7795852/Sorry-Mrs- Whitehouse-I-still-disagree.html. Retrieved 17 April 2012.

55 Bakewell, ibid.

56 Jackson, C., and Tinkler, P., '"Ladettes" and "Modern Girls": "Troublesome" Young Femininities', *Sociological Review*, 55:2, 2007, pp. 251–72. See also Jackson, C., '"Wild" Girls? An Exploration of "Ladette" Cultures in Secondary Schools', *Gender and Education*, 18:4, 2006, pp. 339–60.

57 Jackson and Tinkler, '"Ladettes"', p. 256.

58 Greer, G., 'Long Live the Essex Girl', *Guardian*, 5 March 2001, www. guardian.co.uk/world/2001/mar/05/ gender (retrieved 20 February 2012).

59 Jackson and Tinkler, '"Lad- ettes"', pp. 252–3.

60 Pilditch, D., 'Ladettes ... Or Sadettes?', *Mirror*, 9 July 1998, p. 9.

61 Ibid.

62 David Blunkett, quoted in *Daily Mail*, 19 July 2004, p. 33; cited in Jackson and Tinkler, '"Ladettes"', pp. 260–1.

63 The series *Ladette to Lady* first aired in the UK on ITV in June 2005.

64 Ellen, B., 'Laugh at Essex Girls and You Insult All Women', *Observer*, 7 March 2010, p. 13.

65 Hill, A., 'Today's Girls "Would Rather Look Sexy Than Be Clever"', *Observer*, 9 December 2007, p. 5.

66 Aitkenhead, D., 'Have I Read My Autobiographies? No, Cos I Know What's in Them', *Guardian* (Review section), 16 August 2010, pp. 7–10.

67 See Higgins, C., 'Raw Genius', a tribute to Corinne Day, in the *Guard- ian*, 1 September 2010 (Review sec- tion), pp. 10–11; Watson, L., 'Corinne Day: Photographer Celebrated for Her Ground-breaking Work with Kate Moss', *Independent*, 6 September

2010, www.independent.co.uk/news/obituaries/corinne-day-photographer-celebrated-for-her-groundbreaking-work-with-kate-moss-2071149.html, retrieved 18 April 2012.

68 E.g. 'Peril of Skinny Kate', *Daily Mirror*, 10 November 1994, p. 15; 'Kate's Sick of Taking Stick', *Daily Mirror*, 5 August 1994, p. 17.

69 E.g. 'Cocaine Kate: Her Confession', *Daily Mirror*, 19 September 2005, p. 11; 'F*** OFF! F*** OFF! F*** OFF! F*** OFF! Just F*** OFF', *Daily Mirror*, 16 September 2005, pp. 2–5.

70 Walter, *Living Dolls*.

71 Ibid., pp. 37–8.

72 Ibid., p. 4.

73 Toynbee, P., 'Girlification Is Destroying All the Hope We Felt in 1968', *Guardian*, 15 April 2008, p. 29.

74 www.pinkstinks.co.uk.

75 Russell, R., and Tyler, M., 'Thank Heaven for Little Girls: "Girl Heaven" and the Commercial Context of Feminine Childhood', *Sociology*, 36, 2002, pp. 619–37.

76 Liz Jones, 'Sex and the City and 7 in Heels – the Pathetic Woman's Must-haves' , Mailonline, 26 April 2008, www.dailymail.co.uk/debate/columnists/article-562243/Sex-The-City-7in-heels--pathetic-womans-haves.html, retrieved 18 April 2012.

77 Arnot et al., *Closing the Gender Gap*.

78 Dyhouse, C., 'Gaining Places: The Rising Proportion of Women Students in Universities after 1970', in the same author's *Students*.

79 Ibid., see also Chapter 8.

80 Dyhouse, 'Women Students and the London Medical Schools, 1914–39'.

81 Arnot and Weiner, *Closing the Gender Gap*; see also Arnot, M., *Reproducing Gender?: Essays in Edu-cational Theory and Feminist Politics*, London: Routledge, 2002, pp. 186–92.

82 Epstein, D. (ed.), *Failing Boys?: Issues in Gender and Achievement*, Buckingham: Open University Press, 1998.

83 Blackstone, T., 'Education and Careers: A Rough Road to the Top', in Masson, M. R., and Simonton, D., *Women and Higher Education: Past, Present and Future*, Aberdeen University Press, 1996.

84 The relation between gender and the professions has been usefully examined by Witz,. A., *Professions and Patriarchy*, London: Routledge, 1992.

85 Fawcett Society, 'Job cuts in the public sector hit women worst', www.fawcettsociety.org.uk/index.asp?PageID=1236, retrieved 19 April 2012.

86 For Madonna's impact on young women, see, among others, Turner, K., *I Dream of Madonna: Women's Dreams of the Goddess of Pop*, London: Thames and Hudson, 1993.

87 There has been a tendency to forget some of this: see Strong, C., 'Grunge, Riot Grrrl and the Forget-ting of Women in Popular Culture', *Journal of Popular Culture*, 44:2, 2011, pp. 398–416. See also Budgeon, S., 'I'll Tell You What I Really Really Want: Girl Power and Self-identity in Britain', in Inness, Sherrie A. (ed.), *Millennium Girls: Today's Girls around the World*, Lanham, MD : Rowman and Littlefield, 1998.

88 Phillips, M., 'These "Slutwalks" Prove Feminism Is Now Irrelevant to Most Women's Lives', Mailonline, 13 June 2011, www.dailymail.co.uk/debate/article-2002887/Slut-Walks-prove-feminism-irrelevant-womens-lives.html, retrieved 19 April 2012.

89 Valenti, J., 'Slutwalks and the Future of Feminism', *Washington Post*, 3 June 2011. www.washingtonpost. com/opinions/slutwalks-and-the-future-of-feminism/2011/06/01/ AGjB9LIH_story.html.

8 Looking back

1 Spencer, H., *Principles of Sociology*, London: Williams and Norgate, 1876, vol. 1., pp. 766, 792.

2 Ruskin, *Sesame and Lilies*.

3 Cole, *Marriage, Past and Present*, p. 95.

4 Hughes, M. V., *A London Family, 1870–1900: A Trilogy*, London: Oxford University Press, 1946. Reissued in three parts. This reference from *A London Child of the Seventies*, London: Oxford University Press, 1977, p. 33.

5 Ibid.

6 Davin, A., *Growing Up Poor: Home, School and Street Children in London, 1870–1914*, London: Rivers Oram Press, 1996.

7 Dyhouse, *Girls Growing Up in Late Victorian and Edwardian England*, Chapter 1.

8 Wilkinson, H., for Demos, *No Turning Back: Generations and the Genderquake*, London: Demos, 1994, www.demos.co.uk/publications/ noturningback.

9 Coventry Patmore's poem, *The Angel in the House*, first published in 1854, was a classic and very popular expression of Victorian ideals of femininity.

10 Cohen, S., *Folk Devils and Moral Panics: The Creation of the Mods and Rockers*, London: Routledge, 1980 (1972).

11 Ibid., Introduction to 3rd edn, p. viii; see also p. xxxiv.

12 Ibid., p. 157.

13 It was conflicts over militancy and violent tactics which basically divided 'Suffragists' from 'Suffragettes'; although the divisions were not always clear-cut.

14 Emily Davies famously remarked in 1866, that 'What they call a compromise, we consider a capitulation'. See Delamont, S., 'The Contradictions in Ladies' Education', in Delamont and Duffin (eds), *The Nineteenth Century Woman*.

15 Malos, E., *The Politics of Housework*, London: Allison and Busby, 1980; Himmelweit, S. (ed.), *Inside the Household: From Labour to Care*, London: Palgrave Macmillan, 2000.

16 http://plan-international.org/ girls/campaign/.

17 West, R., 'Mr Chesterton in Hysterics: A Study in Prejudice', originally in *The Clarion*, 14 November 1913, reprinted in Marcus (ed.), *The Young Rebecca*, p. 21.

18 Moran, C., *How to Be a Woman*, London: Ebury, 2012.

SOURCES AND SELECT BIBLIOGRAPHY

Archives and collections

Bishopsgate Institute: Diane Munday papers; James Hemming papers; papers of the National Secular Society

East Sussex County Record Office: coroners' reports for Brighton

National Archives: Home Office papers; Metropolitan Police Files; Ministry of Health papers; Department of Education papers

Salvation Army Heritage Centre: archives and press cuttings, Salvation Army

Tower Hamlets Local History Library: Edith Ramsay Collection

Warwickshire County Record Office: papers relating to Knowle Hill Training School

Whitelands College, University of Roehampton: records relating to the connection with John Ruskin

Women's Library: papers of National Vigilance Association, Traveller's Aid Societies; papers relating to white slave traffic

Books and articles

Aapola, S., Gonick, M., and Harris, A. (eds), *Young Femininity: Girlhood, Power and Social Change*, Houndmills: Palgrave, 2005.

Abrams, M., *The Teenage Consumer*, London: London Press Exchange, 1961.

Alexander, S., *Becoming a Woman and Other Essays in 19th and 20th Century Feminist History,* London: Virago, 1994.

Allen, Grant, *The Woman Who Did*, London: John Lane, 1895.

Allen, M., *The Pioneer Policewoman*, London: Heinemann, 1925.

Amos, Sarah M., 'The Evolution of the Daughters', *Contemporary Review*, 65, April 1894, pp. 515–20.

Anderson, L., *Elizabeth Garrett Anderson, 1836–1917,* London: Faber and Faber, 1939.

Arnot, M., *Reproducing Gender?: Essays in Educational Theory and Feminist Politics*, London: Routledge, 2002.

Arnot, M., David, M., and Weiner, G., *Closing the Gender Gap: Postwar Education and Social Change,* Cambridge: Polity Press, 1999.

Ashworth, A., *Once in a House on Fire*, London: Picador, 1998.

Baden-Powell, O., *Training Girls as Guides: Hints to Commissioners and All Who Are Interested in the Welfare and Training of Girls*, London: Pearson, 1917.

— *Window on My Heart: The Autobiography of Olave, Lady Baden-Powell, as told to Mary Drewery*, London: Hodder and Stoughton, 1973.

Banks, Lynne Reid, *The L-Shaped Room*, London: Chatto and Windus, 1960.

Barber, L., *An Education*, London: Penguin, 2009.

Barlow, J., *Term of Trial,* London: Hamish Hamilton, 1961.

Barnard, A. B., *The Girl's Book about Herself,* London: Cassell, 1912.

Bashkirtseff, M., *The Journal of Marie Bashkirtseff,* translated, with an introduction, by Mathilde Blind, London: Cassell, 1890. Virago Press edition, 1985, offset from 1891 edition, introduced by Rozsika Parker and Griselda Pollock.

Bass, E., and Thornton, L. (eds), *I Never Told Anyone: Writings by Women Survivors of Child Sexual Abuse,* New York: Harper and Row, 1983.

Batchelor, J., *John Ruskin: No Wealth but Life,* London: Chatto and Windus, 2000.

Baumgardner, J., and Richards, A., *Manifesta: Young Women, Feminism and the Future,* New York: Farrar, Straus and Giroux, 2000.

Bechofer Roberts, C. E., *The Trial of Jones and Hulten*, London: Jarrolds, 1945.

Beesley, T., *Our Generation: The Punk and Mod Children of Sheffield, Rotherham and Doncaster 1976–1985,* Peterborough: Fastprint Publishing, 2009.

— *Out of Control,* Rotherham: Days Like Tomorrow Books, 2010.

— *This Is Our Generation Calling,* Rotherham: Days Like Tomorrow Publishing, 2010.

Bell, Ernest A., *Fighting the Traffic in Young Girls; or, War on the White Slave Trade,* G. S. Ball, 1910.

Bell, E. Moberley, *Storming the Citadel: The Rise of the Woman Doctor,* London: Constable, 1953.

Bell, S., *When Salem Came to the Boro: The True Story of the Cleveland Child Abuse Case,* London: Pan, 1988.

Bennett, A., *Our Women,* London: Cassell, 1923.

Berebitsky, J., 'The Joy of Work: Helen Gurley Brown, Gender and Sexuality in the White-Collar Office', *Journal of the History of Sexuality,* 15:1, 2006, pp. 89–127.

Billington-Greig, T., 'The Truth about White Slavery', *English Review,* June 1913, pp. 428–46.

Bingham, A., *Gender, Modernity and the Popular Press in Inter-War Britain,* Oxford University Press, 2004.

Blake, C., *The Charge of the Parasols: Women's Entry to the Medical Profession,* London: Women's Press, 1990.

Blanchard, P., *The Care of the Adolescent Girl,* London: Kegan Paul, 1921.

Bland, L., *Banishing the Beast: English Feminism and Sexual Morality 1885–1914,* London: Penguin, 1995.

— 'White Women and Men of Colour: Miscegenation Fears in Britain after the Great War', *Gender and History,* 17:1, 2005, pp. 29–61.

— 'The Trials and Tribulations of Edith Thompson: The Capital Crime of Sexual Incitement in 1920's England', *Journal of British Studies,* 47, July 2008, pp. 624–48.

Bloom, C., *Bestsellers: Popular Fiction since 1900,* Basingstoke: Palgrave Macmillan, 2002.

Blume, J., *Forever,* London: Pan Horizons, 1986 (1975).

Bonner, T. Melville, *To the Ends of the Earth: Women's Search for Education in Medicine,* London and Cambridge, MA: Harvard University Press 1992.

Bordo, S., *Unbearable Weight; Feminism, Western Culture and the Body,* Berkeley: University of California Press, 1993.

Boston Women's Health Collective, edited by Phillips, A., and Rakusen, J., *Our Bodies, Ourselves*, London: Penguin and Allen Lane, 1978.

Brader, C., '"A World on Wings": Young Female Workers and Cinema in World War I', *Women's History Review*, 14:1, 2005, pp. 99–117.

Braybon, G., *Women Workers in the First World War: The British Experience*, London: Croom Helm, 1981.

Bremner, C. S., *The Education of Girls and Women in Great Britain*, London: Swann Sonnenschein, 1897.

Bristow, Edward J., *Vice and Vigilance: Purity Movements in Britain since 1700*, Dublin, Gill and Macmillan, 1977.

Brittain, V. *Testament of Youth*, London: Gollancz, 1933.

Brown, C., *Lost Girls*, London and Southampton: Camelot Press, 1955.

Brown, H. Gurley, *Sex and the Single Girl*, London: Frederick Mueller, 1963.

Brumberg, J. J., *Fasting Girls: The History of Anorexia Nervosa*, New York: Vintage, 2000 (originally published in Cambridge, MA: Harvard University Press, 1988).

— *The Body Project: An Intimate History of Adolescent Girls*, New York: Random House, 1997.

Burstyn, J. N., 'Education and Sex: The Medical Case Against Higher Education for Women in England, 1870–1900', *Proceedings of the American Philosophical Society*, 117:2, April 1973, pp. 79–89.

Burt, C., 'The Causes of Sex Delinquency in Girls', in British Social Hygiene Council, *Health and Empire*, London: Constable, 1926, pp. 251–71.

Butler, C. V., *Domestic Service; An Inquiry, by the Women's Industrial Council*, London: G. Bell and Sons, 1916.

Butler, J., *Gender Trouble*, New York, London: Routledge, 1990.

Butler-Sloss, E., *Report of the Inquiry into Child Abuse in Cleveland 1987*, London: HMSO, July 1988.

Campbell, B., *Unofficial Secrets: Child Sexual Abuse – the Cleveland Case*, London: Virago, 1988.

Campbell, J. M., 'The Effect of Adolescence on the Brain of the Girl', paper presented to the Association of University Women Teachers in London, 23 May 1908.

Caplan, C., 'The Thorn Birds ; Fiction, Fantasy, Femininity', in Burgin, V., Donald, J., and Caplan, C. (eds), *Formations of Fantasy*, London: Routledge, 1986.

Carey, T., *Where Has My Little Girl Gone?*, Oxford: Lion, 2011.

Cashmore, Ellis, *United Kingdom?: Class, Race and Gender since the War*, London: Unwin Hyman, 1989.

Chernin, K., *The Hungry Self: Women, Eating and Identity*, New York: Times Books, 1985.

Chisholm, C., *The Medical Inspection of Girls in Secondary Schools*, London and New York: Longmans Green and Co., 1914.

Chorley, K., *Manchester Made Them*, London: Faber and Faber, 1950.

Chow, K., 'Popular Sexual Knowledges and Women's Agency in 1920s England', *Feminist Review*, no. 63, 1999, pp. 64–87.

Clarke, Edward H., *Sex in Education; or, A Fair Chance for Girls*, Boston: James R. Osgood, 1875. Project Gutenberg eBook.

Cohen, S., *Folk Devils and Moral Panics: The Creation of the Mods and Rockers*, London: Routledge, 1980 (1972).

Cohler, D., *Citizen, Invert, Queer: Lesbianism and War in Early Twentieth Century England*, Minneapolis: University of Minnesota Press, 2010.

Cole, M., *Marriage, Past and Present*, London: J. M. Dent and Sons, 1938.

— *Be Like Daisies: John Ruskin and the Cult of Beauty at Whitelands College*, St Albans: Brentham Press, 1992.

Collins, M., 'The Pornography of Permissiveness: Men's Sexuality and Women's Emancipation in Mid-Twentieth Century Britain', *History Workshop Journal*, 47, 1999, pp. 99–120.

— (ed.) *The Permissive Society and Its Enemies: Sixties British Culture*, London: Rivers Oram Press, 2007.

Cook, H., *The Long Sexual Revolution, English Women, Sex and Contraception, 1800–1975*, Oxford University Press, 2004.

Cox, P., *Gender, Justice and Welfare; Bad Girls in Britain, 1900–1950*, London: Palgrave Macmillan, 2003.

Crackenthorpe, B. A., 'The Revolt of the Daughters', *Nineteenth Century*, 35, January 1894, pp. 23–31.

Crawford, E., *The Women's Suffrage Movement, a Reference Guide, 1866–1928*, London: UCL Press, 1999.

Crisp, A., Gowers, S., Joughin, N., McClelland, L., Rooney, B., Nielson, S., Bowyer, C., Halek, C., and Hartman, D., 'The Enduring Nature of *Anorexia Nervosa*', *European Eating Disorders Review*, 14, 2006, pp. 147–52.

Currin, L., Schmidt, U., Treasure, J., and Jick, H., 'Time Trends in Eating

Disorder Incidence', *British Journal of Psychiatry*, 186, 2005, pp. 132–5.

'Dane, Clemence' (Winifred Ashton), *Regiment of Women*, London: Heinemann, 1917.

— *The Women's Side*, London: H. Jenkins, 1926.

Dangerfield, G., *The Strange Death of Liberal England*, London: Constable, 1936.

Darlington, R., Margo, J., Sternberg, S., and Burks, B., *Through the Looking Glass*, London: Demos, 2011.

Davin, A., 'Imperialism and Motherhood', *History Workshop Journal*, 5:1, 1978, pp. 9–66.

— *Growing Up Poor: Home, School and Street Children in London, 1870–1914*, London: Rivers Oram Press, 1996.

D'Cruz, S., and Jackson, L., *Women, Crime and Justice in England since 1660*, London: Palgrave Macmillan, 2009.

De Beauvoir, S., *Brigitte Bardot and the Lolita Syndrome* (trans. Bernard Fretchman), London: New English Library, 1962.

— *The Second Sex*, London: Cape, 1953.

De Cruz, S. P., 'Parents, Doctors and Children: The Gillick Case and Beyond', *Journal of Social Welfare Law*, 9:2, 1987, pp. 93–108.

Delamont, S., and Duffin, L. (eds), *The Nineteenth Century Woman: Her Cultural and Physical World*, London: Croom Helm, 1978.

Delaney, S., *A Taste of Honey*, Methuen Modern Plays, London: Eyre Methuen, 1959.

Doezema, J., *Sex Slaves and Discourse Masters: The Construction of Trafficking*, London: Zed Books, 2010.

Donaldson, L. J. and O'Brien, S., 'Press Coverage of the Cleveland Child

Sexual Abuse Enquiry: A Source of Public Enlightenment?', *Journal of Public Health Medicine*, 17:11, pp. 70–6.

Donovan, B., *White Slave Crusades: Race, Gender and Anti-Vice Activism 1887–1917*, Urbana and Chicago: University of Illinois Press, 2006.

Douglas, S. J., *Where the Girls Are: Growing Up Female with the Mass Media*, New York: Times Books, 1994.

Duffy, M., *That's How It Was*, London: Virago, 1983.

Durham, M. Gigi, *The Lolita Effect*, London: Duckworth, 2009.

Dyhouse, C., 'Good Wives and Little Mothers: Social Anxieties and the Schoolgirl's Curriculum, 1890–1920', *Oxford Review of Education*, 3:1, 1977, pp. 21–35.

— *Girls Growing Up in Late Victorian and Edwardian Britain*, London: Routledge and Kegan Paul, 1981.

— 'Miss Buss and Miss Beale: Gender and Authority in the History of Education', in Hunt, F. (ed.), *Lessons for Life: The Schooling of Girls and Women, 1850–1950*, Oxford: Blackwell, 1987.

— *No Distinction of Sex? Women in British Universities 1870–1939*, London: UCL Press, 1995.

— '"Signing the Pledge?" Women's Investment in University Education and Teacher Training before 1939', *History of Education*, 26:2, 1997, pp. 207–23.

— 'Driving Ambitions: Women in Pursuit of a Medical Education 1890–1939', *Women's Historical Review*, 7:3, 1998, pp. 321–44.

— 'Women Students and the London Medical Schools, 1914–39 : The Anatomy of a Masculine Culture',

Gender and History, 10:1, 1998, pp. 110–32.

— *Students: A Gendered History*, London and New York: Routledge, 2006.

— *Glamour: Women, History, Feminism*, London: Zed Books, 2010.

Ehrenreich, B., Hess, E., and Jacobs, G., *Remaking Love: The Feminization of Sex*, New York: Anchor Press/Doubleday, 1986.

Epstein, D. (ed.), *Failing Boys?: Issues in Gender and Achievement*, Buckingham: Open University Press, 1998.

'Erskine, R.' (Roger Erskine Longrigg), *The Passion Flower Hotel: A Novel*, London: Jonathan Cape, 1962.

Evans, M., *A Good School: Life at a Girls' Grammar School in the 1950s*, London: Women's Press, 1991.

Fabian, R., *London after Dark: An Intimate Record of Night Life in London, and a Selection of Crime Stories from the Case Book of Ex-Superintendent R. Fabian*, London: Naldrett Press, 1954.

Faderman, L., *Surpassing the Love of Men: Romantic Friendship and Love Between Women from the Renaissance to the Present*, London: Women's Press, 1985.

Fawcett, M. Garrett, 'The Woman Who Did', *Contemporary Review*, vol. LXVII, 1895, pp. 625–31.

Fletcher, Ian C., 'Opposition by Journalism? The Socialist and Suffragist Press and the Passage of the Criminal Law Amendment Act of 1912', *Parliamentary History*, 25:1, 2006, pp. 88–114.

Foley, W., *A Child in the Forest*, London: Hutchinson, 1978.

Forster, M., *Dames' Delight*, London: Jonathan Cape, 1964.

Fowler, D., *Youth Culture in Modern*

294 | BIBLIOGRAPHY

Britain, c. 1920–1970, Basingstoke: Palgrave Macmillan, 2008.

Francome, C., *Abortion Freedom: A Worldwide Movement*, London: Routledge, 1984.

Fraser, S., *My Father's House*: London: Virago, 1989.

Friedan, B., *The Feminine Mystique*, London: Gollancz, 1963.

Galloway, J., *All Made Up*, London: Granta, 2011.

Garrett Anderson, E., 'Sex in Mind and Education: A Reply', *Fortnightly Review*, 15, 1874, pp. 582–94.

Gelsthorpe, L., and Worrall, A., 'Looking for Trouble: A Recent History of Girls, Young Women and Youth Justice', *Youth Justice*, 9:3, 2009, pp. 209–23.

Geppert, A. C. T., 'Divine Sex, Happy Marriage, Regenerated Nation: Marie Stopes's Marital Manual, *Married Love* and the Making of a Best-Seller, 1918–1955', *Journal of the History of Sexuality*, 8:3, 1998, pp. 389–433.

Gillies, M., *Amy Johnson: Queen of the Air*, London: Weidenfeld and Nicolson, 2003; London: Orion Books, 2004.

Gillis, S., and Munford, R., 'Genealogies and Generations: The Politics and Praxis of Third Wave Feminism', *Women's History Review*, 13:2, pp. 165–82.

Gissing, G., *The Odd Women*, London: T. Nelson and Sons, 1907.

Glendinning, V., *A Suppressed Cry: Life and Death of a Quaker Daughter*, London: Routledge and Kegan Paul, 1969.

Glucksman, M., *Women Assemble: Women and New Industries in Inter-War Britain*, London: Routledge, 1990.

Gonick, M., 'Between "Girl Power" and "Reviving Ophelia": Constituting the Neoliberal Girl Subject', *National Women's Studies Association Journal*, 18:2, 2006, pp. 1–23.

Gorham, D., 'The "Maiden Tribute of Modern Babylon" Re-Examined: Child Prostitution and the Idea of Childhood in Late Victorian England', *Victorian Studies*, 21:3, Spring 1978, pp. 353–79.

— *Vera Brittain: A Feminist Life*, Cambridge, MA: Blackwell, 1996.

Grant, L., *Sexing the Millennium*, London: HarperCollins, 1993.

Greer, G., *The Female Eunuch*, London: Paladin, 1971.

Greig, C., *A Girl's Guide to Modern European Philosophy*, London: Serpent's Tail, 2007.

Grey, D. J., 'Discourses of Infanticide in England, 1880–1922', D.Phil., Department of History, University of Roehampton, 2008.

Griffin, C., *Typical Girls? Young Women from School to the Job Market*, London: Routledge and Kegan Paul, 1985.

Gummer, J. Selwyn, *The Permissive Society: Fact or Fantasy?* London: Cassell, 1971.

Hale, K., *A Slender Reputation: An Autobiography*, London: Warne, 1998.

Hall, G. M., *Prostitution: A Survey and a Challenge*, London: Williams and Norgate, 1933.

Hall, G. Stanley, *Adolescence: Its Psychology and Relation to Physiology, Anthropology, Sociology, Sex, Crime, Religion and Education*, New York: Appleton, 1904.

— *Youth: Its Regimen and Hygiene*, New York: Appleton, 1906.

— *Educational Problems*, New York: Appleton, 1911;

Hamlett, J., '"Nicely Feminine, yet

Learned": Student Rooms at Royal Holloway and the Oxbridge Colleges in Late Nineteenth-century Britain', *Women's History Review,* 15:1, 2006, pp. 137–61.

Hammerton, J., *For Ladies Only? Eve's Film Review, Pathé Cinemagazine, 1921–1933,* Hastings: Projection Box, 2001.

Hampshire, J., and Lewis, J., '"The Ravages of Permissiveness": Sex Education and the Permissive Society', *Twentieth Century British History,* 15:3, 2004, pp. 290–312.

Hardie, J. Keir, *The Queenie Gerald Case: A Public Scandal,* Manchester and London: National Labour Press, 1913.

Harris, Anita, *Future Girl: Young Women in the Twenty-first Century,* London: Routledge, 2004.

— (ed.), *All About the Girl: Culture, Power and Identity,* Abingdon: Routledge, 2004.

Harrison, B., 'For Church, Queen and Family: The Girls' Friendly Society 1874–1920, *Past and Present,* 61:1, 1973, pp. 107–38.

Heath-Stubbs, M., *Friendship's Highway: Being a History of the Girls' Friendly Society, 1875–1925,* London: GFS Central Office, 1926.

Hemery, G., 'The Revolt of the Daughters: An Answer – by One of Them', *Westminster Review,* 141, June 1894, pp. 679–81.

Hemming, J., *Problems of Adolescent Girls,* London: Heinemann, 1967.

Hemmings, S. (ed.), *Girls Are Powerful: Young Women's Writings from Spare Rib,* London: Sheba Feminist Publishers, 1982.

Hill, J., 'The British "Social Problem" Film: "Violent Playground" and "Sapphire"', *Screen,* 26:1, 1985, pp. 34–48.

Hill, M., and Lloyd-Jones, M., *Sex Education: The Erroneous Zone,* London: National Secular Society, 1970.

Himmelweit, S. (ed.), *Inside the Household: From Labour to Care,* London: Palgrave Macmillan, 2000.

Hoffman, Mary M., 'Assumptions in Sex Education Books', *Educational Review,* 27:3, 1975, pp. 211–20.

Holtby, W., *Poor Caroline,* London: Cape, 1931.

Horn, A. M., *Juke Box Britain: Americanisation and Youth Culture, 1945–1960,* Manchester University Press, 2009.

Horwood, C., '"Girls Who Arouse Dangerous Passions": Women and Bathing, 1900–1939', *Women's History Review,* 9:4, pp. 653–73.

Houghton, S., *Hindle Wakes,* London: Sidgwick and Jackson, 1912.

Howes, Annie G., *Health Statistics of Women College Graduates: Report of Special Committee of the Association of Collegiate Alumni, together with Statistical Tables Collated by the Massachusetts Bureau of Statistics of Labour,* Boston, MA: Wright and Potter, 1885.

Hughes, K., *The Victorian Governess,* London: Hambledon Press, 1993.

Hughes, M. V., *A London Family, 1870–1900: A Trilogy,* London: Oxford University Press, 1946.

Hunt, A., *Governing Morals: A Social History of Moral Regulation,* Cambridge University Press, 1999.

Hunt, F. (ed.), *Lessons for Life: The Schooling of Girls and Women, 1850–1950,* Oxford: Blackwell, 1987.

Hutchinson, A. S. M., *This Freedom,* London: Hodder and Stoughton, 1922.

Hutchinson's Women's Who's Who, London: Hutchinson, 1934.

Huxley, E., *Love among the Daughters*, London: Chatto and Windus, 1968.

Ingham, M., *Now We Are Thirty: Women of the Breakthrough Generation*, London: Eyre Methuen, 1981.

Inness, Sherrie A. (ed.), *Millennium Girls: Today's Girls around the World*, Lanham, MD: Rowman and Littlefield, 1998.

Irwin, Mary Ann, '"White Slavery" as Metaphor: Anatomy of a Moral Panic', *Ex Post Facto: The History Journal*, 1996, vol. V, San Francisco State University, www.walnet.org/csis/papers/irwin-wslavery.html.

Jackson, B., *Working Class Community*, London: Routledge and Kegan Paul, 1968.

Jackson, C., ' "Wild" Girls? An Exploration of "Ladette" Cultures in Secondary Schools', *Gender and Education*, 18:4, 2006, pp. 339–60.

Jackson, C., and Tinkler, P., '"Ladettes" and "Modern Girls": "Troublesome" Young Femininities', *Sociological Review*, 55:2, 2007, pp. 251–72.

Jackson, Louise A., '"The Coffee Club Menace": Policing Youth, Leisure and Sexuality in Post War Manchester', *Cultural and Social History*, 5:3, 2008, pp. 289–308.

Jäger, J., 'International Police Co-operation and the Associations for the Fight Against White Slavery', *Paedagogica Historica*, 38:2, pp. 565–79.

Jeffreys, S., *Anticlimax: A Feminist Perspective on the Sexual Revolution*, New York University Press, 1991.

Jephcott, A. P., *Girls Growing Up*, London: Faber and Faber, 1942.

Jeune, M., 'The Revolt of the Daughters', *Fortnightly Review*, 55, February 1894, pp. 267–76.

John, Angela V., *Elizabeth Robins: Staging a Life, 1862–1952*, London: Routledge, 1995.

— *War, Journalism and the Shaping of the Twentieth Century: The Life and Times of Henry W. Nevinson*, London: I. B. Tauris, 2006.

Kamm, J., *Indicative Past: 100 Years of the Girls' Public Day School Trust*, London: Allen and Unwin, 1971.

Kenealy, A., *Feminism and Sex Extinction*, London: T. Fisher Unwin, 1920.

Kent, S. Kingsley, *Sex and Suffrage in Britain, 1860–1914*, London: Routledge, 1995.

Kerr, Rose, *The Story of the Girl Guides 1908–1938*, London: Girl Guides Association, 1976.

Kohn, M., *Dope Girls: The Birth of the British Drug Underground*, London: Lawrence and Wishart, 1992.

La Bern, A. J., *Night Darkens the Streets*, London: Transworld Publishers, 1958 (1947).

Landau, Cécile, *Growing Up in the Sixties*, London: Macdonald Optima, 1991.

Langhamer, C. L., *Women's Leisure in England, 1920–1960*, Manchester University Press, 2000.

Laurie, P., *The Teenage Revolution*, London: Anthony Blond, 1965.

Levine, P., 'Battle Colors: Race, Sex, and Colonial Soldiery in World War I', *Journal of Women's History*, 9:4, 1998, pp. 104–30.

Levy, A., *Female Chauvinist Pigs: Women and the Rise of Raunch Culture*, New York: Free Press, 2005.

Liddington, J., *Rebel Girls: Their Fight for the Vote*, London: Virago, 2006.

Liddington, J., and Norris, J., *One Hand Tied behind Us: The Rise of the Women's Suffrage Movement*,

Virago: London 1978, reprinted Rivers Oram Press, 2000.

Limond, D., '"I never imagined that the time would come"; Martin Cole, the *Growing Up* Controversy and the Limits of School Sex Education in 1970s England', *History of Education*, 37:3, 2008, pp. 409–29.

Lindsey, Shelley Stamp, 'Is Any Girl Safe? Female Spectators at the White Slave Films', *Screen*, 37:1, Spring 1996, pp. 1–15.

Litchfield, M., and Kentish, S., *Babies for Burning: The Abortion Business in Britain*, London: Serpentine Press, 1974.

Littlewood, M., 'Makers of Men: The Anti-Feminist Backlash of the National Association of Schoolmasters in the 1920s and 1930s', *Trouble and Strife*, 5, 1985, pp. 23–9.

Lively, P., *A House Unlocked*, London: Penguin, 2001.

Loncraine, R. 'Bosom of the Nation: Page Three in the 1970s and 1980s', in Gorji, M. (ed.), *Rude Britannia*, London: Routledge, 2007.

Lutzker, E., *Women Gain a Place in Medicine*, New York: McGraw Hill, 1969.

McRobbie, A., '*Jackie*: An Ideology of Adolescent Femininity', Birmingham, Centre for Contemporary Cultural Studies, 1977.

— *Feminism and Youth Culture: From Jackie to Just Seventeen*, Basingstoke, Macmillan Education, 1991.

— *The Aftermath of Feminism: Gender, Culture and Social Change*, London: Sage, 2009.

McRobbie, A., and Garber, J., 'Girls and Subcultures', in Hall, S., and Jefferson, T. (eds), *Resistance through Rituals*, London: Hutchinson, 1976.

McWilliams Tullberg, R., *Women at Cambridge,* London: Gollancz, 1975 (revised edition Cambridge University Press, 1998).

Malos, E., *The Politics of Housework*, London: Allison and Busby, 1980.

Malvery, Olive Christian (Mrs Archibald MacKirdy), and Willis, W. N., *The White Slave Market,* London: Stanley Paul, 1912.

Marcus, J. (ed.), *The Young Rebecca: Writings of Rebecca West, 1911–17,* London: Macmillan and Virago, 1982, p. 122.

Marks, L., and Van Den Bergh, T., *Ruth Ellis: A Case of Diminished Responsibility?* Harmondsworth: Penguin, 1990.

Marshall, D., *The Making of a Twentieth Century Woman: A Memoir* (edited by David Edge Marshall), London: Blazon Books, 2003.

Marshall, M. Paley, *What I Remember,* Cambridge University Press, 1947.

Martin, Courtney E., *Perfect Girls, Starving Daughters: The Frightening New Normalcy of Hating Your Body*, New York: Free Press (Simon and Schuster), 2007.

Martin, J., *Women and the Politics of Schooling in Victorian and Edwardian England,* London: Leicester University Press, 1999.

Martindale, L., *Under the Surface*, Brighton: Southern Publishing Company, 1909.

Masson, M. R., and Simonton, D., *Women and Higher Education: Past, Present and Future,* Aberdeen University Press, 1996.

Matthews, J., 'They Had Such a Lot of Fun: The Women's League of Health and Beauty', *History Workshop Journal,* vol. 30, 1990, pp. 22–54.

Maudsley, H., 'Sex in Mind and in

Education', *Fortnightly Review*, new series, 15, 1874, pp. 466–83.

Maynes, M.-J., Søland, B., and Benninghaus, C. (eds), *Secret Gardens, Satanic Mills: Placing Girls in European History, 1750–1960*, Bloomington: Indiana University Press, 2005.

Melman, B., *Women and the Popular Imagination in the 1920s*, London: Palgrave Macmillan, 1988.

Miller, J., *Relations*, London: Cape, 2003.

Money, A. L., *A History of the Girls' Friendly Society*, London: Gardner, 1897.

Morgan, S., *A Passion for Purity: Ellice Hopkins and the Politics of Gender in the Late Victorian Church*, University of Bristol Press, 1999.

— '"Wild Oats or Acorns?" Social Purity, Sexual Politics and the Response of the Late-Victorian Church', *Journal of Religious History*, 31:2, June 2007.

Mort, F., *Dangerous Sexualities: Medico-Moral Politics in England since 1830*, London: Routledge and Kegan Paul, 1987.

— *Capital Affairs: London and the Making of the Permissive Society*, New Haven, CT: Yale University Press, 2009.

Nabokov, V., *Lolita*, New York: G. P. Putnam, 1958.

National Council for Public Morals, *The Cinema: Its Present Position and Future Possibilities: Being the Report of, and Chief Evidence Taken by the Cinema Commission of Inquiry instituted by the National Council of Public Morals*, London: Williams and Norgate, 1917.

Nava, M., 'Cleveland and the Press: Outrage and Anxiety in the Reporting of Child Sexual Abuse',

Feminist Review, 28, Spring 1988, pp. 103–21.

Newburn, T., *Permission and Regulation: Law and Morals in Postwar Britain*, London: Routledge, 1992.

Newman, A., *A Share of the World*, London: Bodley Head, 1964.

Newsom, J., *The Education of Girls*, London: Faber and Faber, 1948.

Nicholson, V., *Singled Out: How Two Million Women Survived without Men after the First World War*, London: Viking, 2007.

Noakes, L., *Women in the British Army: War and the Gentle Sex, 1907–1948*, London and New York: Routledge, 2006.

Ollerenshaw, K., *Education for Girls*, London: Faber and Faber, 1961.

Orbach, S., *Fat Is a Feminist Issue: The Anti-Diet Guide to Permanent Weight Loss*, New York and London: Paddington Press, 1978.

— *Bodies*, London: Profile, 2009.

Orwell, G., *The Clergyman's Daughter*, London: Gollancz, 1935.

— *The Road to Wigan Pier*, Harmondsworth: Penguin, 1972 (1937).

Osgerby, B., '"The Sexpresso Kids": Coffee Bars and Teenage Culture in Britain, 1945–70', paper given at the 37th Annual Conference of the Social History Society, University of Brighton, 3–5 April 2012.

Ouellette, L., 'Inventing the Cosmo Girl: Class Identity and Girl-Style American Dreams', *Media, Culture and Society*, 21:3, 1999, pp. 359–83.

Palmer, T., *The Trials of Oz*, London: Blond and Briggs, 1971.

Pankhurst, C., *The Great Scourge and How to End It*, London: E. Pankhurst, 1913.

Pearsall-Smith, Alys W., 'A Reply from the Daughters', *Nineteenth Century*, 35, March 1894, pp. 443–50.

Pfeiffer, E., *Women and Work: An Essay*, London: Trübner, 1888.

Phillips, T., *We Are the People: Postcards from the Collection of Tom Phillips*, London: National Portrait Gallery, 2004.

Pipher, M., *Reviving Ophelia: Saving the Selves of Adolescent Girls*, New York: Putnam, 1994.

Plowden, A., *The Case of Eliza Armstrong, 'A Child of 13 Bought for £5'*, London: BBC Publications, 1974.

Priestley, J. B., *English Journey*, London: Heinemann, 1934.

Purvis, J., 'The Prison Experiences of the Suffragettes in Edwardian Britain', *Women's History Review*, 4:1, 1995, pp. 103–33.

— *Emmeline Pankhurst: A Biography*, London: Routledge, 2002.

Purvis, J., and Holton, S. Stanley, *Votes for Women*, London: Routledge, 2000.

Purvis, J., and Joannou, M., *The Women's Suffrage Movement: New Feminist Perspectives*, Manchester University Press, 1998.

Radway, J., *Reading the Romance: Women, Patriarchy and Popular Literature*, Chapel Hill: University of North Carolina Press, 1984.

Rauta, I., and Hunt, A., *Fifth Form Girls: Their Hopes for the Future*, survey carried out on behalf of the Department of Education and Science, London: HMSO, 1975.

Raymond, R. Alwyn, *The Cleft Chin Murder*, London: Claud Morris, 1945.

Rice-Davies, M., *The Mandy Report*, London: Confidential Publications, n.d.

Richardson, A., *The New Woman in Fiction and in Fact: Fin-de-Siècle Feminisms*, London: Palgrave Macmillan, 2001.

Richardson, H. J., *Adolescent Girls in Approved Schools*, London: Routledge, 1969.

Richmond, V., '"It is Not a Society for Human Beings but for Virgins": The Girls' Friendly Society Membership Eligibility Dispute 1875–1936', *Journal of Historical Sociology*, 20:3, 2007, pp. 304–27.

Ringrose, J., 'Successful Girls? Complicating Post-Feminist, Neoliberal Discourses of Educational Achievement and Gender Equality', *Gender and Education*, 19:4, 2007, pp. 471–89.

Robertson, James C., 'Good Time Girl, the BBFC and the Home Office: A Mystery Resolved', *Journal of British Cinema and Television*, 3:1, 2006, pp. 159–63.

Robins, E., *Where Are You Going To?* London: Heinemann, 1913.

Rose, J., *Marie Stopes and the Sexual Revolution*, London: Faber and Faber, 1992.

Rose, S. O., 'Sex, Citizenship and the Nation in World War II Britain', *American Historical Review*, 103:4, 1998, pp. 1147–76.

Rosen, A., *Rise Up Women! The Militant Campaign of the Women's Social and Political Union 1903–1914*, London: Routledge, 1974.

Ross, D., *G. Stanley Hall: The Psychologist as Prophet*, University of Chicago Press, 1972.

Rowbotham, S., *Promise of a Dream*, London: Allen Lane, 2000.

Royden, A. Maude (ed.), *Downward Paths: An Inquiry into the Causes Which Contribute to the Making of the Prostitute*, London: G. Bell and Sons, 1916.

Ruskin, J., *Sesame and Lilies*, London: Smith, Elder and Co., 1865.

Russell, R., and Tyler, M., 'Thank

Heaven for Little Girls: "Girl Heaven" and the Commercial Context of Feminine Childhood', *Sociology*, 36, 2002, pp. 619–37.

Ryle, A., *Student Casualties*, London: Allen Lane, 1969.

Sage, L., *Bad Blood*, London: Fourth Estate, 2000.

Sandbrook, D., *White Heat: A History of Britain in the Swinging Sixties*, London: Little, Brown, 2006.

Savage, G., '"The Wilful Communication of a Loathsome Disease": Marital Conflict and Venereal Disease in Victorian England', *Victorian Studies*, 1990, 34:1, pp. 35–54.

Savage, J., *England's Dreaming: Sex Pistols and Punk Rock*, London: Faber, 2001.

— *Teenage: The Creation of Youth, 1875–1945*, London: Chatto and Windus, 2007.

Saywell, E., *The Growing Girl*, London: Methuen, 1922.

Schofield, M., *Promiscuity*, London: Gollancz, 1976.

Schofield, M., with Bynner, J., Lewis, P., and Massie, P., *The Sexual Behaviour of Young People*, London: Longmans, 1965.

Schrum, K., *Some Wore Bobby-Sox: The Emergence of Teenage Girls' Culture, 1920–1945*, New York: Palgrave Macmillan, 2004.

Self, Helen J., *Prostitution, Women, and the Misuse of the Law: The Fallen Daughters of Eve*, London: Frank Cass, 2003.

Sharpe, S., 'Just Like a Girl': How Girls Learn to Be Women*, London: Penguin, 1976.

Shute, N., *We Mixed Our Drinks: The Story of a Generation*, London: Jarrolds, n.d. (c. 1945).

Sidgwick, Mrs H., *Health Statistics of Women Students of Cambridge and Oxford and of Their Sisters*, Cambridge University Press, 1890.

Simms, M., and Smith, C., *Teenage Mothers and Their Partners: A Survey in England and Wales*, London: HMSO, Department of Health and Social Security Research Report no. 15, 1986.

Singer, B., 'Female Power in the Serial-Queen Melodrama: The Etiology of an Anomaly', in Abel, R. (ed.), *Silent Film*, London: Athlone, 1996.

Slater, E., Cowie, J., and Cowie, V., *Delinquency in Girls*, London: Heinemann, 1968.

Slater, S. A., 'Containment: Managing Street Prostitution in London, 1918–1959', *Journal of British Studies*, 49:2, 2010, pp. 332–57.

Smith, H. L., *The British Women's Suffrage Campaign, 1866–1928*, London and New York: Longmans, 1998.

Sokoloff, B., *Edith and Stepney: The Life of Edith Ramsay*, London: Stepney Books, 1987.

Søland, B., *Becoming Modern: Young Women and the Reconstruction of Womanhood in the 1920s*, Princeton University Press, 2000.

Spencer, H., *Principles of Biology*, London: Williams and Norgate, 1867.

Spencer, S., *Gender, Work and Education in Britain in the 1950s*, Basingstoke: Palgrave Macmillan, 2005.

— 'Girls at Risk: Early School-leaving and Early Marriage in the 1950s', *Journal of Educational Administration and History*, 41:2, May 2009, pp. 179–92.

Spring, J., *Cry Hard and Swim: The Story of an Incest Survivor*, London: Virago, 1990.

Stacey, J., Béreaud, S., and Daniels, J. (eds), *And Jill Came Tumbling After: Sexism in American Education*, New York: Dell, 1974.

Stead, W. T., 'The Journal of Marie Bashkirtseff: The Story of a Girl's Life', *Review of Reviews*, June 1890, pp. 539–49.

Stephen, B., *Emily Davies and Girton College*, London: Constable, 1927.

Stevenson, B., and Wolfers, J., 'The Paradox of Declining Female Happiness', Institute for the Study of Labour (IZA), Discussion Paper no. 4,200, May 2009.

Strachey, R., *Careers and Openings for Women*, London: Faber and Faber, 1935.

— *The Cause: A Short History of the Women's Movement in Great Britain*, Bath: Cedric Chivers, 1974.

Strong, C., 'Grunge, Riot Grrrl and the Forgetting of Women in Popular Culture', *Journal of Popular Culture*, 44:2, 2011, pp. 398–416.

Tabili, L., 'Women "of a Very Low Type": Crossing Racial Boundaries in Imperial Britain', in Frader, Laura F., and Rose, S. (eds), *Gender and Class in Modern Europe*, Ithaca, NY: Cornell University Press, 1996, pp. 165–90.

Tarr, Carrie T., '"Sapphire", "Darling" and the Boundaries of Permitted Pleasure', *Screen*, 26:1, 1985, pp. 50–65.

Taylor, D. J., *Bright Young People: The Rise and Fall of a Generation, 1918–1940*, London: Chatto and Windus, 2007.

Tennant, E., *Girlitude: A Portrait of the 1950s and 1960s*, London: Cape, 1999.

Terrot, C., *The Maiden Tribute: A Study of the White Slave Traffic of the Nineteenth Century*, London: Muller, 1959.

— *Traffic in Innocents: The Shocking Facts about the Flesh Markets of Europe; A Story of Lust and Moral Depravity Unequalled in Civilized Times*, New York: Bantam/E. P. Dutton, 1961.

Thom, D., *Nice Girls and Rude Girls: Women Workers in World War I*, London: I. B. Tauris, 1998.

Thomas, S., 'Crying "the Horror" of Prostitution: Elizabeth Robin's "Where Are You Going To … ?" and the Moral Crusade of the Women's Social and Political Union', in *Women, A Cultural Review*, 16:2, 2005, pp. 203–21.

Thorburn, J., *Female Education from a Physiological Point of View*, Manchester: Owen's College, 1884.

Tickner, L., *The Spectacle of Women: Imagery of the Suffragette Campaign, 1907–1914*, London: Chatto and Windus, 1988.

Tinkler, P., *Constructing Girlhood: Popular Magazines for Girls Growing Up in England, 1920–1950*, London: Taylor and Francis, 1995.

Todd, S., *Young Women, Work and Family in England, 1918–1950*, Oxford University Press, 2005.

Turner, K., *I Dream of Madonna: Women's Dreams of the Goddess of Pop*, London: Thames and Hudson, 1993.

Tweedie, Mrs A., *Women and Soldiers*, London: John Lane, Bodley Head, 1918.

Tweedie, J., *Eating Children*, London: Viking, 1993.

Tylecote, M., *The Education of Women at Manchester University, 1883–1933*, Publications of the University of Manchester no. 277, 1941.

Veness, T., ' A Research Note on Attitudes to Work and Marriage of 600 Adolescent Girls', *British Journal of Sociology*, 12:2, 1961, pp. 176–83.

Voeltz, R. A., 'The Antidote to "Khaki

Fever"? The Expansion of the British Girl Guides during the First World War', *Journal of Contemporary History* 27, 1992, pp. 627–38.

Waites, M., 'Inventing a "Lesbian Age of Consent"? The History of the Minimum Age for Sex Between Women in the UK', *Social and Legal Studies*, 11:3, 2002, pp. 323–42.

Walkerdine, V., 'Sex, Power and Pedagogy', *Screen Education*, no. 38, Spring 1981, pp. 14–24.

— *Schoolgirl Fictions*, London: Verso, 1990.

Walkerdine, J., and Lucey, H., *Democracy in the Kitchen: Regulating Mothers and Socialising Daughters*, London: Virago, 1989.

Walkowitz, J., *Prostitution and Victorian Society: Women, Class and the State,* Cambridge University Press, 1980.

— *City of Dreadful Delight; Narratives of Sexual Danger in Late Victorian London,* Chicago, IL and London: Virago 1992.

Walter, N., *Living Dolls; The Return of Sexism,* London: Virago, 2010.

Weinbaum, E., Thomas, Lynn M., Barlow, Tani E., Ramamurthy, P., Poiger, Uta G., and Yue Dong, M. (eds), *The Modern Girl around the World,* Durham, NC: Duke University Press, 2008.

Weis, R., *Criminal Justice: The True Story of Edith Thompson*, London: Penguin, 1990.

West, P., and Sweeting, H., 'Fifteen, Female and Stressed: Changing Patterns of Psychological Distress over Time', *Journal of Child Psycho-*logy and Psychiatry, 44:3, 2003, pp. 399–411.

Whipple, A., 'Speaking for Whom? The 1971 Festival of Light and the Search for the "Silent Majority"', *Contemporary British History*, 24:3, 2010, pp. 319–39.

Whitehouse, M., *Whatever Happened to Sex?* Hove: Wayland Publishing, 1977.

Whyte, J., Deem, R., Kant, M., and Cruickshank, M. (eds), *Girl Friendly Schooling*, London: Methuen, 1985.

Wilkins, L., *The Adolescent in Britain*, London: Central Office of Information, 1955.

Willcock, H. D., *Report on Juvenile Delinquency*, London: Falcon Press, 1949.

Willis, W. N., *White Slaves in a Piccadilly Flat,* London: Anglo-Eastern Publishing Company, 1915.

Wilson, A., *Finding a Voice: Asian Women in Britain*, London: Virago, 1978.

Witz, A., *Professions and Patriarchy*, London: Routledge, 1992.

Wolf, N., *The Beauty Myth: How Images of Beauty Are Used against Women*, London: Vintage, 1990.

Woollacott, A., ' "Khaki Fever" and Its Control: Gender, Class, Age and Sexual Morality on the British Home Front in the First World War', *Journal of Contemporary History*, 29, 1994, pp. 325–47.

Zweiniger-Bargielowska, I., 'The Body and Consumer Culture', in Zweiniger-Bargielowska (ed.), *Women in Twentieth Century Britain*, London: Longmans, 2000.

INDEX